How to Win at
CONTRACT BRIDGE
in 10 Easy Lessons

by Richard L. Frey

New and Completely Revised

Includes a special section on
4-Deal Bridge (Chicago) and Party Bridge

With an Introduction
by CHARLES H. GOREN

FAWCETT CREST • NEW YORK

A Fawcett Crest Book
Published by Ballantine Books

ISBN 0-449-20995-4

Manufactured in the United States of America

First Fawcett Crest Edition: September 1972
First Ballantine Books Edition: June 1982
Third Printing: February 1986

How many of these can you answer correctly?

		True	False
a.	The higher you bid, the more strength you need.	☐	☐
b.	You need seven points or more to raise partner's suit.	☐	☐
c.	You should never bid if you can be set as much as 500 points.	☐	☐
d.	An opening two no-trump bid is forcing; partner must respond.	☐	☐
e.	Bidding and making a grand slam produces the highest score in contract bridge.	☐	☐

◇　♠　♣　♡　◇　♠　♣　♡

**Whatever your score, this book will show you
how to play better, enjoy more, and win more
at your favorite game.**

ANSWERS TO QUIZ

a. False. Preemptive opening bids (of three or four of a suit) are often made with weaker hands than an opening one bids.

b. Correct. You may respond 1 no-trump with 6. With fewer, you should pass.

c. False. A 500-point penalty may be a profitable sacrifice against the opponents' game; will certainly be profitable against a slam.

d. False. Two no-trump is a limited bid showing 22, 23, or 24 points. With fewer than 3 points, partner may pass.

e. False. A grand slam at no trumps, even when doubled and redoubled, scores at most 3,280 points: 1,500 for the slam; 700 for the rubber; 880 for tricks; 150 for aces; 50 for making contract. The penalty for being set 13 tricks doubled and redoubled vulnerable could amount to 7,600.

Another Fawcett Crest Book
by Richard L. Frey:

ACCORDING TO HOYLE

ACKNOWLEDGMENTS

In addition to the invaluable cooperation of Charles Goren, the author wishes to acknowledge important contributions to this book by the late Albert H. Morehead, former bridge editor of **The New York Times,** by the late Geoffrey Mott-Smith, and especially by Fred Karpin of Silver Spring, Maryland.

INTRODUCTION

BY CHARLES H. GOREN

THIS IS a fine bridge book. In view of its author's fame both as a writer and a player, that will come as no surprise. What will surprise many of his friends is the fact that this is the only complete book on bridge which Dick Frey has ever written.

He has ranked among the bridge greats since 1929, when he won the first of his many tournament victories. He was a star member of the original Four Aces; a favorite partner of Ely Culbertson; one of the first players to be ranked as a Life Master, the highest honor awarded by the American Contract Bridge League.

As a professional free lance writer, he has published five books, scores of entertaining magazine articles on subjects ranging from "Auction Sales" to "Zygotic Twins." He is the author of hundreds of magazine articles about bridge and of a syndicated newspaper column that appeared without interruption for more than thirty years. He has contributed, either in theory or in fact, to some of the best books ever published on contract bridge.

In this book he has combined proven talents as writer and player—with the expected result. Here is a book that is delightfully easy to read and to understand; that quickly imparts the fundamental rules for playing a winning game and, at the same time, reveals the reasons behind these rules in a way that opens wide the doors to a real grasp of the most fascinating card game the world has ever known.

Reading this book is bound to help any player, beginner or experienced, have more fun and win more points in his game of Contract Bridge.

CONTENTS

AUTHOR'S FOREWORD

Many new ideas have come along since I first wrote this "Foreword." The best and most popular of these are included in this revised and expanded edition. But in all other respects, the "Foreword" is as true today as it ever was.

LET'S START off with some long-needed debunking of the false idea that only people with special talents can learn to play bridge well.

Bridge is neither an art nor a science. It is a game. It is played according to *laws,* which govern such things as the way the cards are to be dealt, how tricks are won, how to conduct the bidding auction by which the players compete for the privilege of naming the trump suit. (For new players, these mechanical procedures are reviewed on page 283.)

Bridge is also played according to *rules*—but a rule is not a law. It is simply a way of measuring. A bidding rule, for example, is a way of measuring the trick-taking value of a hand—based on past experience of what similar hands were worth.

However, there are three kinds of trick-winning values. Some tricks are won by *high cards*. Others are won by *long cards:* the smaller cards in the suit that remain after the high cards have slaughtered one another and when all the cards the opponents held in that suit have been exhausted. Still other tricks are won by *trumps*, which can take a trick away from a high card or a long card when a player no longer has any cards in the suit that was led.

Not long ago, when there was no way to measure these three different kinds of trick-winning values with the same kind of ruler, it was much more difficult to learn to play bridge well. Today, thanks to Charles H. Goren, you can easily combine and measure these different values in terms of "points"; you can tell your partner what kind of hand you have and how strong it is by learning how to count points and then selecting the kind of bid that reveals the approximate total to your partner.

The way you do this in bidding is very little different from the way you and a partner might talk over plans for building a house. Your conversation might go like this:

You: "I have some good building material—at least half as much as we'll need to build a house. Plenty of bricks."

Partner: "I have some material, too. Not as much as would take care of my half of the job. And not many bricks; mostly wood."

You: "Never mind. I have wood, too. Much more than half of what we'll need. Tell me what else you have."

So you go on exchanging information about nails and paint and other building supplies you have on hand and pretty soon you know whether you have enough to build a house, how big it should be and even what color.

When you bid in bridge, you exchange exactly the same kind of information, only you must do so in a code. Learning how to bid is simply learning how to measure your strength in terms of points and learning a simple code language in which you describe your holding and also hear what your partner has to say about his hand. Obviously, the one big essential is for partners to use the same code.

The "code" described in this book is the one most universally used by good players everywhere. It is based on the Goren point count. With it, you will be able to swap information with your partner so that you can be sure you have the necessary materials on hand with which to fulfill your contract MOST OF THE TIME. That is all you need to become a winning player.

But enough of bricks, and wood, and nails. Let's get down to brass tacks.

—R.L.F.

PREFACE

(BE SURE TO READ THIS BEFORE YOU COME TO LESSON 2.)

THE MOST important change in this new and revised edition is that it recommends opening the bidding in a major suit only (with rare exceptions) *when the suit contains at least five-card length*. In other words, I now recommend, and have recently been playing,

FIVE-CARD MAJORS AS THE PREFERRED METHOD.

For scores of years, going back to the glory days of the original Four Aces—and even before that—I have played and recommended the traditional method of opening the bidding on four-card majors. Today, however, more and more players (although still not a majority) are learning *not* to open with a bid in a four-card major. Certainly, a vast majority of today's teachers have adopted this method *because it is easier to learn and easier to teach.*

Witness the fact that it has so simplified your choice of opening bid that it requires only two pages of Lesson 2 to explain it in essence.

Note that I have not said that this method is necessarily better. But I have adopted it because more and more of my social game partners are using it, and as time goes by you, too, will find this is the case, especially as Charles H. Goren now recommends it in the latest revision of his *Contract Bridge Complete*.

This does *not* mean that you *must* abandon opening on four-card majors. In fact, the first part of Lesson 2 tells you how to choose your opening bid if you are accustomed to this method, or if your partner prefers it and is unfamiliar with the five-card major method.

It is important, therefore, that you know how to handle opening bids on four-card majors and, indeed, as you will learn, there are certain hands on which you should open a four-card major in preference to some other bid. It is even more important that you know how to play when your partner expects you to have at least five cards in the major suit of your opening bid. Therefore, if your first rebid is in that major, you are promising six-card length unless your partner's response has been a double raise.

If you are a real beginner at the game, I urge you to begin by reading "Goren's Contract Bridge Primer" on pages 283 to 299.

Let me add one encouraging note: The five-card major method is not so very different from the way you may have been playing. It is only easier to learn.

Lesson 1

VALUING YOUR HAND FOR THE BIDDING

OF THE thirteen tricks won in the play of each hand, some are won with *high cards* and the rest with values which are the result of distribution: *long cards,* which win tricks when all the other cards in that suit are exhausted, and *trumps* which win tricks when a player no longer holds a card of the suit that is led.

Here are three different kinds of trick-winning values, yet all are measured in the same currency—points.

HIGH-CARD POINTS

The point values of the high cards are:

$$\text{Ace} = 4$$
$$\text{King} = 3$$
$$\text{Queen} = 2$$
$$\text{Jack} = 1$$

To measure the value of a hand, the first step is to count the high-card points ("x" indicates low card):

♠	A J x x	(5)
♡	K x x	(3)
◇	Q x x	(2)
♣	K J x	(4)
	Total	14

DISTRIBUTIONAL POINTS

That this high-card point value does not in itself give a complete picture is evident when we look at the three following hands, all of which contain the same high cards.

(1)	(2)	(3)
♠ A x x	♠ A J x x	♠ A K J x x
♡ Q J x	♡ A Q x x	♡ A Q J x x
◇ A K x x	◇ K J x x	◇ x x
♣ J x x	♣ x	♣ x

Each hand counts to 15 high-card points. But every experienced bridge player knows that hand (2) is worth more than hand (1), and that hand (3) is worth more than hand (2). In the play of hand (2), the fourth card of each of three suits may become a winning long card, or, if one of the three suits is trump, some of its cards may win tricks by ruffing leads of the short suit, clubs. The same is true of hand (3) only more so. A trump suit of five cards is much more likely to win tricks by ruffing than a suit of four. And the long cards in the second five-card suit are more likely to become established under the protection of the longer trump suit.

There is a simple way to measure this extra distributional value, which produces tricks either by ruffing a short suit or establishing a long suit. It isn't necessary to count *both* the short-suit and the long-suit values. In fact, it would be wrong to do so. To get an accurate picture of your distributional value, all you need do is add points for short suits as follows:

For a void (0 cards in a suit) .... 3 points
For a singleton (1 card in any suit) ..... 2 points
For a doubleton (2 cards in any suit).... 1 point

You count for each short suit.

What you are counting is the extra value your hand will have when it is played at your best trump declaration. And, for this purpose, you arrive at the value of any hand by adding the total of distributional points to the total of the high-card points.

EXAMPLES OF VALUATION

Let us look again at the three "15-point" hands cited, to see how they vary in true value when the proper distributional points are added:

(1)		(2)		(3)	
♠ A x x	(4)	♠ A J x x	(5)	♠ A K J x x	(8)
♡ Q J x	(3)	♡ A Q x x	(6)	♡ A Q J x x	(7)
◇ A K x x	(7)	◇ K J x x	(4)	◇ x x	(1)
♣ J x x	(1)	♣ x	(2)	♣ x	(2)
	15		17		18

Here are additional illustrations of hand valuation:

♠ K J x x	(4)	♠ J x x	(1)	♠ K Q x x x	(5)
♡ —	(3)	♡ x x	(1)	♡ A J x x	(5)
◇ A K x x x	(7)	◇ A Q x x	(6)	◇ x	(2)
♣ Q x x x	(2)	♣ A J x x	(5)	♣ Q x x	(2)
	16		13		14

♠ x	(2)	♠ A J x x x x	(5)	♠ x	(2)
♡ A K x x x x	(7)	♡ A Q x x x	(6)	♡ K x	(3 + 1)
◇ K Q x x x	(5)	◇ x x	(1)	◇ A Q x x x x	(6)
♣ x	(2)	♣ —	(3)	♣ K x x x	(3)
	16		15		15

In summary: the value of a hand is determined by adding the high-card point count to the points assigned for distribution.

EXCEPTIONS IN HIGH-CARD COUNT

Two exceptions will occasionally alter the 4-3-2-1 point count. One exception is the case of a singleton picture card below the rank of ace. To illustrate:

(1)	(2)	(3)
♠ A J x x	♠ A J x x	♠ A J x x
♡ K	♡ Q	♡ J
◇ x x x x	◇ x x x x	◇ x x x x
♣ K x x x	♣ K x x x	♣ K x x x

3

	(1A)	(2A)	(3A)
	♠ A J x x	♠ A J x x	♠ A J x x
	♡ K x	♡ Q x	♡ J x
	◇ x x x	◇ x x x	◇ x x x
	♣ K x x x	♣ K x x x	♣ K x x x

The heart honors in hands (1), (2), (3) are obviously not worth as much as the same cards in hands (1A), (2A), (3A)—being unprotected, they can be felled by higher picture cards. For example, on hand (1), the lead of the ace of hearts by an opponent will capture the king of hearts.

In recognition of this, every singleton picture card other than an ace loses 1 point of its value through being unprotected. If you have a singleton king, reduce it in value from 3 to 2; if you have a singleton queen, reduce it in value from 2 to 1; if you have a singleton jack, treat it as a singleton low card (no high-card value).

Applying the modified count to the first three hands:

(1)		(2)		(3)	
♠ A J x x	(5)	♠ A J x x	(5)	♠ A J x x	(5)
♡ K	(2 + 2)	♡ Q	(1 + 2)	♡ J	(0 + 2)
◇ x x x x	(0)	◇ x x x x	(0)	◇ x x x x	(0)
♣ K x x x	(3)	♣ K x x x	(3)	♣ K x x x	(3)
	12		11		10

The second exception arises when a queen or a jack is accompanied by only one *small* card (Q-x or J-x), as in hands (2A) and (3A). In such case, the queen or jack is reduced in value by one point, just as though it were a singleton. Thus:

(1A)		(2A)		(3A)	
♠ A J x x	(5)	♠ A J x x	(5)	♠ A J x x	(5)
♡ K x	(3 + 1)	♡ Q x	(1 + 1)	♡ J x	(0 + 1)
◇ x x x	(0)	◇ x x x	(0)	◇ x x x	(0)
♣ K x x x	(3)	♣ K x x x	(3)	♣ K x x x	(3)
	12		10		9

Note that the king of hearts in hand (1A) has not been reduced in value, in contrast to the queen and jack of hearts in hands (2A) and (3A), each of which has lost a point.

Two other exceptions to the 4-3-2-1 count apply only to an

opening bid, discussed in Lesson 2. If the opening bidder has no ace, he deducts one point; if he has all four aces, he adds one point.

♠ K Q x	(5)	♠ A x x	(4)
♡ K Q x x	(5)	♡ A J x x	(5)
◇ x x	(1)	◇ A x	(4 + 1)
♣ K Q x x	(5)	♣ A Q x x	(6)
	16 − 1 = 15		20 + 1 = 21

POINT REQUIREMENTS FOR GAMES AND SLAMS

The purpose of the point system discussed thus far is to predict your ability to take tricks during the play: the more points your side owns, the more tricks you are likely to win. And the more accurately you gauge your trick-taking prospects, the greater will be your profit, whether you apply these tricks toward fulfilling your own contract or defeating an over-ambitious contract undertaken by the opponents.

The key to making this profit is proper valuation of your hand. It will tell you with accuracy your own trick-taking potentialities; it will also tell you when the opponents are over their heads and wide open to a penalty double that may pay you more than any bid of your own.

Aside from penalties collected from the opponents, your most profitable contracts are bids for game and slam. For these contracts you need a combined value (your hand and partner's together) as follows:

Game at no trump (9 tricks) or
     at ♠ or ♡ (10 tricks) . . . . 26 points
Game at ◇ or ♣ (11 tricks) . . . . 29 points
Small slam (12 tricks) . . . . 33 points
Grand slam (all 13 tricks) . . . . 37 points

Possession of the required number of points does not guarantee that you will make what you have bid. It simply means that if you have reached the best contract for your combined hands, and if you do not have a misfit, you will make your contract more often than not.

You will rarely have all these points in your own hand, so

5

that you will have to learn how to count partner's points from his bidding, or how to show yours so that he can count them. But for the time being you are concerned only with counting your own hand so that you won't make any mistake in the exchange of information.

Practice! It is a good idea to spend a half hour from time to time, just shuffling a deck, dealing out thirteen cards at random, and determining the value of each hand. Practice until you can do this quickly, accurately and without giving the opponents a reading of your strength by the timing of your count-down.

Point-counting Hint: Together, an ace, king, queen and jack count exactly 10 points. When your hand contains all four of these honors, you can do some wholesale counting that will speed up the job, even though these honors are not all in the same suit.

The quiz that follows will assist you in practicing rapid recognition of the point value of a hand. Don't forget the points you must add or subtract because of unguarded honors, etc. The answers will explain how the count is reached.

QUIZ

What is the value of each of the following hands?

(1)	(2)	(3)
♠ A Q x x x	♠ Q x	♠ Q x x x x x
♡ K J x x	♡ A x x x	♡ A K J
◇ J x x	◇ K Q J x x	◇ x x
♣ x	♣ A J	♣ K x

(4)	(5)	(6)
♠ J x x	♠ x x x x x x	♠ J x
♡ A J x	♡ A x x x	♡ x x x x
◇ K Q x x x	◇ A J	◇ J x x x
♣ Q x	♣ x	♣ A K Q

(7)	(8)	(9)
♠ A K Q x x	♠ —	♠ J x x
♡ Q x x x x	♡ K J x x x	♡ Q x x
◇ K x	◇ J x x x x	◇ Q x
♣ x	♣ A Q J	♣ A K J x x

6

(10)	(11)	(12)
♠ J x x x	♠ K Q J	♠ K J
♡ x	♡ x x x	♡ J x x x x
◇ A K Q J	◇ K J x x	◇ K x
♣ Q J x x	♣ A x x	♣ A Q J x

(13)	(14)	(15)
♠ Q J X	♠ K Q x x x x	♠ Q J
♡ A K x x x x x	♡ A Q x x x x	♡ K J x x x x
◇ K x	◇ —	◇ A x x x
♣ J	♣ x	♣ Q

ANSWERS

1. 13 points. 11 are in high cards, 2 in short-suit valuation for the singleton club.

2. 18 points. The high-card content is 17 points, from which 1 point is subtracted for the unguarded queen of spades. 2 points are added for the short suits: 1 for spades and 1 for clubs.

3. 15 points. 13 points are in high cards, plus 1 each for the doubleton diamond and the doubleton club. Note that no reduction is made for the guarded king of clubs.

4. 13 points. The high cards total 13 points, plus 1 point in distribution for the doubleton club, making 14. 1 point is subtracted for the unguarded queen of clubs. Note that the J-x-x is not reduced in value, since the jack, accompanied by two little cards, is considered guarded.

5. 12 points. 9 are in high cards and 3 in distribution: 2 for the singleton club, and 1 for the doubleton diamond.

6. 11 points. In high cards, the hand contains 11 points, from which 1 point is subtracted for the unprotected jack. 1 distribution point is added for the doubleton spade.

7. 17 points. The high-card content is 14 points. The short-suit variation is 3 points, 1 for the doubleton diamond, and 2 for the singleton club.

8. 15 points. 12 are in high cards, and 3 are in distribution, for the void in spades.

9. 13 points. The hand contains 13 points in high cards and 1 in distribution (the doubleton diamond). But 1 point is subtracted for the unprotected queen of diamonds.

10. 16 points. The high-card content is 14 points, plus 2 for the singleton heart.

11. 14 points. All are in high cards. Since the hand contains no void, no singleton and no doubleton, there is no short-suit valuation to be added. And, in these cases, the worth of the hand is measured exclusively by its *face-value* high-card content, *since there can never be any reduction for an unguarded queen or jack.*

12. 17 points. The high-card content is 15 points. The short-suit valuation is 2 points: 1 for the doubleton spade and 1 for the doubleton diamond.

13. 16 points. The high cards total 14 points, less 1 point for the singleton jack. To these 13 points are added 3 points: 2 for the singleton club, and 1 for the doubleton diamond.

14. 16 points. 11 are in high cards and 5 points are in short-suits: 3 for the void in diamonds, and 2 for the singleton club.

15. 15 points. The high cards total 13 points, less 1 point for the singleton queen of clubs. To the remaining 12 points are added 3 points for distribution: 2 points for the singleton club, and 1 point for the doubleton spade. Note that the Q-J doubleton of spades was not reduced in value. Only when the queen or jack is accompanied by just *one small* card (Q-x or J-x) is a point reduction made for its lack of a guard.

Lesson 2

THE OPENING BID OF ONE IN A SUIT

IT IS much easier to learn *when* to make an opening bid of one in a suit, and *which suit* to bid first when you have a choice, if you fully understand *why* you want to bid and *what* you are bidding for.

Your objective is to win points. The way to win points is by winning tricks. You can win more tricks if your side's best suit is the trump suit, because you will be able to trump the opponents' high cards and you will be better able to establish your own long cards in side suits. *So, you bid for the right to name which suit is to be trumps.*

You win more points if you are able to bid for a game that helps you to win the rubber, or a slam that pays an extra bonus, or by collecting a penalty when the opponents bid too much. (If *you* bid too much, you must pay a penalty, but if you bid too little you will squander your good hands to buy a small gain and you will have to dig into inadequate reserves to pay for what you will lose when the opponents hold the good cards.) *So, you will try to bid for the biggest reward that seems reasonably safe.*

How can you tell which is the best trump suit for your combined hands, and how can you tell how high to bid when you cannot see what partner holds? By bidding in such a way as to convey accurate information about the strength of your hand and the length of your suits. *So, the third reason you bid is to exchange information.*

Every bid you make should be a step toward discovering and reaching your most profitable contract, but it is particularly important that the first bid be correct, because it is the foundation on which the entire auction is built.

WHAT YOU PROMISE

Your opening bid of one in a suit promises three things:

1. That you hold a better-than-average hand—a total of at least 13 points. (You may pass certain 13-point hands but with as many as 14 points you must open the bidding. So, a pass also promises that you have fewer than 14 points.)

2. That the suit you name is at least four cards in length (certain rare exceptions are discussed later) and includes a certain minimum of high-card strength if it is not longer than a four-carder.

3. That if your partner responds in any of the other three suits you will make another bid so as to give him at least one more chance. (That is, if you open with one diamond, you promise to bid again if partner responds one heart or one spade or two clubs.)

With this introduction, you are ready to look at a few hands and decide whether to open the bidding or to pass:

(1)	(2)	(3)
♠ x x	♠ x x x	♠ x x x
♡ A Q x x x	♡ Q x x	♡ x x
◇ A Q x	◇ K x x	◇ A K x x x
♣ x x x	♣ A K x x	♣ A x x

Hand (1) is worth 13 points. You will soon learn to open this hand with a bid of one heart.

Hand (2) contains but 12 points. A pass is the proper call.

Hand (3) also contains but 12 points. Despite the high-card tricks, it should not be opened.

FOUR-CARD MAJORS, THE TRADITIONAL APPROACH: CHOOSING THE CORRECT SUIT

Without a doubt, the selection of the trump suit is the most important single phase in partnership bidding. Once the trump suit is agreed, it becomes a routine matter to determine how high the partnership will go in its contract; that is, whether a game can be made (26 points), or a small slam (33 points), or a mere part score (less than 26 points). The possession of 26 points does not in itself guarantee a game. If, for example, you and your partner have 26 points but you arrive at a contract of four hearts with only five hearts between you, you are not likely to make the game against the opponents' eight trumps. To ensure that your side has a sufficient edge in the all-important trump department, any suit chosen by your side as trumps should have a minimum of *eight* cards in the combined hands.

The first step in insuring that the suit you and your partner agree upon includes at least eight cards is to choose your first bid so that you will tell your partner which is your best suit and, later, just how good it is.

Biddable Suits 1. All five-card, six-card or longer suits are biddable, regardless of their top strength.

2. Not all four-card suits are biddable. The minimum biddable suits should include:

> *In the majors:* Two honors higher than the ten, as A-J-x-x, K-J-x-x, Q-J-x-x. Occasionally, this may be shaded to A-10-x-x, K-10-x-x, Q-10-x-x.

> *In the minors:* A four-card diamond suit should be headed by A, K, or Q, or occasionally J-10-x-x. Almost any four-card club suit is biddable.

3. No three-card major suit is biddable, but a three-card minor may be opened (see pages 18–20).

Rebiddable Suits A rebiddable suit is one that may be bid a second time although partner has not supported it. The primary requirement is that the suit have at least five-card length*; a four-card suit is never rebid unless partner has supported it. To be rebiddable, a five-card suit should be headed by at least two of the four highest honors: A-K-x-x-x, K-Q-x-x-x, K-J-x-x-x, Q-J-x-x-x, etc.

Any six-card or longer suit is rebiddable, regardless of its top strength.

Choosing Which Suit to Bid First When you have more than one biddable suit, the selection of which to bid first is usually easy if one or both is at least a five-card length. In such cases, generally:

---

* But see "Five-Card Majors" on page 23.

(a) Bid your longest suit first. (A five-card suit before a four-card suit; six before five, and so on.)

(b) With suits of equal length (both five cards or six cards) bid the higher-ranking suit first, regardless of relative strength.

♠ Q 9 x x x	♠ A K 9 x x	♠ Q 9 x x x	♠ A K Q
♡ A K x x	♡ x x x x x x	♡ A K x x x	♡ 10 x x x x
◇ A J 9	◇ A x	◇ A x	◇ A Q x x
♣ x	♣ —	♣ x	♣ x
Bid 1 spade	Bid 1 heart	Bid 1 spade	Bid 1 heart

There is a single exception to the rule of bidding the higher-ranking five-card suit first. If the suits are specifically spades and clubs, and the spade suit is not rebiddable, bid clubs first.

♠ A 10 x x x	♠ Q x x x x	♠ A K J x x
♡ x x	♡ A K J	♡ x
◇ x	◇ —	◇ x x
♣ A K x x x	♣ Q x x x x	♣ K J x x x
Bid 1 club	Bid 1 club	Bid 1 spade

In hands that contain no five-card or longer suit, the simple principle of bidding the highest ranking of suits of equal length must be modified.

(a) With two biddable four-card suits:

If the suits are "touching," always bid the higher-ranking suit first. (By "touching" is meant adjacent in rank: specifically, spades and hearts, hearts and diamonds, and diamonds and clubs.)

♠ A K x x	♠ x x	♠ x x
♡ A K x x	♡ A K x x	♡ x x x
◇ x x x	◇ A K x x	◇ A K x x
♣ x x	♣ x x x	♣ A K x x
Bid 1 spade	Bid 1 heart	Bid 1 diamond

If the suits are not touching, bid the lower-ranking suit first.

12

♠ A K x x	♠ A K x x	♠ x x x
♡ x x	♡ x x	♡ A K x x
♢ x x x	♢ A Q x x	♢ x x
♣ A Q x x	♣ x x x	♣ A Q x x
Bid 1 club	Bid 1 diamond	Bid 1 club

(b) With three biddable four-card suits, always bid the suit below the singleton first.

♠ K Q x x	♠ K Q x x
♡ A Q x x	♡ x
♢ x	♢ A Q x x
♣ K J x x	♣ K J x x
Bid 1 club	Bid 1 diamond

♠ x	♠ K Q x x
♡ K Q x x	♡ A Q x x
♢ A Q x x	♢ K J x x
♣ K J x x	♣ x
Bid 1 heart	Bid 1 spade
	(spades are considered to be below clubs)

The reasons for these rules are elucidated in the following sections.

THE PRINCIPLE OF THE GUARANTEED REBID

With certain hands, one bid will convey all the necessary information. But these hands are very much in the minority. Most of the time, the responder will need at least two opportunities to describe his hand adequately. The only way he can be assured of a second chance to bid is if opener promises not to pass when his partner's first response is in a new suit. Without this cardinal principle of bridge bidding, it would be impossible for partners to exchange information at reasonable bidding levels; the contract would get to a high level so fast that there would be no room to give further information without bidding for more tricks than the partnership could win.

This fancy-sounding principle of the guaranteed rebid can be stated quite simply:

"Whenever the bidding is opened at one of a suit, if a partner who has not previously passed responds by naming a *new suit*, the opener must bid again."

Extending this principle to its logical conclusion: If *responder's* rebid names another new suit, opener must bid again. Thus, any time responder names a new suit, opener is forced to keep the bidding open.

However, note that if responder raises partner's suit, or responds with a minimum bid in no trump, opener may pass. Study these bidding situations:

Opener	Responder	Opener	Responder
1. 1 heart ?	1 spade	**4.** 1 spade ?	2 spades
2. 1 club 1 heart ?	1 diamond 1 spade	**5.** 1 heart ?	1 no trump
3. 1 club 2 clubs 3 clubs ?	1 spade 2 hearts 3 diamonds	**6.** 1 club 1 spade ?	1 diamond 1 no trump
		7. 1 heart 2 hearts ?	1 spade 3 hearts

In each of the sequences in the left-hand column, responder has just bid a new suit: opener is thus forced to bid again. In each of the sequences in the right-hand column, responder's last bid was not in a new suit: opener may pass.

It is not necessary, at this point, for you to know what the responder's bids show; as the opener, you need consider only the need to make another bid. And since you must be prepared to make another bid, you must take this into account at the time you select your first bid.

Looking Ahead Since you have to look ahead in the bidding in order to select your opening bid correctly, we'll have to peek ahead just for a moment into the responses that will be discussed in the next lesson.

But first, let's look back for a moment. We can open the bidding with as little as 13 points—but that is in expectation that partner will help us by winning a couple of tricks. We need 26 points for a 9-trick game in no trump. We need 33 points for a 12-trick slam bid. The mathematical shape of these requirements hints that it requires slightly less than 3 points to win a trick.

Peeking ahead, we'll discover that partner can keep the bidding open with as little as 6 points in his hand.

So, if we are going to reach the two-level, contracting to win eight tricks, we should have something like 21-22 points in our combined hands; to be safe at the three-level, we need about 24-25.

Obviously, the higher we force the bidding to go, the more strength we promise to partner. The height to which each player carries the bidding helps his partner gauge the strength of his hand.

We have seen that a five-card suit has some prospect of winning tricks under its own power, so may be rebid once without support.* But a four-card suit may never be rebid, and unless we can find a fit with partner in one of our four-card suits our hand may lose some of the value we have tentatively assigned to it. For example:

♠ K J x x   ♡ x   ◇ A x x x   ♣ K J x x

This hand includes 12 points in high cards. We have added 2 points for the singleton heart, bringing it to 14. But if partner bids hearts, there is danger that he cannot support any of our three suits, and unless one of our three suits is trumps our hand is reduced in value by 2 points. So, until we have found a fit with partner, we must be sure to keep our bidding to a low level.

But suppose we open the bidding with our highest-ranking suit, spades. Over one spade, partner bids two hearts. Now, we cannot rebid spades, we certainly cannot support hearts, and to show one of our other suits we must do so at the three-level with a hand reduced from the 14 points we originally counted to a mere 12. (With a singleton in partner's suit a two no-trump rebid is not desirable.)

---

* But not if you are playing "Five-Card Majors" (see pages 22–23).

So we follow the rule in bidding four-card suits, choosing the suit immediately below the singleton. We open with one diamond. If partner bids one heart, we can make the rebid we promised without actually contracting for more than the seven tricks we undertook with our first bid: we can bid one spade. Of course if partner bids two clubs, or if he bids one spade himself, we can no longer keep the bidding at a low level. But our hand has increased in value because we have already found that eight-card trump suit which is one of our prime goals.

With Two Four-Card Suits Now, let's consider some more examples of hands including two four-card suits.

(1)	(2)	(3)
♠ A Q J x	♠ A Q J x	♠ x x x
♡ x x	♡ x x	♡ A Q J x
◇ x x x	◇ A Q x x	◇ x x
♣ A Q x x	♣ x x x	♣ A Q x x

If you open hand (1) with one spade, partner's two-heart response will drive you to three clubs on your guaranteed rebid.

If you open hand (2) with one spade, partner's two-heart response will force you to three diamonds on your rebid.

If you open hand (3) with one heart, partner's two-diamond response will compel you to three clubs on your rebid.

As is evident, by starting in your highest-ranking suit, you tend to compel partner to make his first response at the two-level, and then force yourself to rebid at the three-level.

But if you properly open hand (1) with one club, partner's "up the ladder" response of either one diamond or one heart will permit you to bid one spade. You will then have shown both of your suits and at this moment will be no higher than you were at the outset.

If you correctly open hand (2) with one diamond, partner's one-heart response will again permit you to bid one spade. If partner had responded to one diamond with two clubs, your rebid would still keep you in the two-level.

If you correctly open hand (3) with one club, partner's one-diamond response would enable you to economically bid one heart.

Another great advantage develops from bidding first the lower of non-touching four-card suits: the transmission to partner of extra distributional information about your hand. To illustrate, we'll peek at a responder's hand.

You
♠ A K x x
♡ Q x x
◇ x x x
♣ A x x

Partner	*You*
1 heart	1 spade
2 clubs	?

What do you bid next? The answer is: four hearts!

How, you may ask, do you know that partner has a minimum of five hearts? Well, if partner had four clubs and four hearts, he would have opened the bidding with one club. But he didn't—he bid one heart first. The only acceptable reason for his opening one-heart bid must be that he held five hearts. You have 13 points in high cards, so you know the combined hands total at least the required 26. You have three hearts and he has five, so you know your combined trumps total at least the desired eight. Ergo, your jump to four hearts.

Extending this principle to cover all three combinations of two non-touching four-card suits (spades and clubs, spades and diamonds, hearts and clubs) we can establish this inference:

Whenever partner opens the bidding in a major suit and follows through on his rebid by bidding a non-touching minor suit, you will know that he has at least five cards in his major suit.

Let's look at some bidding situations.

Partner	*You*
1 spade	1 no trump
2 clubs	

You can visualize partner's hand as (1) or (2) below, but NOT as (3).

(1)	(2)	(3)
♠ A Q 7 6 5	♠ A Q 7 6 5	♠ A Q 7 6
♡ A 2	♡ A 2	♡ A 2
◇ 4 3	◇ 4	◇ 6 5 3
♣ A Q 7 5	♣ A Q 7 6 5	♣ A Q 7 5

He may have four clubs or he may have five, but he cannot have fewer than five spades, else he would have opened the bidding with one club. Likewise, you can be sure that your partner has five cards in his major suit in each of the following examples:

Partner	You	Partner	You
1 spade	2 clubs	1 heart	1 spade
2 diamonds		2 clubs	

No Second Biddable Four-Card Suit Hands of pattern 4-3-3-3 and 4-4-3-2, with no second biddable four-card suit, present a problem in rebidding. For example, suppose that as the opening bidder you hold:

♠ A K J x   ♡ x x x   ◇ x x x   ♣ A Q x

What would be your rebid if you opened this hand with one spade, and your partner made either a two-heart or a two-diamond response? You could not bid spades again (that would show five spades). You cannot raise his hearts (or diamonds) since you have only three cards in his suit and his bid has not promised more than four. Neither can you bid no trump, since you would have no protection in whichever red suit he did not bid. Nor could you, on your rebid, bid a three-card suit. What should you do, then, since you must bid again?

The answer is that one spade is not the proper opening bid. This is the instance referred to on page 11, where an opening bid on a three-card suit is made originally. The correct opening bid is one club.

Three-Card Suit Bids If your four-card suit (or suits) is not biddable, or if it is biddable and in bidding it you may put yourself in an embarrassing position when called upon to provide your guaranteed rebid, you may instead bid a three-card club suit (often referred to as the "short-club" opening bid).

On the hand above, if your partner responds to one club with one heart or one diamond, you move easily to one spade on your rebid. No problem; economy of bidding space has been achieved.

Let us look at a few more illustrations of proper "short-club" openings.

(1)	(2)	(3)
♠ Q x x x	♠ A K x x	♠ x x x x
♡ x x x x	♡ x x x	♡ x x x
◇ A K	◇ K J x	◇ A K Q
♣ A x x	♣ K x x	♣ A J x

On hands (1) and (2) if the opening bid is one spade, partner's new suit response will have to be at the two-level. In (1) if he responds with two diamonds or two clubs, you have no adequate rebid. In (2) if he responds with either two clubs or two hearts, you have no adequate rebid.

On hand (3) you cannot open your 14-point hand with one spade, since the spade suit is not biddable. So, either you pass (and nobody holds such good hands that he can afford to pass a 14-point hand) or you make the tactical, temporizing bid of one club. No matter what your partner responds, your rebid will be easy. If he responds with one diamond or one heart, you will rebid (as you will learn) one no trump; if he responds in spades you will raise him to two spades. And if he responds with one no trump or two clubs, you will have the right to pass, since neither of these bids is a new suit.

Do not open a minor suit of less than three-card length or one that is not headed by at least the queen. If these requirements rule out a one club opening, it is permissible to open a three-card diamond suit. Partner is entitled to raise your opening bid in a minor suit if he holds good support (but never with fewer than four cards), or to expect at least the queen in the suit you have bid if he elects to lead that suit should an opponent become declarer. It is correct to open one diamond, not one club, with any of the following:

(1)	(2)	(3)
♠ A x x x	♠ x x x x	♠ x x x x
♡ J x x x	♡ K Q x	♡ x x x x
◇ A Q x	◇ A K J	◇ A K J
♣ K x	♣ J x x	♣ A K
(14 pts)	(14 pts)	(15 pts)

As between biddable three card minors, however, always prefer to open one club. For example, in (1) above, if the hand included one more club and one fewer card in either major, you would open one club, ignoring the greater strength in the diamond suit.

19

Note that short suit distribution points are not counted when deciding to open with a three-card minor. Optional 13-point opening bids should be passed; usually an opening bid in a three-card minor should include 14-15 high-card points.

Don't go out of your way to open the bidding with a three-card suit. This device is intended only for a mediocre hand in which an opening bid of the longest suit would turn out to be either misleading or embarrassing as the bidding progresses to higher levels. All good hands, and all hands where an "easy" rebid can be anticipated, should be bid naturally—longest suit first. To illustrate:

♠ x x x	♠ A K x x	♠ x x x
♡ A K J x	♡ x x x	♡ A K Q
◊ A Q x	◊ A K x	◊ A Q x x
♣ A J x	♣ K Q x	♣ K J x
Bid 1 heart	Bid 1 spade	Bid 1 diamond

♠ A J x x	♠ x x x
♡ A Q x x	♡ Q J 10 x
◊ x x	◊ A K x
♣ A K x	♣ A J x
Bid 1 spade	Bid 1 heart

Third-Position Opening Bids In third position, you are permitted to open the bidding with as few as 11 points. The reason for the waiving of the 13-point requirement in this instance is: *you are not required to provide a guaranteed rebid,* since your partner, who has passed originally, has denied holding 13 points. Therefore, if he has less than 13, and you have less than 13, a game cannot be made.

Extending this, whenever you open in third position on 11 or 12 points (or even 13), you must pass any non-forcing response that your "passed" partner may make. To bid again, when you know that your side can make no more than a part-score, is losing bridge.

The third-position opening with sub-minimum values is made for one of the following three reasons:

(a) As a lead-director, in the event that the opponents purchase the contract.

(b) As a guide to taking a possible sacrifice in lieu of letting the opponents make a game or slam.

(c) As a try for a part-score, or even a game contract if a "fit" is found with partner.

Let us look at a few illustrations of third-position opening bids:

(1)	(2)	(3)
♠ x x x	♠ J x x x	♠ A K x x
♡ x x	♡ J x x	♡ x x x
◇ A K Q J x	◇ x x	◇ x x x
♣ x x x	♣ A K Q x	♣ A J x

(1) An opening bid of one diamond is proper as a lead-director. Of course, as you open with one diamond, you intend to pass whatever response partner makes.

(2) Bid one club, with intention of passing partner's response of one of a suit, one or two no trumps, or two clubs.

· (3) Bid one spade, intending to pass on the next round. In first or second position, you would open this hand with one club (the "short-club" bid), since you would then be compelled to provide a guaranteed rebid. But in third position you are not under obligation to rebid; therefore bid your best suit as a lead-director.

In fourth position, the same opening requirements prevail as for first and second positions, namely, a minimum of 13 points. However, the fourth-position opener need not provide a guaranteed rebid, since his partner has already passed, denying 13 points. To open on fewer than 13 points in fourth position is silly: to tell partner what to lead, or in what suit to sacrifice, when both opponents have already passed, serves no purpose. By passing with a subnormal opening hand you'll never get a minus score—which score, of course, is worse than the zero you get if you pass. When you open in fourth position, it will be because you feel that your hand is good enough to snare a plus score.

We come now to the major change in modern bidding trends: The avoidance of opening the bidding in a four-card major suit, and the adoption of the principle that when your opening bid is one heart or one spade you are telling partner you have at least five cards in that suit.

FIVE-CARD MAJORS:
THE MODERN APPROACH

A substantial number of bridge players prefer not to open with one heart or one spade unless they hold at least *five* cards in the bid suit. Otherwise they bid their longer minor; or, if the minors are equal in length, one club is chosen unless the diamonds are very much stronger. For example, you are playing five-card majors and hold any of these hands:

(1)	(2)
♠ A J x x	♠ A K x x
♡ A K x x	♡ x x x
◇ A x x x	◇ K J x
♣ x	♣ K x x

(3)	(4)
♠ A K x x	♠ x x
♡ A Q x x	♡ A K x x
◇ Q x x	◇ Q J x x
♣ x x	♣ K x x

(1) Bid one diamond: you have agreed not to open in a major suit unless it has at least five cards.

(2) Bid one club. Here, the traditional and five-card major approaches produce the same result.

(3) Bid one diamond. You have agreed not to open a four-card major, and a two-card suit is never opened.

(4) Bid one diamond, choosing your longer minor.

When your major suit includes five or more cards, the procedures for opening the bidding are identical to those discussed previously. For example:

(1)	(2)	(3)
♠ x x	♠ Q 9 x x x	♠ A K 9 x x
♡ A Q x x x	♡ A K x x x	♡ Q x x x x x
◇ A Q x	◇ A x	◇ A x
♣ x x x	♣ x	♣ —
Bid one heart	Bid one spade	Bid one heart

A primary advantage of opening five-card or longer majors is that it enables partner to give an immediate raise with only three-card support, knowing that your side has at least an eight-card fit. This not only simplifies the problem of what to bid first, but, as you will see, it makes it easier for partner to choose his response and for both players to rebid.

If you do not have a five-card major but your hand meets the other requirements—at least 13 points and a guaranteed rebid—you open with a minor suit, if necessary with a three-card suit. This will often provide you with an easy rebid if you can show your major at the one level. But remember: You should avoid rebidding a five-card major; an immediate rebid of a major usually shows six-card length, unless partner has responded with a jump raise, promising four-card support or three very strong ones (for example: A-K-x, A-Q-x, A-J-x, K-Q-x, etc.).

Be aware that this method is not quite as simple as it seems. Opener may be forced to suppress a good four-card major or may encounter rebid problems later. For example, if you open one club and partner responds one spade, you may have to rebid one no trump even with four good hearts and no stopper in diamonds. You need a very strong hand, 16-17 points, to show your four-card heart suit at the two-level.

Another disadvantage is that partner may have to respond one no trump to one spade even though his hand is something like:

♠ x   ♡ x x   ◇ K J x x   ♣ Q 10 x x x x

To overcome this, many play that a one no trump response is forcing. If opener does not have a six-card suit or a five-card heart suit, he must rebid in his better minor, preferring clubs with equal three-card minors.

It is *not* essential that you play one no trump forcing, which makes it impossible to play a one no trump contract when responder has 6 to 9 points in a balanced hand. Indeed, many who play five-card majors do not play the forcing no trump, and, in teaching beginners, many teachers do not recommend it, even though it is better and they use it themselves.

The opening bidder rebids over one trump in the same way he would if he were playing the four-card major method and is free to rebid a good five-card major or to rebid two hearts with 5-4-2-2 distribution. So until you are thoroughly familiar with the five-card major method, it may be easier not to play one no trump forcing and to explain to your partner that you will feel free to pass a one no trump response.

However, most of the examples in the remainder of this book, unless noted otherwise, assume that you are bidding five-card majors.

23

Lesson 3

RESPONSES TO THE OPENING BID OF ONE IN A SUIT

THE PREVIOUS lessons have discussed the problems of the opening bidder. Let us now direct our attention to the partner of the opener, known as the *responder*.

CAPTAINCY

Responder as Captain   The responder's everyday problems will be greatly simplified if he constantly bears in mind the principle that *an opening bid facing an opening bid will yield a game.* In terms of the point-count: 26 points will usually produce a game. Opener announces a holding of 13 points. If responder also holds at least 13 points (an opening bid), he knows that the combined assets equal the 26 points required to produce a game.

As is apparent from the above, the responder, holding 13 or more points, is the first one to know that the combined hands will yield a game. Therefore, he should assume captaincy of the team, and direct the further bidding to arrive at the proper trump suit (or no trump).

More often than not, responder is the "key" man of the partnership. Opener has announced at least 13 points, leaving not more than 27 to the other three hands. If responder holds his average share of 9, the opener's side has a majority of the 40-odd high-card points in the deck. Thus, whether the responder can assume captaincy or not, his first action is likely to disclose which side holds the balance of power.

Opener as Captain   If responder has fewer than 13 points, he is in no position to assume captaincy. The making of a game will depend on how many points above 13 the opener has. The captaincy of the team in these cases is turned over to the opener who, upon learning how many points responder has (from 6-12, inclusive), adds this number to his own to determine whether the total reaches 26.

With fewer than 13 points, responder should seek to transmit to the opener the precise details of his hand, both in terms of points and the distributional pattern. And then the opener takes control, by adding his 16 to the responder's 10; or his 20 to responder's 6; or his 18 to responder's 9; etc. Of course, at the same time that responder is showing points, he is also showing his suit or suits, with the object of arriving at the proper trump suit, the suit in which the partnership has eight or more cards.

RESPONDER'S TABLE

As a permanent guide for the responder's bidding, he employs the following table:

> With 6 to 9 points, responder plans to make *one* forward-going bid.
>
> With 10 to 12 points, responder plans to make *two* forward-going bids.
>
> With 13 or more points, responder plans to make as many bids as may be required to get to game. In this situation, responder knows immediately that a game exists, and the only issue to be resolved is where the game will be played.

This table serves not only the responder but also the opener, who, as he hears responder speak once, twice, or three times, knows precisely how many points responder possesses. (The reader should appreciate that these "ranges," 6-9, 10-12, etc., are not to be adhered to slavishly. Situations will arise where judgment will tell you that a bid based on a one-point deviation is proper.)

How these ranges are applied by the responder, and how the knowledge of these significant bids is utilized by the opener, can be observed in the following examples:

Partner opens with one heart, and you respond with one spade, holding:

	(1)			(2)			(3)	
♠	A Q x x x	(6)	♠	A Q x x x	(6)	♠	A Q x x x	(6)
♡	x x	(0)	♡	A x x	(4)	♡	A x x	(4)
◇	x x x	(1)	◇	x x	(1)	◇	x x	(1)
♣	x x x	(0)	♣	x x x	(0)	♣	K x x	(3)
		7			11			14

On hand (1), if opener rebids two hearts, you *pass*. (7 points permit only one forward-going bid.)

On hand (2), if opener rebids two hearts, you bid *three hearts*. (11 points permit two forward-going bids.)

On hand (3), if partner rebids two hearts, you bid *four hearts*. (14 points, game assured, and trump suit established.)

You, as opener, hold the following hand:

♠	x x	(1)
♡	A K Q x x	(9)
◇	K J x	(4)
♣	Q x x	(2)
		16

The bidding has proceeded:

You	Partner
1 heart	1 spade
2 hearts	3 hearts
?	

Your correct bid now is four hearts. You are looking at 16 points. Your partner, who has responded twice, has indicated 10 points (10-12). He has raised your hearts, thereby indicating that hearts is the trump suit. Both conditions for making a game are fulfilled: 26 points and the proper trump suit.

Another illustration. You hold:

♠ K 10 x x   ♡ x x   ◇ A x x   ♣ A K x

The bidding has proceeded:

(a)

You	Partner
1 club	1 heart
1 spade	2 spades
?	

Your proper bid is now four spades. Your partner, in bidding twice, has shown 10 points. You have 17. In raising your spades, partner has announced that spades is the trump suit.

(b)

You	Partner
1 club	1 heart
1 spade	2 hearts
?	

Three no trumps is your proper bid. Partner, who has spoken twice, has at least 10 points, and you have 16. Game is assured. There is no trump suit: you don't care for his heart suit, and he doesn't care for either of yours. But between you, each of the four suits is protected. Hence, three no trumps.

One final illustration, from opener's point of view. You, as opener, hold:

$$
\begin{array}{ll}
\spadesuit \ x \ x & (1) \\
\heartsuit \ A \ K \ J \ x \ x & (8) \\
\diamondsuit \ K \ x \ x & (3) \\
\clubsuit \ J \ x \ x & \underline{(1)} \\
& 13
\end{array}
$$

The bidding has proceeded:

You	Partner
1 heart	1 spade
2 hearts	3 hearts
?	

Your correct action is now to *pass*. You are looking at 13 points. Responder has 10-12. Between you, the partnership holds 23, 24, or 25 points—short of the 26 required for a game. Responder cannot have 13 points, for if he did he would have bid four hearts, knowing that you, as opener, hold at least 13 points. He likes hearts—but obviously, the points for a game are lacking.

27

The above illustrations indicate how the "responder's table" guides both responder and opener in their partnership bidding. This table, and its application by both opener and responder, will be discussed at greater length in Lesson 5.

CHOOSING THE CORRECT RESPONSE

Now let us turn our attention to the specific categories of responses which responder is continually called upon to make. There are four kinds of basic responses:

    I.   The single raise of partner's suit.
    II.   The one no trump response.
    III. The one-over-one response.
    IV.   The two-over-one response.

I. THE SINGLE RAISE OF PARTNER'S SUIT

This is a most specific-type bid, announcing that responder possesses: (1) exactly 7-10 points and (2) trump support, a minimum of x-x-x if partner has opened one heart or one spade, and x-x-x-x if partner has opened one club or one diamond. Opener promises at least five cards in his suit by opening one heart or one spade, so three-card support is sufficient to produce an eight-card fit. But an opening bid of one club or one diamond may be made with a four- or perhaps only a three-card suit.

Responder's Valuation   The value of the responding hand, for a direct raise, is determined by adding the points assigned for (a) high cards, and (b) short suits. The regular table is modified as set forth below.

(a) High cards in side suits are valued as usual. But there is an adjustment for the high cards in the trump suit, for the reason that picture cards in partner's trump suit are worth a little more than the same cards in side suits. The king of partner's suit becomes promoted to an ace, and is considered to be worth 4 points. In similar fashion, the queen of partner's suit is promoted to the value of a king, worth 3 points; the jack of partner's suit becomes the equivalent of a queen, worth

2 points. However, there is an upper limit to the promotion: if 4 points have already been counted in the trump suit alone, no promotion is made.

The following holdings are valued as shown, opposite a diamond bid by partner:

(1) ◇ Q x x x (2 + 1 = 3)		(4) ◇ A x x x (4 + 0 = 4)	
(2) ◇ J x x x (1 + 1 = 2)		(5) ◇ Q J x x (3 + 1 = 4)	
(3) ◇ K x x x (3 + 1 = 4)		(6) ◇ K J x x (4 + 0 = 4)	

Note in the last three examples that a maximum of 1 point is allowed for promotion of trump honors.

(b) Short suits in the dummy-to-be are increased in value as follows:

—Add 1 point for each doubleton.
—Add 3 points for each singleton.
—Add 5 points for each void.

It will be observed that the distributional count in the dummy hand differs from the distributional count in the opener's hand: a more liberal allowance is made for short suits in dummy's hand.

Deductions of one point must be made for each defect when the dummy hand contains a flaw. The most common flaws are:

1. A 4-3-3-3 distribution.
2. Insufficient guards for a counted high card (Q-x, J-x, K alone).
3. Only three trumps if partner opens one club or one diamond.

Examples of the Single Raise   Here are some examples of valuation by the responder, in support of an opening one-spade bid. You will observe that each hand falls in the 7-10 range, and so calls for a raise to two spades.

(1)		(2)		(3)	
♠ Q x x x	(2 + 1)	♠ K x x x	(3 + 1)	♠ A x x x	(4)
♡ x x	(1)	♡ x	(3)	♡ —	(5)
◇ A J x x	(5)	◇ J x x x	(1)	◇ x x x x x	(0)
♣ x x x	(0)	♣ Q x x x	(2)	♣ x x x x	(0)
	9		10		9

(4)		(5)		(6)	
♠ A x x x	(4)	♠ K x x	(3+1)	♠ Q x x	(2+1)
♡ K x x	(3)	♡ x	(3)	♡ Q x	(2+1)
◇ J x x	(1)	◇ K x x x x	(3)	◇ K x x x	(3)
♣ x x x	(0)	♣ x x x x	(0)	♣ x x x x	(0)
8 − 1 = 7		10 − 1 = 9		9 − 1 = 8	

(7)	
♠ K J x	(4)
♡ K	(3+3)
◇ x x x x	(0)
♣ x x x x x	(0)
10 − 1 = 9	

(1) High cards: 7 points, plus 1 point for the promotion of the queen of trumps. One distributional point is added for the doubleton heart.

(2) High cards: 6 points, plus 1 point for the promotion of the king of trumps. Three distributional points are added for the singleton heart.

(3) High cards: 4 points. No promotion is made for the ace of trumps. Five points are added for the void in hearts.

(4) High cards: 8 points. No distributional points. A one-point deduction is made for the defect of a 4-3-3-3 distribution.

(5) High cards: 6 points, plus 1 point for the promotion of the king of trumps. Three points are added for the singleton heart. One point is deducted because the queen is unguarded.

(6) High cards: 7 points, plus 1 point for the promotion of the queen of trumps. One distributional point is added for the doubleton heart.

(7) High cards: 7 points. There is no promotion in the trump suit, since four points have already been counted. Three points are added for distribution (the singleton heart). One-point deduction is made for fact that the king is unguarded.

The Single Raise: a Limit Bid As was stated, the direct single raise is a precise bid showing exactly 7 to 10 points. *Never make this single raise on more than 10 points.* If you do, you may easily miss a makable game. Let me illustrate how this might happen.

The single raise is known as a "limit bid." When you make this response, your partner is permitted to pass. If he holds 13 to 15 points he *should* pass. There would be no object in bidding further: your hands lack the 26 points requisite for game, and you have already found your eight-card trump suit.

But suppose that you have incorrectly given a single raise with an 11-point hand. With 15 points, your partner dutifully passes—and you miss a probable game.

So, always bear in mind that over your single raise your partner may pass and will do so with a hand of 15 points or less. Later, you will learn the ways of informing him that you have 11, 12, or more points in addition to adequate trump support for his suit.

II. THE ONE NO-TRUMP RESPONSE

The one no-trump response, like the single raise, is a limit bid. It is made on hands that contain exactly 6 to 10 points.

Holding 6 points or more it is your duty to respond to partner's opening bid of one in a suit. If you do not possess the requirements to raise his suit, or to respond with one of another suit,* the accepted practice is to respond with one no trump. This response is made to keep the bidding open for partner in case he has a good hand or a second suit.

The 6-10 points shown by a one no-trump response must always be in high cards, *for distributional points are not counted in valuing the hand for no trump bids.*

The one no-trump response is correct only if you have no biddable suit that can be shown at the one-level. As far as *responder* is concerned, any major or minor four-card suit is biddable at the one-level when it is headed by at least the J-10 or the Q (J-10-x-x, Q-x-x-x). This differs slightly from the opener's requirements for a biddable suit.

Examples of Minimum Responses Let us look at some examples of the one no-trump response and the single raise. Partner opens with one heart and you hold:

---

* One-over-one bidding, which is discussed in the next section.

(1)	(2)	(3)
♠ J x x	♠ 10 x x x	♠ J x x
♡ x x	♡ x x	♡ x x x x
◇ J x x x	◇ x x x	◇ J x
♣ A Q x x	♣ A Q x x	♣ A Q x x

(4)	(5)	(6)
♠ K x	♠ x x x	♠ x x x
♡ x x	♡ A K	♡ A x x x
◇ J x x x	◇ J x x x	◇ x x x
♣ A x x x x	♣ x x x x	♣ x x x

(1) Bid one no trump, showing 6-10 points.

(2) Bid one no trump, showing 6-10 points.

(3) Bid two hearts, showing 7-10 points and adequate trump support. In support of hearts this hand is worth 8 points: 8 in high cards, less 1 for the unguarded jack of diamonds, plus 1 for the doubleton diamond.

(4) Bid one no trump on your 8 points (no value assigned for any short suit when a no-trump response is made).

(5) Bid one no trump. Do not let the top hearts mislead you into raising partner. Two cards, even A K, are not adequate support for a suit in which partner might have only four cards.

(6) Pass. For no trump the hand is valued at 4 points. For hearts, it is valued at only 3 points (1 point is deducted for the defect of a 4-3-3-3 distribution). Do not respond to partner's opening bid of one in a suit with less than 6 points.

As with the single raise, opener has the right to pass the limit response of one no trump, since this bid shows a maximum of 10 points. If the opener holds 15, 14, or 13 points, he will know immediately that the combined hands cannot contain the 26 points necessary for game.

In summary: both the single raise and the one no-trump response show mediocre hands, not more than 10 points. The single raise shows 7-10, counting distributional values; one no trump shows 6-10 in high cards exclusively. Opener has the right to pass either of these two limit responses. Whenever opener has 13, 14, or 15 points, he knows after a limit response that the combined hands cannot reach to 26 points; consequently, bidding a game is out of the question.*

---

* An exception occurs when opener has a second suit, in support of which a responder who bids one no trump may be able to furnish additional distributional values.

Let us now turn our attention to the responses which offer more hope: the one-over-one response and the two-over-one response.

III. THE ONE-OVER-ONE RESPONSE

The one-over-one response is the bid of a higher-ranking suit at the one-level, as one diamond over opener's one club. While this response may be made on as few as 6 points, it may also be made with as many as 18 points! So, this one-over-one response does not immediately promise any more strength than does a response of one no trump: 6 points is all opener will expect you to have. But there is a great difference. The one no-trump response indicates a maximum of 10 points, while the one-over-one response is not so limited.

Examples of One-over-One Response Let us look at some illustrations of this open-end one-over-one response. Partner opens with one diamond, and you hold:

(1)	(2)	(3)
♠ Q J x	♠ x x x x x	♠ K x
♡ K J x x	♡ A K J	♡ A Q x x x
◊ x x x	◊ Q x x	◊ A Q x
♣ x x x	♣ x x	♣ x x x

(1) Bid one heart, with the intention of passing on the next round. As responder, you are guided by the "responder's table": with 6-10 points you are entitled to one forward-going bid; with 10-12 points to two forward-going bids; with 13 or more points, to as many bids as may be required to get to game in the proper trump suit. Your partner, the opener, is aware of the fact that you are bidding according to this table, and *that your first bid may be your last.*

(2) Bid one spade, intending to make a second bid on the next round. The opportunity to make this second bid will be available since opener must bid again whenever responder names a new suit.

(3) Bid one heart, knowing full well that your partnership can make at least a game. Opener cannot pass. The sole issue to be resolved is where the game will be played: in a suit, and if so, which, or in no trump.

In summary: the one-over-one response in a new suit may show as few as 6 points, and, from opener's point of view, might be just as weak as either the single raise or the one no-trump response. But the bid might also be made on a good hand. If it is made on a good hand, responder will speak again (and again); if it is made on a minimum hand, responder has the right to pass at his next turn.

Important note: never respond with one no trump when you can conveniently show a biddable suit at the one-level. The specific information that you possess a biddable suit can be of great assistance to your partner.

IV. THE TWO-OVER-ONE RESPONSE

Whenever you name a new suit at the two-level, you are making what is called a two-over-one response. To make this response, you need at least 10 points (an average hand, since there are 40 high-card points in the deck).

The primary reason for this minimum requirement is that the response increases the level of the contract and also compels partner to bid again. From a business point of view, you don't want to drive the contract higher unless you can afford it. To afford it, you need more than a bare minimum of points, otherwise you'll go broke. Even though you have a respectable suit, if you have fewer than 10 points and cannot bid that suit at one, content yourself with a one no-trump response. Your partner will then be relieved of his promise to provide a guaranteed rebid over any but non-forcing responses.

Responses with 10-Point Hands You may be puzzled by the fact that a one no-trump response shows 6-10 points, while a two-over-one response is also made on 10 points. The natural question, of course, is when should you content yourself with a one no-trump response and when should you bid two of a new suit?

The answer is: with a 10-point hand that offers a genuine choice, prefer the one no-trump response, because it does not force partner to speak again with a minimum hand. For example, partner opens with one heart and you hold:

(1)	(2)	(3)
♠ A x x	♠ x x	♠ x x x
♡ x x	♡ x x	♡ J x x
◇ K J x x	◇ x x x x	◇ K x x
♣ Q x x x	♣ A K Q x x	♣ A K x x

(1) Bid one no trump.

(2) Bid two clubs.

(3) A bid of two clubs is mandatory, for one no trump would say falsely that the hand holds no more than 10 points.

Generally speaking, you should favor the one no-trump response with a reasonably balanced 10-point hand (no voids or singletons). When your hand is unbalanced (with a void, a singleton, or two doubletons), prefer to respond with two of a suit.

Examples of Responses Partner opens with one diamond, and you hold:

(1)	(2)	(3)
♠ A Q x x x	♠ x x x	♠ K J x
♡ x x x	♡ J x x	♡ x x
◇ x x	◇ x x	◇ x x x
♣ x x x	♣ A Q x x x	♣ A Q x x x

(4)	(5)	(6)
♠ x x x	♠ K J x	♠ x
♡ x x	♡ x x	♡ x x x
◇ x x x x	◇ x x x x	◇ K Q x
♣ A K x x	♣ A K x x	♣ A K J x x x

(1) Bid one spade.

(2) Bid one no trump. The hand lacks the 10 points for a two-over-one response.

(3) Bid two clubs; you have 10 high-card points, plus 1 point for distribution.

(4) Bid two diamonds, showing 7-10 points and normal trump support for partner. Do not make the mistake of bidding two clubs, for partner would then (a) rely on you for at least 10 points and (b) be compelled to bid again even with a minimum hand.

(5) Two clubs is mandatory. With 11 points in high cards, the hand is too good for one no trump (6-10 points). With 10-12 points, you are entitled to make two forward-going bids. After your partner bids again, you will present your second bid, which will probably be a raise in diamonds. Partner will then know that you have 10-12 points, because you voluntarily spoke twice; that you have a club suit; and that you have support for his diamonds.

(6) Bid two clubs. You have more than enough strength to show your fine suit at the two-level.

In summary: the two-over-one response, based on *a minimum of 10 points,* informs partner that you have an "upper middle class" type of hand, as opposed to the "lower class" type of hand which a one no-trump response indicates (*a maximum of 10 points*).

THE FREE BID

Hitherto, we have dealt only with situations in which your side has opened the auction and the opponents have remained silent. The subject of competitive bidding will be discussed at length in Lesson 7. But at this juncture we must consider how an adverse bid affects the action of the responder.

A "free bid" is one made *voluntarily* by you, the responder, after your partner has opened the auction and your right-hand opponent has overcalled. To illustrate:

Partner	*Opponent*	*You*
1 diamond	1 heart	1 spade, etc.

Thus far, the bidding requirements have assumed that your right-hand opponent passed your partner's bid. If he comes into the auction however, any bid you make immediately is a *free bid.* That is to say, you are not forced to bid in order to give partner a second chance in case he has a very strong hand; opponent's bid has provided him with that chance. Therefore you will pass on all the hands with which your only object in bidding would be to keep the auction open.

When you make a free bid *in a new suit,* the number of points which you will require will depend on whether you make that free bid at the one-level or the two-level. However, even if you give only a free raise in partner's suit, or a free bid of one no trump, partner will know that you have more than the barest of minimums.

When your partner opens the bidding, you know that he has a minimum of at least 13 points. However, it is conceivable that he may have 20 or more points. When you respond with just 6 points, you are in a sense making a courtesy bid, so that if he does possess 20 or more points, he can promptly bid a game. He doesn't figure to hold 20 or more points—but who are you to decide arbitrarily that he doesn't? Should you, with 6 points, elect to pass, you are making a decision which you have no right to make. In the absence of an intervening bid by the opponents, you will make some response, for if you don't the bidding is apt to proceed:

Partner	Opponent	You	Opponent
1 diamond	Pass	Pass	Pass

And, if your partner happens to have 20 or more points, you will have failed to arrive at a makable game—not to mention incurring the everlasting mistrust of partner.

However, when an opponent overcalls your partner's opening bid, you are relieved of the necessity of making a "courtesy-type" response, for no game can be missed if you pass. Suppose your partner opens with *one diamond*, and the next opponent bids *one heart*. Should you now pass, *your partner will have another chance to bid,* which he will do if he possesses a good hand. But he can also pass, which he will do with a minimum-type holding. Had you freely bid in a new suit, you would have forced partner to provide his guaranteed rebid even if he held a minimum hand—and your free bid of one spade on, say, 6 points, might well have pushed the partnership to an unmakable contract.

Requirements for Free Bids The requirements for a free bid depend upon the character of the bid and upon the bidding level, as follows:

For a free bid in a new suit:

1. At the one-level: a minimum of 8 points.

2. At the two-level:

(a) In a suit lower-ranking than partner's suit: a minimum of 10 points in high cards.

(b) In a suit higher-ranking than partner's suit: a minimum of 11 points, of which at least 10 are in high cards.

For a free raise of partner's suit: a minimum of 8 points (and a maximum of 11 points).

For a free response of one no trump: a minimum of 8 points (and a maximum of 11 points).

The reason for the distinctions (a) and (b) under the free bid of a new suit at the two-level can be observed from the following:

Partner	Opponent	You
(a) 1 diamond	1 spade	2 clubs
(b) 1 diamond	1 spade	2 hearts

In case (a), your partner can rebid his diamonds, if he wishes, at the two-level. In case (b), if he cannot support your hearts and can only rebid diamonds, he will be pushed to the three-level. Your hand should have additional strength to cover this contingency.

Examples of Free Bids You are South, holding:

♠ x x   ♡ A Q x x x   ◇ Q x x   ♣ x x x

The bidding has begun:

North	East	South
1 spade	2 clubs	?

Your proper action is to pass. Your hand counts 8 points in high cards, less than the 10 required for a free bid in hearts, which rank lower than your partner's spades. But if the bidding had been:

North	East	South
1 club	1 diamond	?

you could freely bid one heart.

Another illustration: you are South, and the bidding has begun:

North	East	South
1 heart	1 spade	?

Your hand is one of the following:

(1)	(2)
♠ Q x x	♠ A x x
♡ x x x x	♡ x x x x
◇ A x x x	◇ A x x x
♣ x x	♣ x x

With (1) you should pass. You have only 7 points (6 in high cards plus 1 for distribution). For a free raise to two hearts, you need 8 points.

With (2), you may freely raise to two hearts, having the requisite 8 points.

When an opponent has interjected a bid, a free raise by you

should guarantee that you have a bit more than the usual 7-point minimum. In fact, the free raise of partner's suit may be made on as many as 11 points, for the responder will often have no better bid available. For example, you are South, holding:

$$
\begin{array}{lr}
\spadesuit \text{ J x x} & (1) \\
\heartsuit \text{ Q x x x} & (2+1) \\
\diamondsuit \text{ A x} & (4+1) \\
\clubsuit \text{ Q x x x} & \underline{(2)} \\
& 11
\end{array}
$$

The bidding has begun:

North	East	South
1 heart	1 spade	?

You should bid two hearts. Although this is a slight underbid of your 11-point hand, you have no good alternative.

The Free No-Trump Response You are South, holding:

♠ J 10 x ♡ x x ◇ J x x x ♣ A x x x

The bidding has begun:

North	East	South
1 heart	1 spade	?

Your proper call is pass. Had East not bid, you would properly have responded one no trump, as a courtesy-bid showing 6-10 points. But you are short of the 8 points for a free bid.

Had you held the following hand, however, a free bid no-trump response by you would have been proper.

♠ K 10 x ♡ x x ◇ J x x x ♣ A Q x x

It stands to reason that when you bid no trump over an adverse suit bid, you must have at least one stopper in that suit. Otherwise, you may find yourself in a contract at which the opponents take the first five (or more) tricks.

Specifically, the free bidder of one no trump (or two no trump or three no trump) states that he has at least the ace, K-x, Q-x-x, or J-x-x-x in the opponent's suit.

39

For example:

North	East	South	West
North	*East*	*South*	*West*
1 heart	1 spade	?	

South holds:

♠ Q 10 x   ♡ x x   ◇ K J x x   ♣ K x x x

With 9 high-card points and a stopper in spades, the opponent's bid suit, South makes a free bid of 1 no trump, knowing this will make it easy for North to gauge the value of the combined hands. With a minimum 13 points opener can pass. With 14-15 points, opener can try 2 no trumps, hoping that South has 11. With 16-plus opener can bid 3 no trumps. Any other bid by opener will tend to show a shortage in spades.

LENGTH OF THE TRUMP SUIT

"How does the partnership ascertain with accuracy that they have between them at least eight cards of a suit and can select it as trumps?"

Assuming for the moment that you are still opening four-card majors, whenever partner opens with one heart or one spade you know he has at least four of that suit. If he bids that suit for a second time, you know he has at least five. (Playing five-card majors, his rebid would announce at least six.) To illustrate:

North	East	South	West
North	*East*	*South*	*West*
1 heart	Pass	1 spade	Pass
2 hearts	Pass	2 spades	

North's opening bid told partner he had at least 13 points and at least four hearts. When, at his second opportunity, he bid two hearts, he guaranteed at least five. (Playing five-card major openings, his rebid would announce at least six.)

Likewise, when South bid one spade he guaranteed that he had at least four spades; and his rebid announced that he held at least five spades and at most two hearts.

Consider this bidding sequence:

North	East	South	West
1 club	Pass	1 diamond	Pass
1 heart	Pass	1 spade	

When North opens the bidding with one club, he is assumed to have a minimum of four clubs. South's response of one diamond, shows at least four diamonds. North now introduces the heart suit, announcing that he also has four hearts. When South then bids one spade, he says that, in addition to at least four diamonds, he also holds four spades. As yet, the partnership has not found any suit of eight or more cards; in fact, it begins to appear that the combined hands contain no such suit. In such a case, no trump will tend to become the final contract. But the initial quest will always be for a (major) suit of eight or more cards; no trump will be the last resort if the quest fails.

Suppose your partner, North, opens the bidding with one heart. East passes. You hold:

$$
\begin{array}{ll}
\spadesuit \ \text{A J x x x} & (5) \\
\heartsuit \ \text{A x x} & (4) \\
\diamondsuit \ \text{K x x} & (3) \\
\clubsuit \ \text{x x} & \underline{(1)} \\
& 13
\end{array}
$$

You say to yourself: "I have 13 points. My partner has opened the bidding, so he has at least 13 points. Between us we have the 26 points required for a game bid. But do we have an eight-card trump suit?" Over partner's one-heart bid, you bid one spade. (Don't worry that this tiny bid will cause you to miss a game; your partner is required to rebid.) Next North bids two hearts. Now you know that he has at least five hearts (six if you are playing five-card majors), so that the combined hands contain at least eight. Without further ceremony, you bid for game—four hearts.

Try another example. Your partner opens the bidding with one spade and the next hand passes. You hold:

```
♠ x x        (1)
♡ J x x x    (1)
◇ K x x      (3)
♣ A K Q x    (9)
            ——
            14
```

Once again, you say to yourself: "He has 13 points; I have 14 points; between us we have at least 27 points. We should bid a game. Now the only question is where."

You respond two clubs, showing that you have at least four clubs. Suppose that your partner next bids two hearts. Now you're all set; you know that he holds at least four hearts; you also have four; your partnership has the ideal eight of a major suit. Therefore you now contract for the game at four hearts, recognizing that the requisite points are there (with at least one extra), and that the trump suit is the proper one.

In the next example, you are South, holding:

```
♠ A K x x    (7)
♡ A K x x    (7)
◇ x x x      (0)
♣ x x        (1)
            ——
            15
```

The bidding proceeds:

North	East	South	West
1 diamond	Pass	1 spade	Pass
2 clubs	Pass	2 hearts	Pass

Suppose North now bids two no trumps. What does this show? Let us analyze the situation to bring out the logical inferences that are the essence of good bidding.

You know that North has at least four cards each in diamonds and clubs. With nine or ten cards in two suits he would have an unbalanced distribution, and would probably rebid a five-card suit in preference to proposing no trump. You also know that North does not have four cards in spades or hearts, else he would have confirmed one of your suits. The pattern of his hand is 4-4-3-2.

Thus you know that the combined hands hold no eight-card

suit. But there should be a game, since you hold 15 points opposite his minimum of 13. So your next bid is clearly indicated—three no trumps.

JUMP BIDS BY RESPONDER

A jump bid is one for more tricks than are legally necessary to overcall the last previous bid, as three hearts over one heart, two no trumps over one spade, etc. Any such bid by the responder can be warranted only by a hand of at least 13 points; it therefore says primarily, "Partner, we have a game. Keep going until we get there." In addition to a certain minimum of points, each of the various jump bids conventionally shows something about the distribution of the hand.

I. Jump Raise from One to Three This double raise states: "Partner, I have at least four supporting trumps and exactly 13-15 points. I guarantee game."

Take note that this double raise requires a minimum of four trumps; only three including a face card if partner has opened a five-card major.

On each of the following hands, your proper response is three hearts over partner's opening one-heart bid:

(1)	(2)
♠ A J x x	♠ K x x x
♡ x x x x	♡ A x x x x
♢ A Q x x	♢ K Q x
♣ x	♣ x

(1) In support of hearts, this hand is valued at 14 points: 11 in high cards, plus 3 for the singleton.

(2) In support of hearts, this hand is valued at 15 points: 12 in high cards and 3 for the singleton.

The thought may stir in your mind: "Why do I bid only three hearts when I know that we can make a game at four hearts?" Here is the explanation: for purposes of reaching a slam, the three-heart response will give the partnership more bidding space to interchange information than would an immediate jump to four hearts. To reiterate: this single-jump response cannot be passed—at least a game will always be reached. The maximum number of points for the bid is 15.

Limit Jump Raises Some play that a double-raise of partner's suit is not forcing. It shows a hand of about 11 points, including distributional values, and with a near-minimum hand partner can pass. It is never made with fewer than four good trumps.

The limit jump raise gives up the advantage of being able to set the trump suit, insist on reaching game, showing a hand of precisely 13-15 points and allowing partner to explore slam prospects below the game level if his hand warrants. In return, it affords a descriptive bid for the hand with which you would like to be more encouraging than a single raise but do not quite have the values for a game-forcing double-raise. For example:

♠ x x   ♡ A Q J x x   ◇ K x x   ♣ x x x

This hand does not warrant a double raise in hearts if you are playing forcing double raises showing 13-15 points. It also includes so much length and strength in partner's suit that the defensive value of the combined hands is decreased alarmingly; if an opponent has a singleton or a void in hearts, it will wipe out from 6 to 10 high-card points. A jump to three hearts therefore has pre-emptive value that may possibly be important.

This is not a new concept. It was a part of the original Culbertson System, but was abandoned because players found it awkward to describe hands such as:

♠ x x   ♡ A Q J x x   ◇ A Q x   ♣ x x x

Playing non-forcing limit raises, it is necessary to manufacture a forcing first response, then jump in hearts. This is done by first responding two diamonds.

II. Jump Raise to Game in a Suit   The occasion for such a leap as four hearts over one heart is an unbalanced hand that contains either a void or a singleton, very rich in trump support (usually five trumps or more), but definitely lacking in high cards and defensive tricks. *The hand should never contain more than 9 points in high cards.*

Responder believes the contract has a reasonable chance to be made; at the same time he tries to prevent the opponents from getting together. Even if the contract should go down, the loss figures to be slight, in absolute terms. But, in many cases when defeat is incurred, there is actually a relative gain. Had the opposition been able to enter the auction, they would have found a makable game or slam contract worth more to them than the small penalty they collect from you.

In short, this direct leap to game in a suit is *pre-emptive:* Here are some examples:

(1)	(2)	(3)
♠ x x x x x	♠ —	♠ x
♡ x	♡ K x x x x x	♡ x
◇ A Q x x x	◇ Q x x x x	◇ K x x x
♣ x x	♣ x x	♣ Q x x x x x x

On each of the above hands, you are the responder. On (1), partner opens with one spade; on (2), partner opens with one heart; on (3), partner opens with one club. Your response on each hand should be an immediate leap to game in partner's suit.

Don't ever make this jump to game on more than 9 points, for if you do, you may fail to arrive at a makable slam contract. With the following hand, it would be wrong to jump to four spades over partner's opening one-spade bid:

♠ Q x x x   ♡ x   ◇ A x x x   ♣ K Q x x

In support of spades, this hand is worth 15 points, 11 points being in high cards. The correct response is three spades.

III. Jump Response of Two No Trumps This bid shows 13-15 points in high cards; a balanced hand (4-4-3-2; 4-3-3-3; 5-3-3-2); and positive protection in each of the three unbid suits. Generally speaking, the bid states: "Partner, I have both the desire and the strength to play the game at three no trumps."

To illustrate, your partner opens the bidding with one spade, and you hold:

(1)	(2)	(3)
♠ x x	♠ x x	♠ Q x
♡ A J x	♡ A Q x	♡ K Q x
◇ K J x x	◇ K J x x	◇ K J x x x
♣ K Q x x	♣ A J x x	♣ K x x

On each of these hands your proper response is two no trumps.

Why do you jump to only two no trumps when you know

you can make a game? Why not jump directly to three no trumps, where you want to be?

Well, *you* might want to be in three no trumps, but perhaps your partner doesn't. Also, as you will learn immediately, the jump to three no trumps is used to show a stronger hand. The major reason for the two no-trump response is that this below-game jump gives opener the opportunity to rebid at the three-level to show an unbalanced hand, and warn against no-trump play. Responder can then decide whether to go on to three no trumps or to play the contract in opener's suit.

Suppose you held the following hand:

♠ A K x x x ♡ x ♢ A Q x x ♣ x x x

You open with one spade. Let's assume that your partner, with a balanced hand of 13-15 points, jumps to three no trumps. What would you do now?

Well, you might lift your eyes skyward in supplication, but no aid or reply would be forthcoming. And there is no answer: on Mondays, Wednesdays and Fridays, four spades might be the superior contract. On Tuesdays, Thursdays and Saturdays, three no trumps might be the only makable game.

Over responder's assumed three no-trumps bid, there simply is no room to move, no room to find out which is the superior contract. So you pass, since the burden of proof is upon you to demonstrate that ten tricks at spades will be won more easily than nine tricks at no trump.

But if your partner responds with two no trumps, you can rebid three diamonds; now partner can make a more informed decision.

You may have noticed a similarity between the jump to two no trumps and the double raise of partner's suit. Each of the bids is made on 13-15 points, and each is of course forcing to game. But the similarity ends there. The double raise of a suit always affirms at least four supporting trumps, and is usually made on an unbalanced hand. In addition, the 13-15 points almost always include distributional points. The two no-trumps response, on the other hand, denies four supporting trumps, shows a balanced hand with each of the unbid suits protected; and its 13-15 points are always in high cards exclusively.

IV. Jump to Three No Trumps over a Suit This most precise bid is made only on a hand divided 4-3-3-3, containing 16-18 points in high cards, and having protection in each of the three unbid suits. The response strongly suggests the possibility of a slam, for at the moment the bid is made responder guarantees that the combined hands have at least 29 points between them.

If partner opens with one diamond, each of the following hands calls for a response of three no trumps.

(1)	(2)	(3)
♠ A J x	♠ A Q x	♠ K Q x
♡ K J x	♡ Q J x x	♡ K Q x
◇ x x x	◇ Q x x	◇ J x x
♣ A K x x	♣ A Q x	♣ K Q J x

V. Jump Bid in a New Suit   This bid is made on a hand that contains at least 19 points, plus either a self-sustaining suit of its own or excellent support for partner's suit. Since opener has at least 13 points, the combined assets are known to be a minimum of 32 points, nearly in slam zone (33 points).

This so-called *jump-shift* response is probably the strongest single bid that responder can make, stating as it does that the partnership is no more than one point removed from a small slam. Here are some examples:

(1)	(2)	(3)
♠ x	♠ A K Q 10 x	♠ A Q x x
♡ K Q x x x	♡ x	♡ x
◇ K x x	◇ A K J x x	◇ A K x x
♣ A K J x	♣ x x	♣ K J x x

(1) Partner opens one heart. Respond with three clubs. You know that the final contract will be in partner's suit. In support of hearts, your hand is valued at 19 points: 16 in high cards plus 3 for the singleton.

(2) Partner opens one heart. Respond with two spades. Although you have no support for partner's suit, there is a distinct promise of a slam in one of your two excellent suits. (You have 17 points in high cards and 3 in distribution.)

(3) Partner opens one club. Respond with two diamonds, to tell your partner that you have at least 19 points and that either (1) you have an excellent suit of your own or (2) you love his suit. In support of his clubs, your hand is valued at

20 points (17 in high cards plus 3 points for the singleton heart in combination with four trumps).

VI. Jump Bids After Responder Has Passed Originally
These encompass the following types of situations:

(1)		(2)		(3)	
You	*Partner*	*You*	*Partner*	*You*	*Partner*
Pass	1 heart	Pass	1 diamond	Pass	1 heart
2 spades		3 clubs		2 no trump	

In each case your previous pass has denied possession of the 13 points required to open the bidding. Therefore, your jump response at your next turn tells your partner that you have *almost an opening bid*. Let us look at the following examples:

(1)		(2)		(3)	
♠ K Q x x x		♠ K J x x		♠ x x	
♡ x x x		♡ x x		♡ Q J 10 x x x	
◇ A Q x		◇ K J 10 x		◇ K x	
♣ x x		♣ K J x		♣ A x x	

You	*Partner*	*You*	*Partner*	*You*	*Partner*
Pass	1 heart	Pass	1 heart	Pass	1 club
2 spades		2 no trumps		2 hearts	

Each of these hands warrants a jump response to partner's opening bid, to inform him that you have a "maximum" pass.

When you have originally passed, and your partner subsequently opens in a suit in which you have four or more supporting cards for him, you will jump with even greater enthusiasm, since your hand will have been increased in value by virtue of his bid. For example:

(1)		(2)	
♠ x		♠ x	
♡ K x x x		♡ Q x x x	
◇ x x x x x		◇ x x x x	
♣ A K x		♣ A Q x x	

You	Partner	You	Partner
Pass	1 heart	Pass	1 heart
4 hearts		3 hearts	

(1) This hand was valued at 12 points originally, 10 in high cards and 2 for the singleton. But after partner's heart bid the hand counts 14 points: 10 in high cards, 3 for the singleton, and 1 for the promotion of the king of trumps.

When responder, after having passed originally, jumps to game, you can be assured that his hand has been transformed to the equivalent of an opening bid or better, by virtue of partner's opening bid. Observe that this is different from the weak pre-emptive type jump by a player who has not passed.

The direct jump to game is essential, for partner could and might pass a mere jump to three hearts, since he knows from your original pass that you don't have 13 points.

(2) This hand was worth 10 points when you originally passed. It is now worth 12 points in support of hearts: 8 in high cards, 3 for the singleton, and 1 for the promotion of the queen of trumps. Your jump to three hearts will inform partner that you have *almost* an opening bid in support of hearts (12 points). He will know that you don't have 13 or more points, else you would have opened the bidding or would have jumped him to four hearts. Over your three-heart response, he can determine whether to pass or to go on.

To summarize these jump bids by a responder who has previously passed: they show (a) a near-opening bid, or (b) a hand that has increased to the equivalent of an opening bid (or better) by virtue of partner's opening bid.

QUIZ

I. *The Opening Bid* You are the dealer. What do you call on each of the following hands?

(1)	(2)	(3)
♠ A J x x	♠ K J x x x	♠ A x x x x
♡ x x x	♡ A K x x x	♡ K x
◇ A J x x	◇ x x	◇ x
♣ Q x	♣ x	♣ A x x x x

(4)	(5)	(6)
♠ A Q J x	♠ A Q J x	♠ A Q J x
♡ A K J x	♡ x x	♡ x x x
◇ x x	◇ A K J x	◇ x x
♣ x x x	♣ x x x	♣ A K J x

(7)	(8)	(9)
♠ x x	♠ A K x x	♠ x x
♡ A x x x x	♡ A x x x	♡ A K Q x x
◇ A K Q x	◇ x	◇ Q x x
♣ x x	♣ Q J x x	♣ x x x

(10)	(11)	(12)
♠ Q J x x x x	♠ x x x	♠ A x
♡ x	♡ A K Q J	♡ Q x x x
◇ A K x x x x	◇ x x x	◇ Q x x x
♣ —	♣ A x x	♣ A Q x

(13)	(14)	(15)
♠ Q x x x x	♠ x x x	♠ x x x x x x
♡ K J x	♡ A K x x	♡ A K x x x
◇ x x	◇ K x	◇ A x
♣ A K x	♣ A x x x	♣ —

II. *The Response.* You are South, and the bidding has proceeded as indicated. What do you bid?

North	*East*	*South*
1 diamond	Pass	?

(1)	(2)	(3)
♠ x x	♠ x x	♠ Q x x
♡ A x x	♡ K J x x	♡ A x x
◇ x x x x	◇ A K x	◇ x x x x
♣ K x x x	♣ x x x x	♣ x x x

(4)	(5)	(6)
♠ x x x	♠ A K x x x	♠ A K Q
♡ x x x	♡ x x x	♡ x x x x x
◇ x x	◇ x x	◇ x x
♣ A K x x x	♣ x x x	♣ x x x

50

(7)	(8)	(9)
♠ x x x	♠ x x x	♠ Q J x x
♡ A J x x	♡ x x x	♡ x x x
◇ x x x	◇ A Q x	◇ x x x
♣ x x x	♣ x x x x	♣ A x x

(10)	(11)	(12)
♠ A K x x x	♠ A Q	♠ Q x x
♡ K x x	♡ K Q x x x	♡ x
◇ x x	◇ x x	◇ x x x x x
♣ K x x	♣ K Q x x	♣ Q x x x

You are South and the bidding has proceeded as follows.
What do you bid?

North	East	South
1 diamond	1 heart	?

(13)	(14)	(15)
♠ A Q x x	♠ A Q x x	♠ x x x
♡ x x x	♡ x x x	♡ K x
◇ x x	◇ x x x	◇ x x x x
♣ x x x x	♣ K x x	♣ A Q J x

(16)	(17)	(18)
♠ A K	♠ Q x x	♠ x x x
♡ x x x	♡ x x	♡ A K x
◇ J x x x	◇ x x x	◇ x x x
♣ x x x x	♣ A Q x x x	♣ x x x x

(19)	(20)	(21)
♠ K Q x x	♠ K Q x x x	♠ K Q x x x
♡ K J x	♡ Q x x x	♡ Q x x
◇ x x x	◇ x x x	◇ x
♣ A x x	♣ x	♣ A Q x x

You are South, and the bidding has proceeded as indicated.
What do you bid?

North	East	South
1 spade	2 diamonds	?

(22)	(23)	(24)
♠ x x x x	♠ J x x x	♠ x x
♡ 10 x x	♡ K x x	♡ Q x x
◇ A x	◇ K x	◇ x x x
♣ x x x x	♣ x x x x	♣ A K x x x

(25)	(26)	(27)
♠ x x	♠ A K x	♠ A K x x
♡ A K x x x	♡ x x x	♡ x x
◇ Q x x	◇ x x x	◇ x x x x
♣ x x x	♣ x x x x	♣ K x x

ANSWERS

I. *The Opening Bid*. (1) Pass. Your hand is worth but 12 points: 12 in high cards, plus one for distribution, less one for an insufficiently-guarded queen.

(2) One spade. With two five-card suits, bid the higher-ranking first.

(3) One club. This is the exception to the principle of bidding the higher-ranking of two five-card suits first. With five spades and five clubs, the spades not being rebiddable, open with one club.

(4) One club. Playing five-card majors, you may not open one heart or one spade.

(5) One diamond. Your stronger minor.

(6) One club. For the same reason as in (5).

(7) One heart. Bid the longer suit first, quality notwithstanding.

(8) One club. Four-card major bidders would also choose one club, the suit below the singleton.

(9) Pass. Your hand counts to but 12 points: 11 in high cards plus 1 for the doubleton.

(10) One spade. As with two five-card suits, so it is with two six-card suits: the higher-ranking suit should be bid first.

(11) One club. If you do not open four-card, clubs should be chosen with three-card minors of about equal strength.

(12) One diamond. The longer minor.

(13) One spade.

(14) One club. Compare with (5) and (6).

(15) One spade. The longer suit, quality notwithstanding. You will show your hearts on the next round, giving partner his choice of your two suits.

II. *The Response.* (1) Two diamonds, showing 7-10 points and adequate trump support. Your hand contains 8 points: 7 in high cards and 1 in distribution.

(2) One heart. With 11 high-card points, you intend to make a second bid later, but first show your suit.

(3) One no trump. Your hand contains but 6 points, and you need a minimum of 7 points to raise partner. (Actually in support of diamonds, your hand contains but 5 points, 1 point being deducted for a 4-3-3-3 distribution.)

(4) One no trump. You cannot name a new suit at the two-level without at least 10 points.

(5) One spade. The normal response, showing 6 points and a biddable spade suit.

(6) One heart. Any five-card suit is considered biddable.

(7) Pass. You have 5 points, less 1 for 4-3-3-3.

(8) One no trump. Do not make the mistake of raising partner's diamonds. He will expect at least 7 points, and you have but 5, deducting 1 point for a 4-3-3-3 distribution.

(9) One spade. In responding, a major suit headed by the queen or jack ten is biddable. (Q-x-x-x, J-10-x-x). Do not respond with one no trump, for in so doing, you would conceal from partner a biddable four-card spade suit.

(10) One spade. You have 14 points, and know you can make a game. Bide your time, interchange information, find the proper trump suit (or no trump) first—and then bid the game where it belongs. Partner cannot pass your "temporary" one-spade response.

(11) One heart, for the same reason as in (10). Game is a certainty—exploration will reveal where it is to be.

(12) Two diamonds, a single raise. Your hand counts to 7 points: 4 in high cards, and 3 for distribution (a singleton plus four supporting trumps).

(13) Pass. A minimum of 8 points is required to bid "freely" at the one-level.

(14) One spade. You have the requisite 8 points for a free bid.

(15) Two clubs. You have just enough, 10 points, for the

free bid at the two-level of a new suit which ranks below your partner's suit.

(16) Two diamonds. Your hand contains 10 points: 8 points in high cards, plus 1 for distribution, plus 1 for the promotion of a picture card in partner's trump suit.

(17) Pass. You have 9 points, and need a minimum of 10 to name a new suit at the two-level.

(18) Pass. You can never bid anything freely unless you have at least 8 points.

(19) One spade, with the intention of ultimately arriving at a game contract (you have 13 points). Do not make the mistake of bidding one no trump (9-11 points), since your partner could and might then pass.

(20) One spade. You have 9 points, enough to make a free bid at the one-level (7 in high cards, plus 2 for the singleton).

(21) One spade, with the intention of ultimately contracting for a game. Partner cannot pass your new-suit response.

(22) Pass. To raise partner freely you need 8 points. You have only 5 points: 4 in high cards and 1 in distribution.

(23) Two spades. You have the requisite 9 points: 7 in high cards, 1 in distribution, and 1 for the promotion of the jack of partner's trump suit.

(24) Pass. The free bid of a new suit at the three-level always requires a minimum of 11 points, as does the naming of a new suit at the two-level if that suit is higher ranking than partner's.

(25) Two hearts. Your 10 points permit a free bid since your suit ranks lower than partner's.

(26) Pass. The quality of your spades is gorgeous—but you do not have the 8 points necessary for a free raise.

(27) Two spades. You have 11 points: 10 in high cards and 1 in distribution.

Part-Score Bidding   A part-score affects the bidding in one important way: the conventional meaning of some bids is revised "for the duration," since a below-game contract will suffice to yield a game. Let us look at some examples of strategy and tactics in part-score situations.

When you have a part-score, and your partner's opening bid will not suffice to produce a game, you should go out of your way to keep the bidding open for him. To illustrate: you have a part-score of 60, and your partner opens with one heart. You hold:

(1)	(2)	(3)
♠ x x	♠ K J x x	♠ Q x x
♡ Q x x x	♡ x x	♡ x x
◇ J x x x	◇ 10 x x x	◇ Q x x x
♣ x x x	♣ 10 x x	♣ J x x x

(1) Raise to two hearts. Of course, partner will pass your response, since he knows that two hearts is "game." Admittedly, you might go down an extra trick because of your shaded raise, but the risk is worth the potential gain.

(2) Scratch up a one-spade response, since whatever rebid partner makes will put you into a game.

(3) Bid one no trump with your 5-points-that-should-have-been-6-points. You're no higher than you were at the start, and one no trump, if made, will net you a game.

Whenever you have a part-score and partner's new-suit (one-over-one, or two-over-one) response gives you enough for a game, you are under no compulsion to rebid. Suppose that you hold the following hand, you have a part-score of 60, and the bidding has proceeded as indicated.

♠ Q x x   ♡ A x x   ◇ A K x x   ♣ Q x x

You open with one diamond and:

(a) If partner responds with two clubs, you will pass.

(b) If partner responds with one heart or one spade, you will bid one no trump, since you need 40 points to make a game.

Do not make a normal conventional jump to game if a more economical non-jump bid will yield a game. For example, you have 40 on score: partner opens with one no trump and you hold:

(1)	(2)
♠ A x x	♠ A Q x x x x
♡ K x x	♡ K x x
◇ J x x	◇ x x x
♣ K x x x	♣ x

(1) Bid only two no trumps with your 11 points (instead of the normal three no trumps).

(2) Bid only two spades (instead of four) since two spades will yield a game.

Where you envision the possibility of a slam, any jump bid over the score needed to yield a game will be recognized by partner as a slam try. To illustrate: you hold the following hands and the bidding has proceeded as indicated; you have a part score of 40.

Partner		Opponent	You
1 no trump		Pass	?

(1)			(2)	
♠ A J x	(5)		♠ A x x	(4)
♡ Q x x	(2)		♡ Q x x	(2)
◇ K x x x	(3)		◇ K x x	(3)
♣ A J x	(5)		♣ A x x x	(4)
	15			13

(1) Bid three no trumps. Partner will know that this is a slam try, telling him to bid a slam if he has a maximum hand (18 points). Normally, without the part-score, you would have raised from one to four no trumps.

(2) Bid two no trumps. No slam can be made, since you have only 13 points opposite partner's 16-18 (33 being required for a small slam).

Any jump-shift bid by responder is forcing for one round, with or without a part-score. Thus, you are North with a part-score of 40 and the bidding has proceeded as indicated:

(1)	North	East	South	West
	1 heart	Pass	2 spades	Pass
	?			

(2)	1 diamond	Pass	3 clubs	Pass
	?			

In both cases you cannot pass, even though a game has been reached. If, on the next round, South either rebids his own suit, supports your suit, or bids three no trumps, you have the right to drop him. But if he again names a new suit, you must bid again, until he lets you go by not naming a new suit.

An opening bid of two in a suit is a one-round force, even if the making of the two-bid contract is sufficient for game.

If, on the second round of bidding, the original two-bidder names a new suit, responder must bid once more; if opener bids anything other than a new suit, responder can drop him. For example, you are North with a part-score of 40, and the bidding proceeds:

	South	West	North	East
(1)	*South*	*West*	*North*	*East*
	2 spades	Pass	2 no trumps	Pass
	3 spades	Pass	Pass	
(2)	2 spades	Pass	2 no trumps	Pass
	3 hearts	Pass	?	

(1) Even with a barren hand, you must make the negative two no trumps bid. You cannot pass. When partner then rebids three spades, you can pass.

(2) When South names a new suit, you *must* bid again, by rebidding three no trumps, supporting hearts or spades, or naming a new suit of your own.

Summarizing the subject of part-score bidding, let me again point out that when a part-score exists, a temporary new game goal has been created, and the bidding is now directed towards the attainment of this revised goal. The normal, conventional bids are, in these situations, withdrawn from circulation, and are superseded by the logic behind the specific situation at hand. Be aware of the score at all times, so that you'll never turn to partner in apologetic fashion, and say: "Partner, I forgot we (or 'they') had a part score."

Lesson 4

OPENING NO TRUMP BIDS AND THE RESPONSES

IF I wanted to convince somebody that bridge is a *very easy* game to play, I would begin by presenting the *no-trump opening* bids and the responses thereto. As the reader will see, this subject is the simplest to master.

"No-trump bidding" means the exploration and selection of the final contract after an original opening bid of one, two, or three *no trumps*.

In studying this lesson, the reader should never lose sight of the goals:

—26 points in the partnership hands will usually yield a game at either three no trumps or four of a major suit (29 points for five in a minor suit).

—33 points in the combined hands will usually produce a small slam.

—37 partnership points will bring a grand slam.

No-trump bidding differs from suit bidding in one important respect: when your partner opens with one in a suit, you know he has a minimum of 13 points, but his maximum is unknown— he may have 14, 15, etc. But when he opens with either one, two, or three *no trumps*, you know *exactly* what he has to *within one point!*

When he opens with one of a suit, your responses are governed by the responder's table: with 6-9 points, you make one forward-going bid; with 11-12 points, two forward-going bids; and with 13 or more points, as many bids as may be required to get to game or slam in the proper trump suit. In other words, after an opening bid of one in a suit, responder conveys information to opener; then opener conveys information to responder; then responder conveys further information to opener, etc., etc.

But when the opening bid is one, two, or three no trumps, opener tells you *not only his minimum* number of points, *but also his maximum*. So the responder's table, for purposes of no-trump bidding, is put aside. Since the opener's first bid tells you *precisely* how many points he has, you need not tell him exactly how many points you have. You can decide at once whether a game or a slam or a mere part-score can be made.

In virtually every situation where your partner has opened with either one, two, or three no trump, you, the responder, will assume captaincy of the team. You will be the one to select the final contract, whether you have a good hand or a bad hand.

In valuing a hand for an opening no-trump bid, only high cards are counted: no points are assigned for distribution. Likewise, responder's hand is valued on the basis of high cards, exclusively. However, when the responder has a "workable" five-card suit, he will add 1 point. A workable suit must be headed by at least the queen, e.g., Q-x-x-x-x. When responder has any six-card suit, he will add 2 points; with a seven-card suit, 4 points. Responder's actions will be discussed later in this lesson.

Generally speaking, then, in no-trump bidding, only high cards are assigned a point value.

THE OPENING BID OF ONE NO TRUMP

To open the bidding with one no trump, your hand must fulfill each of the following three requirements:

——The point-count must be 16-18 inclusive, in high-card strength. (Note: some bridge players prefer to use a 15-17 point one no trump opening bid. If you should happen to partner one of these individuals, just add 1 point to each of the requirements for responder's bids. For example, to raise to two no trumps, you now need 9-10 points instead of 8-9 points. Thus, since opener's bid shows one point less on the average, responder needs one point more for each possible action. Also, if you are the one no trump opener and responder makes an invitational bid, remember that 17 points is now your best possible hand, 15 points is your worst, and 16 points is in between. To illustrate, if you open with one no trumps and partner raises to two no trumps, go on to three no trumps with 16 or 17 points but pass with 15 points.)

——The hand must be of balanced distribution, namely 4-3-3-3; or 4-4-3-2; or 5-3-3-2. (Put in negative fashion: no voids, no singletons, and no two doubletons.)

——At least three suits must have positive protection (A-x, K-x, Q-x-x, or J-x-x-x); and the fourth suit should be no worse than Q-x or x-x-x.

Flaws and Plus Values When counting the value of your hand for no trump openings, *deduct* one point each for any of the following flaws:

—Unstopped suit
—Insufficiently guarded honor(s)
—No aces
—Fewer than six honor cards

Add one point each for:

—All four aces
—A five-card suit including four honors (A K J 10 x, K Q J 10 x, etc.)

Whenever your hand counts to *more* than 18 points, either by adding for these plus values or by counting a distributional point for a doubleton, prefer to open with one in a suit.

On the following hands, one no trump is the proper opening bid:

(1)		(2)		(3)	
♠ K J x	(4)	♠ Q J x x	(3)	♠ A Q x	(6)
♡ A Q x	(6)	♡ K x	(3)	♡ A x	(4)
◇ J x x x	(1)	◇ A K x	(7)	◇ A J x x x	(5)
♣ A J x	(5)	♣ A x x x	(4)	♣ Q 10 x	(2)
	16		17		17

(4)		(5)		(6)	
♠ Q x	(1)	♠ x x x	(−1)	♠ Q x	(1)
♡ A J x x	(5)	♡ A K Q x	(9)	♡ K x x	(3)
◇ K Q x x	(5)	◇ A J x	(5)	◇ A Q x x	(6)
♣ A Q x	(6)	♣ K J x	(4)	♣ A Q x x	(6)
	17		17		16

In hands (4), (5), and (6), note that the spade suit is unprotected. This is acceptable, since the other three suits are fully protected. In hands (4) and (6), deductions have been made

for the insufficiently-guarded honors. Do not deduct for a second flaw in the same suit.

The following hands should NOT be opened with one no trump:

(1)		(2)		(3)	
♠ A J x x	(5)	♠ A K x x	(7)	♠ A x x	(4)
♡ A Q x	(6)	♡ A K J x	(8)	♡ A J x x x x	(5)
◇ K x x	(3)	◇ Q x	(1)	◇ A x	(4)
♣ A J x	(5)	♣ x x x	(−1)	♣ K x	(3)
	19		15		16

(1) This hand contains 19 points, and so is outside the range of the 16-18 points fixed for a one no-trump opening bid.

(2) This hand does not have three suits fully protected (the diamonds and the clubs being unguarded).

(3) This hand, though it has the requisite high-card points and all suits protected, is unbalanced (6-3-2-2). The proper opening bid is one heart.

RESPONSES TO AN OPENING BID OF ONE NO TRUMP

To repeat: whether responder has a good hand or a bad hand, he will usually become the captain of the partnership. He is in position to sum up the joint assets, by adding his points to those which the opening bidder has announced. If the total reaches 26, he will bid a game; if 33, a small slam; if 37, a grand slam.

Note well: Responder will count all high cards at *full face value*. No reduction is made for singleton or insufficiently guarded picture cards, e.g., singleton king counts 3, Q-x counts 2, and so on.

I. Responses with Balanced Hands Holding a balanced hand (no void, no singleton, no two doubletons) opposite your partner's opening bid of one no trump, raise him (or pass) according to the following scale:*

—With 7 or fewer points, pass.

—With 8 or 9 points, bid two no trumps.

—With 10-14 points, bid three no trumps.

---

* However, see "Conventional Club Response (Stayman)" Page 76.

—With 15 or 16 points, bid four no trumps.

—With 17 or 18 points, bid six no trumps.

—With 19 or 20 points, an immediate bid of six no trumps is not quite adequate. First jump to three in your longest suit, and follow up with a leap to six no trumps. Your partner will then bid a grand slam if he holds a maximum hand.

—With 21 or more points, bid seven no trumps.

Let us look at some illustrations. You hold each of the following hands, and your partner has opened the bidding with one no trump.

(1)	(2)	(3)
♠ x x x	♠ x x x	♠ A x x
♡ K x x	♡ K x x	♡ Q x x
◇ K J x x	◇ K J x x x	◇ Q x x
♣ x x x	♣ x x	♣ J x x x

(4)	(5)	(6)
♠ A x x	♠ A x x	♠ Q x
♡ K x x	♡ J x x	♡ K Q x
◇ Q x x x	◇ K Q x	◇ A x x x
♣ J x x	♣ K x x x	♣ A x x x

(7)	(8)	(9)
♠ A Q x	♠ K Q x	♠ A K x
♡ K x x	♡ A J	♡ A J x
◇ A x x	◇ A J x x x	◇ A Q x
♣ K J x x	♣ K J x	♣ Q x x x

(10)	(11)	(12)
♠ A Q x	♠ x x x	♠ Q x x
♡ K J x x	♡ x x x	♡ Q J x
◇ A K x x	◇ A J x x x	◇ Q x x
♣ A J	♣ x x	♣ Q x x x

(1) Pass. You have 7 points opposite partner's 16-18. You know it is impossible for the partnership to have more than 25 points, even if partner has a maximum hand. Game is out of the question.

(2) Raise to two no trumps. You have 8 points: 7 high-card points, plus 1 point for a "workable" five-card suit. In such situations, the fifth card of your workable suit is likely to develop into a winning trick.

(3) Bid two no trumps, which opener will carry to three if he has more than absolute minimum (that is, if he has 17 or 18 points).

(4) Bid three no trumps. Your 10 points, added to partner's guaranteed minimum of 16, counts up to 26 points.

(5) Bid three no trumps. Partner's maximum is 18 points. You have 13. The total can never reach to the 33 points needed for a small slam.

(6) Bid four no trumps. If opener holds a maximum hand (18 points), he will bid six (33 points in the combined hands). If opener passes, four no trumps will easily be fulfilled, since the combined hands can have no fewer than 31 points.

(7) Bid six no trumps. You have 17 points, partner has 16-18. A small slam is assured (33 points); a grand slam is impossible, since the combined assets cannot reach 37.

(8) Jump to three diamonds first, then leap to six no trumps on your rebid. If partner has 18 points, he will bid the grand slam.

(9) Jump to three clubs first, then six no trumps.

(10) Bid seven no trumps. Your 22 points opposite partner's 16-18 guarantee a grand slam. It is impossible for the opponents to have more than 2 points: either one queen or two jacks.

(11) Pass. Game is out of the question: you have only 6 points opposite partner's maximum of 18.

(12) Bid two no trumps. You have 9 points, and if partner has more than a bare minimum, he will accept your invitation to game, and will bid three no trumps. When responder raises to two no trumps (on 8 or 9 points), he relinquishes captaincy of the team. He does not know whether or not a game can be made: it all depends on whether opener has just 16 points, or 17-18 points.

You may be disturbed by what seems to be an unmathematical twist in the above: that if responder raises to two no trumps on 8 or 9, and opener accepts the invitation by bidding three on 17 or 18, then the partnership may find itself in game with only 25 points (17 + 8).

Admittedly, this will happen on occasion, but the partnership will still have an excellent chance to fulfill the contract. As a matter of fact, the expert player is guided in all bidding sequences by the experience-proven tenet: "Whenever the combined hands contain *at least* 25 points, with a positive chance that they may well contain more, a game should be bid." If the "uncertain-of-26 points" bidder were always to pass, he would lose thousands of points in the long run. The policy of "taking a chance" and bidding the close games, making approximately half of them and being defeated on half, gains on net.

But please note: *don't* go setting 25 points as your new goal! It is still, and always will be, 26 points.

II. Responses with Unbalanced Hands   If your partner opens with one no trump and you have an unbalanced hand (a void, a singleton, or two doubletons), your natural inclination is to bid a suit rather than raise the no trump. Certainly this is your proper course if your suit is a major and you are strong enough to insist on game (10 points or more). But when your suit is a minor, generally raise the no-trump rather than bid it, if your hand is not too unbalanced.

Remember that responder adds one point for a "workable" five-card suit (Q-x-x-x-x); he adds 2 points for a six-card suit; 4 points for a seven-card suit.

An important caution: never respond with two of a suit if your hand contains 8 or more points, for any suit response in the two-level begs opener to pass.* The responses of two diamonds, two hearts, and two spades are made on hands of 7 or fewer points, and assert that the combined hands cannot contain 26 points.

Your partner opens with one no trump, next hand passes, and you hold:

(1)			(2)	
♠ A x x	(4)		♠ x x	(0)
♡ x x	(0)		♡ J x	(1)
◇ K J x x x x	(4 + 2)		◇ x x x	(0)
♣ x x	(0)		♣ A Q J x x x	(7 + 2)
	10			10

(3)	
♠ x x	(0)
♡ x x	(0)
◇ x x	(0)
♣ A Q x x x x x	(6 + 4)
	10

---

* A two-club response over one no trump, as used by many players, has an artificial meaning, explained later in this lesson.

65

On each of the above hands, your proper response is to bid three no trumps. Do not make the mistake of bidding two or your suit—partner has the right to pass. Nor should you jump to five diamonds on hand (1) or five clubs on hands (2) and (3). Remember that 29 points are needed to win eleven tricks; these uneconomical contracts should never be undertaken except as a last resort, when all else has failed.

Partner opens with one no trump and you hold:

(1)	(2)	(3)
♠ x	♠ x	♠ x x x x x
♡ x x x x x x	♡ x x	♡ —
◇ x x x	◇ J x x x x x x	◇ x x x x x
♣ x x x	♣ x x x	♣ x x x

(4)	(5)	(6)
♠ x x x	♠ Q x x x x	♠ —
♡ x	♡ x	♡ Q x x x
◇ K Q J x x	◇ x x x x	◇ x x x x x
♣ K x x x	♣ x x x	♣ x x x x

(1) Bid two hearts, which opener will usually pass. A response of two in a suit (except clubs) over one no trump shows less than 7 points—and the hand may contain no high-card points whatsoever. At no trump, hand (1) will probably not take a trick. At hearts, it will probably add two or three tricks to partner's high-card tricks.

(2) Bid two diamonds, at which contract your diamonds will produce anywhere from four to seven tricks.

(3) Bid either two diamonds or two spades—but bid one of them! Don't pass one no trump, at which contract your hand is utterly useless. Which suit to bid is an out-and-out guess, so the recommended course is to bid two spades, which will give your side more points below the line if the contract is fulfilled, and will have a better chance to shut out opponent's heart suit.

(4) Bid three no trumps. You have 10 points, and partner has at least 16. Do not run the risk of bidding two diamonds, which partner will probably pass.

(5) Bid two spades—it will be the best possible contract.

(6) Bid two diamonds, showing your "weakness" (7 or fewer points).

As stated previously, a response of two diamonds, two hearts, or two spades over one no trump denies the point-count needed to produce a game. The logic behind these responses should be evident from the preceding illustrations: why play a doomed-to-defeat one no-trump contract when it is perfectly apparent that two of a suit will be a superior contract?

The two-of-a-suit response serves as a danger-signal to opener, and he must usually heed the signal by passing. But, in a certain situation, opener is permitted to proceed with caution: he may raise responder to the three-level in responder's suit. Opener will make this single-raise only if he holds a maximum hand of 18 points AND an excellent fit in responder's suit, specifically, at least two of the three top cards (A-K-x, A-Q-x, or K-Q-x*). Responder may, of course, pass this raise to the three-level, but on occasion he will have a hand with which he might gamble a three no-trump bid, in the knowledge that his suit has been consolidated. For example:

North
♠ A x x
♡ A x x
◇ A K x
♣ Q J x x

West
♠ Q x x x x
♡ J x x x
◇ x
♣ A K x

East
♠ K J x x x
♡ Q x x
◇ J x x
♣ x x

South
♠ —
♡ K x x
◇ Q 10 x x x x
♣ x x x x

North	East	South	West
1 no trump	Pass	2 diamonds (a)	Pass
3 diamonds (b)	Pass	3 no trumps (c)	

---

* The high-card trump support must always be accompanied by a little card in a suit, to use as an entry to the responder's hand. See the illustration which follows.

(a) Denying more than 7 points, and expressing the desire to play the hand at two diamonds.*

(b) Announcing 18 points and at least two of the three top diamonds (accompanied by a small diamond).

(c) South knows that North has at least the A-K-x of diamonds; on the proper assumption that six diamond tricks will be won, South gambles three no trumps with the hope that three more tricks will be made in the other three suits.

III. Jumps to Four Hearts or Four Spades This is a shut-out bid—opener must pass. The bid is made on an unbalanced hand, containing a suit of at least six-card length, and no more than 9 points in high cards. To make this jump with more than 9 high-card points risks missing a makable slam.

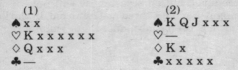

```
        (1)                        (2)
  ♠ x x                      ♠ K Q J x x x
  ♡ K x x x x x x            ♡ —
  ◇ Q x x                    ◇ K x
  ♣ —                        ♣ x x x x x
```

(1) Bid four hearts. Deficient as is the hand in points, at least six trump tricks should be won, and the Q-x-x-x of diamonds will tend to consolidate partner's diamond holding.

(2) Bid four spades. The spade suit should be absolutely solid, since partner figures to have the spade ace, and the five clubs should prove a strong asset with partner's top cards.

IV. Jumps to Three of a Suit This bid is made on a five-card or longer suit, with at least 10 points in the hand. It guarantees a game, with slam possibilities. The jump asserts a positive desire to play the final contract in that suit. Here are some illustrations:

```
     (1)                 (2)                  (3)
 ♠ Q x x          ♠ K J x x x x       ♠ x x
 ♡ A K x x x x    ♡ A x x             ♡ A J x x
 ◇ x x            ◇ J x               ◇ A Q J x x x
 ♣ x x            ♣ Q x               ♣ x

 Bid 3 hearts     Bid 3 spades        Bid 3 diamonds
```

Over the jump bid, the opener should (a) raise that suit, if

—————————
* Exception: "Two-way" Stayman. See page 90.

68

he has more than minimum support for it; or (b) bid three no trumps. To illustrate:

You have opened the bidding with one no trump, and your partner has responded with three hearts. You hold:

(1)	(2)	(3)
♠ K J x	♠ Q x	♠ K x x
♡ Q x	♡ K J x	♡ A Q
◇ A J x x	◇ A J x x	◇ A x x x
♣ A Q x x	♣ A Q x x	♣ A x x x

(1) Bid three no trumps. You have "sub-minimum" support in hearts.

(2) Bid four hearts. You have more support than your partner could have expected you to have.

(3) Bid four hearts.

REBIDS BY THE OPENING NO-TRUMP BIDDER

The opening no-trump bidder should bear in mind that his first call almost completely describes his hand in terms of points, distribution, and "protection." Responder knows within 1 point what opener holds. Consequently, opener should not take aggressive action in rebidding, unless invited to do so by responder.

The situations where opener *must pass* are as follows:

——When responder jumps to three no trumps.

——When responder jumps to game in a suit.

——When responder raises to two no trumps and opener has exactly 16 points.

——When responder bids two diamonds, hearts, or spades, and opener has 16 or 17 points. However, with 18 points *and* excellent trump support (A-K-x, A-Q-x, K-Q-x) opener may raise responder's suit to three.

——When responder jumps to four no trumps (15 or 16 points) and opener has a minimum hand. With a maximum hand, opener should bid six no trumps.

——When responder jumps to three of a suit, and follows up with six no trumps, opener passes with 16 or 17. If opener has 18, he should bid seven no trumps.

THE OPENING BID OF TWO NO TRUMPS

For an opening bid of two no trumps, your hand must fulfill all these requirements:

——The point-count must be 22-24 in high cards.

——All suits must have positive protection (at least A-x, K-x, Q-x-x, or J-x-x-x).

——The hand must be balanced (4-3-3-3; 4-4-3-2; or 5-3-3-2).

Two no trumps is the correct opening bid on the three following hands:

(1)	(2)	(3)
♠ A Q x	♠ K x	♠ A K J
♡ A J x	♡ A Q x x	♡ K J x
♢ K Q x x	♢ A Q J x	♢ A Q
♣ A K x	♣ A Q J	♣ A J x x x

RESPONSES TO TWO NO TRUMPS

Note well: Any suit response over two no trumps is forcing to game—opener cannot pass.

Responses with Balanced Hands With a balanced hand, respond as follows:

—With fewer than 4 points, pass.

—With 4-8 points, bid three no trumps. (A small slam is out of the question. Opener has at most 24 points. Even if you have 8 points, the combined total cannot possibly exceed 32 points.)

—With 9 points, raise to four no trumps. If partner has a maximum two no-trumps bid (24), he will bid six no trumps.

—With 10 points, first bid three of your longest suit, then raise to four no trumps. This procedure shows a stronger hand than does the immediate raise to four no trumps.

—With 11 or 12 points, bid six no trumps. Since partner has a minimum of 22 points for his bid, a small slam is sure (33); at the same time, you know that a grand slam (37) cannot be made.

—With 13 or 14 points, first bid a suit and then jump to six no trumps. This is stronger than bidding six no trumps directly.

The former sequence commands opener to bid the grand slam if he has a maximum hand.

—With 15 or more points, bid a grand slam.

To illustrate the above. Partner opens with two no trumps and you hold:

(1)		(2)		(3)	
♠ K x x	(3)	♠ K x x	(3)	♠ K x x	(3)
♡ x x x	(0)	♡ x x	(0)	♡ K x x	(3)
◇ J x x x	(1)	◇ K J x x x	(4 + 1)	◇ Q x x x	(2)
♣ x x x	(0)	♣ x x x	(0)	♣ J x x	(1)
	4		8		9

(4)		(5)		(6)	
♠ K x	(3)	♠ K x x	(3)	♠ A x	(4)
♡ K x x	(3)	♡ K x	(3)	♡ Q x x	(2)
◇ K x x x	(3)	◇ K x x x	(3)	◇ K x x x	(3)
♣ J x x x	(1)	♣ Q x x x	(2)	♣ A x x x	(4)
	10		11		13

(7)	
♠ K Q x	(5)
♡ A x x	(4)
◇ Q J x x	(3)
♣ K x x	(3)
	15

(1) Bid three no trumps.

(2) Bid three no trumps. With your 8 points opposite partner's maximum of 24, the combined hands cannot total the 33 required for a small slam. Do not bid three diamonds, for nothing can be gained by bidding the suit and something might be lost—the bid might elicit a four-diamond rebid by opener, bypassing the chance to play for game at three no trumps.

(3) Bid four no trumps, showing 9 points. If partner has a maximum hand, he will bid six no trumps.

(4) Bid three diamonds, then four no trumps on your rebid. Partner will then know that you have 10 points, and with 23 or 24 he will bid six no trumps.

(5) Bid six no trumps.

(6) Bid three clubs (or three diamonds), then jump to six no

71

trumps on your rebid. Opener with then know you have 13 or 14 points, and if he has a maximum hand he will bid seven no trumps.

7) Bid seven no trumps. The combined partnership hands have at least 37 points.

Responses with Unbalanced Hands   With an unbalanced hand, respond to partner's opening bid of two no trumps as follows:

——With a five-card major suit, headed by any honor (A, K, Q, or J), and at least 3 points in high cards, bid that major suit.

——Bid any six-card major suit at the three-level, regardless of the point-count of your hand.

——With a five- or six-card minor suit, if the hand contains but 3-7 points, bid three no trumps.

——Jump to four in a major suit with a good six-card suit and a hand containing about 7-8 points in high cards. Here are some examples of the above:

(1)	(2)	(3)
♠ K x x x x	♠ x	♠ Q x x x x x
♡ x	♡ A x x x x	♡ x x x
◇ x x x x	◇ x x x x	◇ x x
♣ Q x x	♣ x x x	♣ x x

(4)	(5)	(6)
♠ x x	♠ x x	♠ A Q J x x x
♡ Q x x	♡ x x x	♡ x
◇ Q x x x x x	◇ A J x x x x	◇ x x x
♣ x x	♣ x x	♣ x x x

(1) Bid three spades, which is forcing to game (partner is not permitted to pass any suit response at the three-level). Opener will then take over by bidding either four spades or three no trumps; and whichever bid he makes you will pass.

(2) Bid three hearts, for the same reasons as above.

(3) Bid three spades. If opener raises to four, you will pass. If opener bids three no trumps, rebid four spades, since your hand may produce no tricks at no trump but is a cinch to yield at least four tricks at a spade contract. Partner will know, if you insist on four spades, that you don't have a good hand, else you would have jumped directly to four spades. Compare hand (6).

(4) Bid three no trumps, with a figurative shrug of the shoulders. A try for a minor-suit game (11 tricks) is not warranted on your meager holdings. A better gamble is to indulge in the wishful thinking that at three no trumps partner will be able to establish and cash your diamond suit.

(5) Bid three no trumps, on the same logic as in (4).

(6) Bid four spades, informing partner that you have a very good spade suit (of at least six cards), and 7-8 high-card points. With this knowledge, he may be able to contract for a small slam, as for example if he holds:

♠ K x x   ♡ A K x   ◇ A K x x   ♣ A K x

THE OPENING BID OF THREE NO TRUMPS

The requirements for the bid are:
——25-27 points in high cards.
——Balanced distribution (4-3-3-3; 4-4-3-2; 5-3-3-2).
——All suits protected (A-x, K-x, Q-x-x, or J-x-x-x). Examples of the opening bid of three no trumps:

♠ A Q x	♠ K J x	♠ A K x
♡ K Q x	♡ A Q x x	♡ A K J
◇ A K J x	◇ A K Q x	◇ A J x x x
♣ A K x	♣ A K	♣ A Q

The reader may think the above hands unrealistic. He is right: they are not everyday, run-of-the-mill hands. They are tremendous hands *by definition:* 25-27 points. Looking at it another way, opener says he has enough to make a game all by himself.

RESPONSES TO THREE NO TRUMPS

In responding to three no trumps, any bid is an invitation to a slam. The following is the responder's guide:
——With 7 points and no workable five-card suit, raise to four no trumps.
——With 7 points and a workable five-card suit (Q-x-x-x-x or better), raise to five no trumps.
——With 8 or 9 points, jump to six no trumps.

——With 10 or 11 points, bid four diamonds* and on your rebid follow up with a jump to six no trumps. Opener will then bid seven if he has a maximum hand.

——With 12 or more points, bid seven no trumps.

Let us look at some examples. You hold the following hands, and partner has opened with three no trumps.

(1)	(2)	(3)
♠ Q x x	♠ K x x	♠ K x x
♡ K x x	♡ K J x x x	♡ K x x
◇ Q x x x	◇ x x	◇ Q x x
♣ x x x	♣ x x x	♣ x x x x

(4)	(5)	(6)
♠ K x x	♠ A J x	♠ A J x
♡ A x x	♡ Q x	♡ Q x x
◇ J x x	◇ K x x x	◇ K Q x
♣ Q x x x	♣ Q x x x	♣ K x x x

(1) Bid four no trumps (7 points).

(2) Bid five no trumps (7 points and a workable five-card suit).

(3) Bid six no trumps.

(4) Bid four diamonds (artificially) and follow up with a jump to six no trumps, thereby showing 10 or 11 points.

(5) Bid seven no trumps.

(6) Bid seven no trumps.

HANDS OF 19-21 POINTS

In terms of the high-card point-count, the opening no-trump bids show the following: one no trump, 16-18 points; two no trumps, 22-24; three no trumps, 25-27. You will notice that the continuity of points from 16 to 27 is broken by the absence of 19, 20, and 21. You may have wondered what one bids with balanced hands that have all suits protected, but have 19-21 points. For example:

---

* The four-diamond bid is artificial. Four of a major suit cannot be bid, since opener has the right to pass this game bid. Nor can four clubs ever be bid, since this bid originates a convention discussed later. (Gerber Four-club Convention.)

```
♠ A J x        (5)
♡ K Q x        (5)
◇ K J x        (4)
♣ A Q x x      (6)
              ────
               20
```

Such a hand cannot be opened with one no trump, for it is too good; nor with two no trumps, for it is not good enough; nor with 1½ no trumps, for that is illegal.

The way to deal with such hands 19-21 is to open with a bid of one in the longest suit (one club in the above hand). After partner responds, jump to either two or three no trumps. The distinction is as follows:

——When opener's hand contains 19 or 20 points, his rebid is two no trumps.

——When opener's hand contains 21 points, his rebid is three no trumps.

The jump rebid to two no trumps will be passed by responder only if his hand contains fewer than 6 high-card points. The jump to three no trumps, on 21 points, speaks for itself: even if responder had only 5 high-card points, the partnership will have the 26 points required for game.

Here are three examples of these 19-21 point hands:

```
     (1)              (2)              (3)
♠ A Q x          ♠ A J x          ♠ A Q J
♡ A Q x          ♡ A K x          ♡ A Q x
◇ K J x x        ◇ K Q x          ◇ K J x
♣ K x x          ♣ Q J x x        ♣ A x x x
```

(1) One diamond is the proper opening bid, to be followed up with a jump to two no trumps, which responder will carry to game if he has at least 6 high-card points.

(2) One club is the proper opening bid, to be followed up with a jump to two no trumps.

(3) One club is the correct bid. Whatever partner's non-jump response happens to be, opener will then jump to three no trumps, showing 21 points.

The point-count range for opening hands of the no-trump family is now complete, with no break:

16-18 points, one no trump.

19-20 points, one of a suit, followed by a jump to two no trumps.

21 points, one of a suit followed by a jump to three no trumps.

22-24 points, two no trumps.

25-27 points, three no trumps.

A no-trump type hand with 28 or more points should be opened with either a two-bid in a suit, or the less frequent opening bid of four no trumps, which shows 28-29 points. The powerhouse bid of two in a suit is discussed in Lesson 6.

THE STAYMAN CONVENTION

The universal employment of the "Stayman convention" arises from the demonstrated fact that, when the partnership has eight or more cards of a major suit, the superior final contract is in that suit, as opposed to no trump.

Hence, whenever the responder to an opening one no trump is unable to bid a major suit, but sees that the partnership may have a major suit of eight or more cards between them, he initiates the quest by bidding *two clubs*.

This two-club bid means absolutely nothing with respect to responder's club suit—he may have no clubs whatsoever. It says to opener: "Partner, if you have a four-card (or five-card) major suit, headed by the queen or better, please bid it!"

If opener holds neither four spades nor four hearts he rebids with *two diamonds*, artificially. This two-diamond rebid says nothing about the suit itself: opener may have two, three, four or five diamonds.

The following is an illustration of these artificial bids:

North	East	South	West
1 no trump	Pass	2 clubs (a)	Pass
2 diamonds (b)			

(a) "Partner, I'm interested in getting together in a major suit. If you have a biddable spade suit or a biddable heart suit, please bid that suit."

(b) "I have no biddable major suit."

If the opening bidder happens to have two four-card major suits, he first bids the spades, and, if it is expedient to do so, he shows the hearts later. Consequently, if the opener's first rebid is two hearts, he denies having a biddable spade suit;

but if his rebid is two spades, it does not rule out a biddable heart suit.

To bid two clubs, the responder must hold at least 8 points. That is, he must have a hand with which, were the convention not employed, he could have bid at least two no trumps. Naturally, if responder does not have at least four spades or four hearts, he will not employ the two-club bid.

Your partner opens with one no trump and you hold:

(1)	(2)	(3)
♠ Q J x x	♠ K Q x x	♠ A K x x
♡ K x x x	♡ K Q x x	♡ x x
◊ A x x x	◊ x x	◊ K x x x
♣ x	♣ x x x	♣ x x x

(1) Bid two clubs. If partner rebids two spades, or two hearts, you will raise him to four; if he rebids two diamonds, you will bid three no trumps.

(2) Bid two clubs. As in (1), if opener bids either spades or hearts, you will raise him to game in his suit. And if he rebids two diamonds, you will jump to three no trumps.

(3) Bid two clubs. If opener bids two spades, you will raise him to four; if he bids two hearts or two diamonds, you will jump to three no trumps.

(4)	(5)	(6)
♠ A x x x	♠ K J x x	♠ A Q x x
♡ A x x x	♡ K J x x	♡ x x
◊ J x x x	◊ x x	◊ Q x x x
♣ x	♣ x x x	♣ x x x

The above hands are, without the use of the two-club convention, normal raises of one no trump to two (8 or 9 points). With the convention, two clubs is the correct bid on each of them.

(4) If, over two clubs, opener bids two spades or hearts, you will raise to four. Although you have but 8 points in high cards, the four supporting trumps and a singleton give you 3 additional distributional points. The total value is therefore 11 points. If, over two clubs, opener bids two diamonds, you will now bid two no trumps, the same bid you would have made originally had the convention not been employed. Opener

will know you have exactly 8 or 9 points, since with 10 or more you would have leaped to three no trumps on your rebid.

(5) If opener, over two clubs, bids spades or hearts, you will raise to three. Your hand is worth 9 points, having 1 distributional point for four supporting trumps and a singleton. Again, opener will know (a) that you "like" the major and (b) that you have exactly 8 or 9 points. If over two clubs, opener bids two diamonds, you will bid two no trumps, informing him that you have 8-9 points, and leaving the final decision to him.

(6) If, over two clubs, opener bids two spades, you raise him to three. Your hand is worth 9 points in support of spades. If, over two clubs, opener bids two hearts, you will bid two no trumps, knowing that opener cannot have a biddable spade suit (else he would have bid spades first). If opener bids two diamonds over two clubs, the spade suit is similarly forgotten, and you will bid two no trumps.

With *none* of the following hands should the response of two clubs be made, since responder has no interest (or ability) to play the final contract in a major suit.

(1)	(2)	(3)
♠ x x x	♠ K x	♠ A x x
♡ x x	♡ K x x	♡ Q x x
◇ A Q x x	◇ K x x x	◇ Q J x
♣ A x x x	♣ J x x x	♣ x x x x

(1) Bid three no trumps.
(2) Bid three no trumps.
(3) Bid two no trumps.

As is apparent, whenever responder has neither four or more spades, nor four or more hearts, he will make the same bid he would have made before learning the two-club conventional bid.

Opener's Rebid Let us now look at a few examples of how the opener handles the artificial response of two clubs. Opener bids one no trump on each of the following hands, and partner responds with two clubs.

(1)	(2)	(3)
♠ A K x	♠ A x x	♠ K J x
♡ K x x	♡ K x x	♡ K J x
◇ K x x	◇ K x x	◇ A x
♣ A J x x	♣ A Q x x	♣ A J x x x

(4)	(5)	(6)
♠ A Q x x	♠ A Q x x	♠ K x x
♡ A x x	♡ K J x x	♡ K J x x
◇ K x x	◇ K x	◇ A J x
♣ A J x	♣ K x x	♣ A x x

(7)	(8)
♠ K x	♠ A Q x x
♡ K J x x	♡ K J x x
◇ A J x	◇ A x
♣ A Q x x	♣ K J x

(1) Bid two diamonds, denying a four-card or longer major suit. If responder then bids two no trumps, you carry on to three (as you would have done had he bid two no trumps directly over your one).

(2) Bid two diamonds, for the same reason as in (1). If responder then bids two no trumps, you will pass, just as you would have passed a direct raise to two no trumps.

(3) Bid two diamonds. Don't become enamoured with your club support and forget that the two-club was conventional. Responder is not interested in clubs. If, over two diamonds, responder bids two no trumps, go to three.

(4) Bid two spades. If responder then bids four spades, you automatically pass; if he bids three spades, you bid four with your maximum hand; if he bids two no trumps, bid three no trumps.

(5) Bid two spades. If he bids three spades, you will pass; if he bids two no trumps, you will pass, just as you would pass a direct raise to two no trumps.

(6) Bid two hearts. You will then pass his next bid of either three hearts or two no trumps.

(7) Bid two hearts. If partner raises to three, you will bid four; if partner, instead, bids two no trumps, you will carry on to three no trumps.

(8) Bid two spades, knowing that you have a game somewhere (you have 18; partner has at least 8). If partner raises to three spades you, of course, bid four; if he bids two no trumps, you should bid *four* hearts. If you bid only three hearts, he has the right to pass—which right you shouldn't give him since you know you belong in a four-heart contract. Similarly, if over your two-spade bid, he bids three no trumps, you should

79

bid four hearts, knowing that his denial of spades must simultaneously be an affirmation of hearts.

Further Uses of the Stayman Convention   You may have noticed that, in every example thus far presented, the opening no-trump bidder has become the declarer. It will usually be thus, for the two-club response asks opener to name his major suit; responder then raises or else returns to no trump. If the opener bids a major suit which responder fails to raise, responder may bid the other major only if he holds five or more cards in it. Responder's denial of opener's first major acknowledges that responder has the other. So, if the opener happens to have both major suits, over responder's denial of his first major suit, opener can always name his second, recognizing in advance that responder must like it (else he would not have bid two clubs).

There are circumstances, however, when *responder* becomes the declarer after the conventional two-club response. These circumstances will arise when responder has a *five-card* major suit. Let me introduce this situation by presenting you with a problem. As opener, you hold the following hand:

♠ A J x   ♡ A x x   ◇ K Q x x   ♣ A x x

You open with one no trump. Partner responds with two clubs, asking you to name a biddable major suit. You bid two diamonds, denying both hearts and spades. Suppose your partner bids two spades. Now what do you say?

Your proper bid is four spades! First, you know you have a game, since responder's two-club response indicated a minimum of 8 points. Secondly, your two-diamond rebid denied both majors. Would responder bid two spades, holding only four spades, when he already knows you don't have four spades? Obviously not. Therefore, he must have *at least five spades*. You have the best you could be expected to have both in spades and in points. Consequently, four spades becomes your bid. His hand might have been:

♠ K x x x x   ♡ x   ◇ A J x x   ♣ x x x

The practical significance of the two-club convention can be seen from the above bidding sequence. Without the convention, you might have arrived at the distinctly inferior contract of three no trumps. Against no trump, either a heart or a club opening lead by the opponents would place the contract in distinct jeopardy.

The use of this convention does not affect the normal jump responses to one no trump. Holding:

♠ x ♡ A Q x x x ◇ x x x ♣ A Q x x

the correct response is a jump to three hearts, which is forcing to game. With the above type of hand (game being assured), nothing can be gained by employing the two-club convention. But where responder has a hand of moderate strength, including a decent five-card suit, he is often in a dilemma. To respond with two spades or hearts proclaims weakness; to bid two no trumps abandons the possible eight-card major. The two-club convention provides a way out. He first bids two clubs, then (if opener's response was two diamonds) shows his five-card major suit.

For example, responder holds:

♠ K x x ♡ K Q x x x ◇ x x x x ♣ x

After the opening one no-trump bid, responder cannot be sure of the proper final contract—it may be in no trump or it may be in spades. Responder therefore bids two clubs, forcing opener to bid. If opener rebids two diamonds (denying a four-card major suit), responder now bids two hearts. *This bid is not forcing.* If opener has a minimum 16-point hand, a pass is in order. However, the opening no-trump bidder should strive to keep the bidding open by bidding either two no trumps or, preferably, by raising partner's suit to the three-level if opener has three cards of partner's suit. The raise to three of partner's suit or to two no trumps should be made with a hand that contains 17 points. With 18 points, opener should jump to game in either partner's suit or in no trump, since 26 points are guaranteed.

To illustrate, the bidding has proceeded:

You	Partner
1 no trump	2 clubs
2 diamonds	2 hearts
?	

(1)	(2)	(3)	(4)
♠ A x x	♠ A x x	♠ A x x	♠ A J x
♡ K x	♡ K x x	♡ K J x	♡ K x
◇ K J x x	◇ K Q x	◇ K Q x	◇ K Q x x
♣ A J x x	♣ A J x x	♣ A J x x	♣ A J x x

(1) Pass.
(2) Bid three hearts.
(3) Bid four hearts.
(4) Bid three no trumps.

Bear in mind that, in the foregoing sequence, partner's two-heart bid is always made on 8 or 9 points and is, in a sense, the equivalent of a direct raise from one no trump to two. If responder holds 10 or more points, he should insist on a game by jumping to three hearts or spades over the two-diamond bid, even though he has previously made a two-club response. For example, you hold:

♠ A J x   ♡ K Q x x x   ◇ x x x x   ♣ x

Partner	You
1 no trump	2 clubs
2 diamonds	3 hearts

Partner will now know (a) that you are forcing him to a game, and (b) that you have at least five hearts. Trust him to make the right decision.

There will inevitably be hands on which you would like to bid two clubs over one no trump, inviting opener to pass, but hesitate to do so for fear that opener will "misinterpret" your two-club call. With the following hand you would like to get out of no trump and into clubs:

♠ —   ♡ x x x   ◇ x x x   ♣ x x x x x x x

The solution to your problem is simple. Bid two clubs, which your partner *will* assume is the conventional bid. And what will he do? He must bid two diamonds, hearts, or spades, his only three possible rebids. Then you bid three clubs and the cat is out of the bag—he will know that you "misled" him and that all you have is a broken-down club suit. He knows that because three clubs in this situation has no conventional meaning.

Admittedly, in the above sequence, you have taken the partnership to the three-level on a horrible hand. But you will learn, as experience will demonstrate, that the given hand will play better at three clubs, where it will produce five or six winning club tricks, than at no trump, where it will produce zero tricks.

The club convention is also employed over an opening two no trumps bid, and is initiated by a bid of three clubs, asking partner to show a biddable four-card major suit. The purpose, of course, is the same: to play the hand in a major suit, if eight-card agreement can be found. If opener has no biddable major suit, he bids three diamonds. If he has a major suit, he bids it.

To illustrate, partner opens with two no trumps, and you hold:

(1)	(2)	(3)
♠ Q x x x	♠ Q x x x	♠ x x
♡ Q x x x	♡ x	♡ J x x x
◇ x x x x	◇ K x x x x	◇ J x x x
♣ x	♣ x x x	♣ x x x

(1) Bid three clubs. If opener bids three diamonds, go to three no trumps.

(2) Bid three clubs, asking for spades. If opener bids diamonds or hearts, go to three no trumps.

(3) Pass, being thankful that partner, and not the opponent, opened with two no trumps!

The club convention is used sparingly over an opening three no trumps bid, since opener has already contracted for a game. It may be employed whenever responder intends to contract for a slam, but desires to play the slam in a major suit, if agreement can be reached. This application is discussed in Lesson 6.

"TWO-WAY" STAYMAN

Some play that a two club response to one no trump shows a hand of fewer than 10 points, allowing responder to pass opener's rebid or to make a non-forcing rebid of his own; a two diamond bid is artificial, asks partner to show a four-card major, and guarantees game. Opener bids two no trumps without a four-card major but he may bid a five-card minor or jump to three in a five-card major. The use of this bid prevents a sign-off two diamond response with a weak hand and a diamond suit. However, partners may agree that a response of two clubs followed by responder's rebid of three diamonds shows such a hand. (This method is NOT considered in the following Quiz.)

QUIZ

You are the dealer, holding each of the following hands. What is your opening bid?

(1)	(2)	(3)
♠ A Q x	♠ A Q x	♠ A x
♡ A Q x x	♡ A Q x	♡ Q x x
◇ x x	◇ x x x	◇ A J x x x
♣ A Q x x	♣ A Q x x	♣ A x x

(4)	(5)	(6)
♠ A x	♠ K Q x	♠ A Q 10
♡ A x	♡ A x	♡ A K x
◇ A J x x x	◇ K J x x	◇ A K Q x
♣ K J x x	♣ A K Q x	♣ K Q x

(7)	(8)	(9)
♠ A J x	♠ A K x x	♠ A K x
♡ A Q x	♡ A Q x x	♡ A K x x
◇ A K x	◇ K x	◇ Q J x
♣ Q x x x	♣ Q x x	♣ A J x

Your partner has opened the bidding with one no trump. What is your response with each of the following hands?

(10)	(11)	(12)
♠ x x	♠ x x x	♠ x x x
♡ x x x	♡ J x x	♡ J x x x x x
◇ A K Q x x	◇ A x x x x	◇ x x x x
♣ x x	♣ x x	♣ —

(13)	(14)	(15)
♠ x x x	♠ J x	♠ x x x
♡ J x x x x	♡ K x x	♡ x x x
◇ x x	◇ J x x x x	◇ A K J x
♣ x x x	♣ K x x	♣ x x x

(16)	(17)	(18)
♠ K Q J x x x	♠ J x x x	♠ x
♡ —	♡ K Q x x x	♡ A x x
◇ x x x	◇ A x x	◇ J x x x
♣ Q J x x	♣ x	♣ K Q x x x

(19)	(20)	(21)
♠ A x x x	♠ x x	♠ J x x x
♡ A x x x	♡ A Q J x x	♡ J x x x
◇ x x x x	◇ x x	◇ A K J x
♣ x	♣ A x x x	♣ x

(22)	(23)	(24)
♠ A x x	♠ A x x	♠ K Q x
♡ K Q x	♡ K Q x	♡ K x
◇ A J x	◇ A J x	◇ A Q x x
♣ K x x x	♣ J 10 x x	♣ A J x x

(25)	(26)	(27)
♠ A Q x x	♠ K J x	♠ x
♡ A Q x x	♡ A K	♡ x x x
◇ A J x	◇ A Q J x	◇ x x
♣ x x	♣ Q J x x	♣ x x x x x x x x

Your partner has opened the bidding with two no trumps. What is your response with each of the following hands?

(28)	(29)	(30)
♠ x x	♠ Q x x x	♠ x x x
♡ x x x	♡ Q x x x	♡ x x x
◇ Q x x x	◇ x x	◇ A x x x
♣ Q x x x	♣ x x x	♣ x x x

(31)	(32)	(33)
♠ J x x x	♠ K Q x x x x	♠ K J x x x x
♡ J x x x	♡ K x x	♡ x x x
◇ x x	◇ x x	◇ x x
♣ x x x	♣ x x	♣ x x

(34)	(35)	(36)
♠ A x x	♠ K Q x x	♠ K Q x
♡ K x x	♡ K Q J x	♡ K Q x
◇ Q J x x	◇ x x x	◇ x x x x
♣ J x x	♣ x x	♣ x x x

Your partner has opened the bidding with three no trumps. What is your response with each of these hands?

(37)	(38)	(39)
♠ Q x x	♠ K x x x x	♠ x x x
♡ Q x x	♡ x x	♡ A x x
◇ Q x x	◇ x x x	◇ K x x
♣ Q x x x	♣ x x x	♣ x x x x

(40)	(41)	(42)
♠ A x x	♠ x x x	♠ K x x
♡ K Q x	♡ x x x x	♡ Q x x x
◇ K x x x	◇ x x x	◇ x x
♣ x x x	♣ x x x	♣ x x x

You, as opener, hold each of the following hands, and the bidding proceeds as shown. What do you next say?

You	*Partner*
1 no trump	2 clubs
?	

(43)	(44)	(45)
♠ A Q x x	♠ A Q x	♠ K J x x
♡ K J x	♡ K J x	♡ A Q x x
◇ Q J x	◇ Q J x x	◇ Q J x
♣ A x x	♣ A x x	♣ A x

(46)	(47)	(48)
♠ x x x	♠ J x x x	♠ J x x x
♡ A x x	♡ A Q	♡ A J x x
◇ A J x	◇ A Q x	◇ A Q
♣ A K Q x	♣ K J x x	♣ K Q x

You, as opener, hold each of the following hands, and the bidding proceeds as indicated. What do you say now?

You	Partner
1 no trump	2 clubs
2 diamonds	2 no trumps
?	

(49)	(50)	(51)
♠ A Q x	♠ K J x	♠ A 10 x
♡ Q x x	♡ K x x	♡ A 10 x
◇ A Q 10	◇ A x x	◇ A 10 x x
♣ K J 10 x	♣ K Q x x	♣ A 10 x

You, as opener, hold each of the following hands, and the bidding proceeds as indicated. What do you say now?

You	Partner
1 no trump	2 clubs
2 diamonds	2 hearts
?	

(52)	(53)	(54)
♠ A J x	♠ A Q x	♠ A J x
♡ K x	♡ K x	♡ K x x
◇ K J x x	◇ A x x x	◇ A J x
♣ A J x x	♣ A J x x	♣ A x x x

(55)	(56)	(57)
♠ A x x	♠ A x x	♠ A x x
♡ K x x	♡ K x	♡ K x x
◇ A x x	◇ K x x x	◇ K 10 x x
♣ A Q x x	♣ A Q x x	♣ A Q 10

You open the following hand with one no trump, and your partner responds as indicated. What is your rebid?

♠ A Q x x
♡ A x x
◇ K x x
♣ K J x

(58)	
You	*Partner*
1 no trump	2 clubs
?	

(59)	
You	*Partner*
1 no trump	2 no trumps
?	

(60)	
You	*Partner*
1 no trump	3 hearts
?	

(61)	
You	*Partner*
1 no trump	4 spades
?	

(62)	
You	*Partner*
1 no trump	2 clubs
2 spades	2 no trumps
?	

(63)	
You	*Partner*
1 no trump	2 clubs
2 spades	3 clubs
?	

(64)	
You	*Partner*
1 no trump	2 clubs
2 spades	3 hearts
?	

(65)	
You	*Partner*
1 no trump	2 clubs
2 spades	3 spades
?	

ANSWERS

(1) One club. To open with one no trump, you must have
16-18 points (which you do); a balanced hand (which you do);
positive protection in at least three suits (which you do); and
the fourth suit must contain a minimum of x-x-x (which you
do not have). An opening one no-trump bid is never made if
one suit contains but two little ones. Therefore, one club should
be bid (with two, non-touching, four-card suits, the lower
ranking is bid first).

(2) One no trump, since the hand conforms to the requirements in all aspects.

(3) One diamond. To open with one no trump your hand
must contain 16-18 points in high cards. You have only 15
points.

(4) One diamond. To open with one no trump, your hand must be a balanced one (4-3-3-3; 4-4-3-2; 5-3-3-2). Your hand is unbalanced (5-4-2-2).

(5) Two no trumps, showing 22-24 high-card points within a balanced hand, and all suits protected.

(6) Three no trumps, showing 25-27 points, with a balanced hand, plus protection in all suits.

(7) One club, with the intent of jumping to two no trumps over partner's one-over-one suit response. The two no trumps rebid shows 19-20 points.

(8) One no trump. If the partnership belongs in spades or hearts, responder's use of the "two-club convention" will get you to the major suit contract.

(9) Two no trumps, as per definition.

(10) Three no trumps. You have 10 points (9 in high cards plus one for the fifth card of your "workable" diamond suit. If you bid two diamonds, partner will pass; if you jump to three diamonds, you may get to the uneconomical game contract of five diamonds.

(11) Pass. You do not have enough points to yield a game, and with your reasonably balanced hand there is no assurance that a two-diamond contract will prove better than one no trump.

(12) Two hearts, which partner will almost always pass (if he doesn't, he can bid only three hearts, which you will pass). This type of worthless unbalanced hand will invariably play better in a suit than at no trump.

(13) Two hearts. Even with one fewer heart, two hearts is likely to play better than one no trump.

(14) Two no trumps, showing 8-9 points. Do not ever bid two diamonds, two hearts, or two spades over one no trump with 8-9 points, since partner will almost surely pass. Over two no trumps partner, with 17 or 18 points, will bid three no trumps, where you belong.

(15) Two no trumps, for the same reason as in (14) above.

(16) Four spades. This jump to game shows a good six-card suit with less than 10 points in high cards.

(17) Two clubs, the initiation of the two-club convention. If opener rebids either two spades or two hearts, you will raise him to game in his suit. If opener rebids two diamonds, you will jump to three hearts, announcing a game and a five-card heart suit.

(18) Three no trumps. The points for a game are there—

and five clubs or five diamonds contracts are never first-choice contracts.

(19) Two clubs, the conventional bid. If opener rebids two hearts or two spades, you will raise to game in his suit (8 high-card points plus 3 in distribution, for a singleton with four supporting trumps). If, instead, opener rebids two diamonds, you will bid two no trumps on your 8 points.

(20) Three hearts, forcing to game and announcing a good heart suit plus an aversion to no trump.

(21) Two clubs, the conventional bid. If opener rebids two hearts or two spades, you will raise to game in his suit. If, instead, he rebids two diamonds, you will jump to three no trumps.

(22) Six no trumps. Your partner's 16 plus your 17 totals 33, a small slam.

(23) Four no trumps, showing 15-16 points. Opener will then make the final decision as to whether a small slam is the proper contract.

(24) Bid three clubs or three diamonds, to be followed by a jump to six no trumps. Opener will recognize this bidding sequence as showing 19-20 points.

(25) Two clubs, the conventional bid, with the full intention of bidding a small slam on the next round. If opener rebids two spades, you bid six spades; if opener rebids two hearts, you rebid six hearts; and if opener rebids two diamonds, rebid six no trumps.

(26) Seven no trumps (21 + 16 = 37).

(27) Two clubs, to which opener will respond conventionally with either two diamonds, two hearts, or two spades. When you then rebid three clubs, opener will recognize that you have nothing except a broken-down club suit; and that you were not employing the two-club convention.

(28) Three no trumps (22 + 4 = 26).

(29) Three clubs, the conventional bid asking for a major suit. If opener rebids three hearts or three spades, you will raise him to game; if opener rebids three diamonds, you will bid three no trumps.

(30) Three no trumps (22 + 4 = 26).

(31) Pass. The major suits are there, but the points aren't.

(32) Four spades, showing a good six-card suit with about 8 high-card points throughout the hand.

(33) Three spades, and if partner rebids three no trumps,

you will bid four spades. He will know you are not "slam-conscious," for if you were you would have taken more aggressive action on your rebid.

(34) Six no trumps (22 + 11 = 33).

(35) Three clubs, conventionally. With your 11 points you are going to get to a slam. If opener rebids three hearts, you will bid six hearts; if opener rebids three spades, you will bid six spades; and if opener rebids three diamonds you will bid six no trumps.

(36) Three diamonds, to be followed up with four no trumps. The sequence informs partner that you have a balanced hand containing 10 points.

(37) Six no trumps (25 + 8 = 33).

(38) Pass. Slam cannot be made, and there is no assurance whatsoever that four spades will be superior to three no trumps.

(39) Four no trumps, showing 7 points. Opener will bid a small slam if he has 26 or 27 points.

(40) Seven no trumps (25 + 12 = 37).

(41) Pass, with a "Thank you, dear partner, for holding such good cards. I'll go get the sandwiches and drinks."

(42) Pass. Slam cannot be made, for partner has at most 27 points opposite your 5 points. The club convention asking for major suits is not used over three no trumps, except where slam is assured and it's merely a question of whether to play the slam in a major suit or in no trump.

(43) Two spades, in response to partner's conventional bid asking you to show a biddable four-card major suit.

(44) Two diamonds, a denial of a biddable major suit.

(45) Two spades, the higher-ranking major suit. Hearts will be shown on the next round, if partner fails to support spades.

(46) Two diamonds, a denial of major suits. Don't forget that responder's two-club bid did not ask you for club support.

(47) Two diamonds, since your major suit is not a biddable one (you need at least the Q-x-x-x for the major suit to be biddable).

(48) Two hearts, this being your biddable major suit. If responder rebids spades, you will, of course, support his spades by raising him.

(49) Three no trumps. Partner has 8-9 points.

(50) Pass. The combined hands do not warrant being in game.

(51) Three no trumps. Although you have but 16 points in

high cards, the four aces are worth an additional point. And the four tens, although having no positive numerical values, are positive assets.

(52) Two no trumps. Partner has 8 or 9 points, and a five-card heart suit. You have the option of passing his two-heart bid, which is not forcing. So, when you rebid two no trumps, responder will know you have more than 16 points, and don't particularly care for his hearts. Let him make the final decision.

(53) Three no trumps, showing a maximum hand (18 points) with but two hearts. (If you had three hearts, knowing he had five of them, you would have raised to four hearts).

(54) Four hearts. Three hearts plus five hearts equals eight hearts.

(55) Three hearts, showing three hearts and 17 points (with 16 points, you would have passed; with 18 points you would have raised to four hearts).

(56) Pass. There is no future with your 16 points opposite his 8 or 9 points.

(57) Three hearts, announcing three supporting hearts. In a sense, you might pass, since you have but 16 high-card points. However, your two tens are assets; and, generally speaking, wherever possible, you should give partner another chance in case he has a maximum response (like 9 points, with a couple of extra ten-spots floating around).

(58) Two spades, in response to partner's conventional two-club bid asking you for a biddable major suit.

(59) Three no trumps, which you will always bid in this sequence whenever you hold 17 or 18 points.

(60) Four hearts. Partner has guaranteed a game, and has indicated at least five hearts.

(61) Pass. This is automatic. When partner jumps to game over one no trump, you will always pass.

(62) Three no trumps, which is what you would have bid had he responded directly with two no trumps.

(63) Pass. The rascal wasn't using the two-club convention.

(64) Four hearts. Partner has five hearts, and he has voluntarily bid at the three-level. He must also have at least 9 points, for with 8 points he would have rebid two no trumps rather than push towards a game.

(65) Four spades. Partner likes spades, and he has 8-9 points. Since you know you have at least 25 between you, with a 50-50 chance that the combined assets total 26, the game contract should be undertaken.

Lesson 5

REBIDS BY OPENER AND RESPONDER

GENERALLY SPEAKING, the easiest bids to make are the opening bid and the initial response: the opener, having 13 or more points, bids his longest suit; the responder, with 6 or more points, usually names his longest suit. The problems, if you want to call them that, arise when opener is called upon to make his second bid; and when responder is called upon to make his rebid. These problems arise because judgment replaces definition: what has partner's rebid told me concerning how much more he has *over and above* this minimum as defined by his first bid? How many points does he have? How many of each of his bid suits does he have? Does he like my suits? Do we have enough for a game? If so, in what suit? etc., etc. In other words, *interpretation* becomes predominant.

Let us now discuss the subject of rebids by both opener and responder, in order to properly understand the precise meaning and significance of the messages that are being interchanged across the table.

PART ONE: REBIDS BY OPENER

It is an accepted fact that probably the most important single bid made in any bidding sequence is the *second bid made by the opener*. Opening bids of one in a suit are necessarily ambiguous: they do not pretend to give a precise description of either the strength of the hand, or of its type. They may range from as little as 13 points to as many as 23. In this respect, they differ from opening bids of one, two, and three no trumps, which are precisely descriptive.

Opener's second bid will usually state to which class of openings the particular hand belongs. Roughly speaking, the opener's hand will fall within one of the following four classes:

I. The minimum range.

II. The good hand. This is just above the minimum range.

III. The very good hand. This is the type of hand on which the opener will make some jump rebid. He wishes to reach a game if responder has the values announced by responder's first bid.

IV. The rock-crusher. This is the type of hand with which, after responder has spoken once, a game is absolutely guaranteed; and the only thing remaining to be resolved is *where* the guaranteed game should be played.

Opener is continually aware that responder is bidding according to the responder's table: he makes one voluntary response on 6-10 points; with 11-12 points, he will voluntarily make two forward-going bids; with 13 or more points, he will bid a game sooner or later.

The opener must realize that responder's first bid may well be his last. Consequently, if opener has a hand with which he can envision the possibility of making a game based on this first response, he should make some vigorous rebid to coerce responder into bidding involuntarily. Conversely, if responder's first bid doesn't indicate sufficient points for opener to visualize the possibility of making a game, opener will not jump on his rebid. Instead, he will rebid as economically as possible, awaiting responder's second voluntary bid (11-12 points).

To put it in figures: if opener has 20 points and responder shows 6 on his first response, opener will make sure of getting to game (the various bids available to opener in these situations will be presented in a moment). If opener has, say, 15 points, he will know that game cannot be made if responder has but 6-10 points. Opener will therefore rebid in economical fashion (not jumping), awaiting responder's second voluntary bid (showing 11-12 points). If no second response is forthcoming, then no game can be made.

Let us now examine in detail the four types of hands opener may have, and consider the appropriate courses of action.

I. The Minimum Range   The minimum range encompasses hands containing 13, 14, or 15 points. With such hands, opener should not bid again unless responder makes a *forcing* response. If responder single-raises opener's suit, thereby showing 7-

10 points, opener should pass, since he knows the partnership does not have sufficient points for a game. Similarly, if responder bids one no trump, showing 6-10 points, opener should pass.

When responder names a new suit, opener must bid again, but he should do so as economically as possible, by:

(1) naming a new suit at the one-level;
(2) rebidding one no trump;
(3) making a simple rebid of his own suit;
(4) single raising responder's suit; or
(5) bidding a new suit at the two-level.

To illustrate:

	(1)		(2)
Opener	*Responder*	*Opener*	*Responder*
1 diamond	1 heart	1 diamond	1 heart
1 spade		1 no trump	

	(3)		(4)
Opener	*Responder*	*Opener*	*Responder*
1 diamond	1 heart	1 diamond	1 spade
2 diamonds		2 spades	

	(5)
Opener	*Responder*
1 diamond	1 spade
2 clubs	

II. The Good Hand   This category includes hands containing 16, 17, or 18 points. Opener should make a constructive and aggressive rebid of some kind. He should avoid making a rebid that may lead responder to conclude that opener has a minimum holding. In other words, opener should not rebid one no trump, nor simply rebid his own suit, nor merely single-raise responder's suit, etc. The rest of this lesson is concerned with specifically what he should do.

III. The Very Good Hand   This covers hands containing 19, 20, or 21 points. Opener should rebid most vigorously, to make certain that the partnership arrives at a game contract. As will be illustrated soon, opener will make some *jump* rebid.

IV. The Rock-Crusher   These will be hands containing 22 or more points; game is guaranteed, with slam in the offing.

Opener's rebid will be what is called a *jump-shift* bid (to be described shortly).

Now let us look at illustrations of the various specific-type bids which opener is called upon to make on his rebid.

Rebids by Opener over a Single Raise In addition to all the points which you (as opener) counted originally for high cards and distribution, make the following adjustment whenever your partner directly raises your suit:

——Add 1 additional point for the fifth trump.

——Add 2 additional points for the sixth and each subsequent trump.

Your proper procedure now depends on the revised count of your hand, as set forth in the following paragraphs.

(a) If you have 13-15 points, pass.

For example, you hold the following hand:

♠ A Q x x x   ♡ A Q x   ◇ x x   ♣ x x x

The bidding has proceeded:

You	Partner
1 spade	2 spades
?	

You should pass. Your hand was worth 13 points originally (12 in high cards and 1 for the doubleton). With partner raising, the fifth spade becomes worth 1 additional point. With 14 points opposite 7-10, a game does not exist.

(b) If you have 16-18 points, rebid three of your suit. To illustrate, your hand is:

♠ A K x   ♡ A Q x x x x   ◇ x x   ♣ x x

You	Partner
1 heart	2 hearts
3 hearts	

Your hand is currently worth 18 points, 1 point being added for the fifth heart and 2 points for the sixth heart. The hand was worth 15 points at the outset, 13 in high cards and 1 point for each of the doubletons.

What responder will do next is discussed in detail later.

Your partner will know that you had the right to pass the two-heart response. Your actual three-heart bid says: "Partner, I know you have just 7-10 points, but I don't know exactly how many you have. If you have the upper half of your announced range, either 9 or 10 points, carry on to game; if you have the lower half, either 7 or 8 points, pass."

(c) If you have 19-21 points, bid game in your major suit.

This is a clear-cut situation, with no interpolation necessary: partner's 7-10 points added to your 19-21 points guarantee a combined holding of at least 26 points. To illustrate, you hold:

$$
\begin{array}{ll}
\spadesuit \text{ A J x x x} & (5) \\
\heartsuit \text{ A K x} & (7) \\
\diamondsuit \text{ A J x} & (5) \\
\clubsuit \text{ x x} & (1) \\
\hline
& 18
\end{array}
$$

You	Partner
1 spade	2 spades
4 spades	

Your hand was worth 18 points at the outset. It is now worth 19 points, 1 point being added for the fifth spade. Even if partner holds only 7, the total must be at least 26.

Rebids by Opener over One No Trump This response indicates precisely 6-10 points. You, as opener, have the option of passing this bid. Generally speaking, if you have a minimum hand, you will pass. However, there are some situations where you will bid again, simply because you "can't stand" playing the hand at one no trump.

Let us examine these circumstances in which you will bid again (at the two-level) despite the fact that you know a game is unattainable.

There are three types of distributions conducive to no-trump play: 4-3-3-3; 4-4-3-2; and 5-3-3-2. If your hand contains a void, a singleton or two doubletons (an unbalanced hand), you have a valid reason for getting out of no trump, but even in these situations it is not obligatory for you to do so. However, if your hand is unbalanced, you may either rebid your suit or name some other suit, even with a minimum hand (13-15 points). If your hand is of the "good" class (16-18 points) there may well be a game, since partner may have 9 or 10 points.

If you have 19 or 20 points, you will insist on a game, since at least 25 points are guaranteed, and you may well have 26-30 points between you.

To illustrate the above, you hold each of the following hands with the given bidding:

	(1)		(2)
	♠ K x x		♠ x x
	♡ Q x x		♡ A Q x x x
	◇ A K J x x		◇ A K x
	♣ x x		♣ J x x

You	Partner	You	Partner
1 diamond	1 no trump	1 heart	1 no trump
?		?	

(1) Pass, despite your rebiddable diamond suit. Game is out of the question, and you have a balanced hand suitable for play at no trump.

⁺(2) Pass. You're not going anywhere with your minimum hand facing partner's mediocre hand (6-10 points). The best place to play mediocre hands is at one no trump.

You hold the following hands, and the bidding has proceeded as indicated:

	(1)		(2)
	♠ A K x x x x		♠ x x
	♡ A x x		♡ A Q x x x
	◇ x x x		◇ A Q x x x
	♣ x		♣ x

You	Partner	You	Partner
1 spade	1 no trump	1 heart	1 no trump
?		?	

(1) Bid two spades. You can't stand one no trump, and the six-card spade suit offers more safety as the trump suit.

(2) Bid two diamonds. You can't stand one no trump, and wish to play the hand at either diamonds or hearts, depending on which suit partner likes best.

You hold the two following hands and the bidding has proceeded as stated:

	(1)		(2)
	♠ A K 10 x x		♠ A K 10 x x
	♡ K J x		♡ K J x
	◇ A Q x		◇ A Q x
	♣ x x		♣ K x

You	Partner	You	Partner
1 spade	1 no trump	1 spade	1 no trump
?		?	

(1) Bid two no trumps, asking partner to bid three if his one no trump response was in the upper range (9 to 10 points as opposed to 6 or 7 points).

(2) Bid three no trumps. You have 20 high-card points; partner has at least 6 points. Note that this hand was too good to be opened with one no trump (16-18) and not good enough for two no trumps (22-24 points).

Non-Jump Bids by Opener after a One-over-One Response
When you open with one of a suit, and partner responds with one of another suit, you must bid again (your guaranteed rebid). Your first opportunity has now arisen to clarify the nature of your opening bid, both as to the point-count strength and as to the distributional pattern. If your opening bid was a minimum, this is the time to inform partner of the fact. This information is transmitted to partner by a rebid of (a) one no trump, (b) one of another suit, (c) two of your own suit, (d) two of a new suit, or (e) two of partner's suit. Any of these rebids conveys the following message:

"Partner, proceed with caution. I may have an absolute minimum hand, and I don't figure to have more than 15 points (although on infrequent occasions, feeling conservatively inclined, I may have 16 points, at best)."

Let us look at some illustrations of the above. You hold the following hands, and the bidding has proceeded as stated:

	(1)		(2)
	♠ J x x		♠ J x x
	♡ A J x		♡ A J x x
	◇ K x x		◇ K x
	♣ K Q x x		♣ K Q x x

You	Partner	You	Partner
1 club	1 diamond	1 club	1 diamond
?		?	

99

	(3)		(4)

(3)
♠ x x
♡ A J x
◇ K x x
♣ K Q x x x

(4)
♠ x x
♡ A J x x x
◇ A K x x x
♣ x

You	*Partner*	*You*	*Partner*
1 club	1 diamond	1 heart	1 spade
?		?	

(5)
♠ x x
♡ J x x x
◇ A Q x
♣ A Q x x

You	*Partner*
1 club	1 heart
?	

(1) Bid one no trump.
(2) Bid one heart.
(3) Bid two clubs.
(4) Bid two diamonds.
(5) Raise partner to two hearts.

Raising Partner's One-over-One Response to Two Whenever your partner responds with one of a new suit for which you have adequate trump support, you should promptly raise him in his suit. How high you should raise him will depend on how many points you have. With a minimum holding, you will raise him to the two-level; with "good hands" and "very good hands," to the three-level and four-level, respectively.

For example:

(1)
♠ Q x x x
♡ x x
◇ A Q x
♣ K Q x x

(2)
♠ x x x x
♡ x
◇ A Q x x
♣ A Q x x

You	*Partner*	*You*	*Partner*
1 club	1 spade	1 diamond	1 spade
?		?	

(3)

♠ A x x
♡ x x x x
♢ x
♣ A K J x x

You	Partner
1 club	1 spade
?	

(1) Raise to two spades.

(2) Raise to two spades.

(3) Raise to two spades (although a two-club rebid would not be subject to any sharp criticism).

Note well: As opener, whenever you are about to raise your partner in his suit, you drop the original value assigned for distribution, and revalue your distribution as though you were the responder who was about to raise the opener. That is, with four or more supporting trumps and a void, add 5 points; for four or more supporting trumps and a singleton, add 3 points; and for four or more supporting trumps and a doubleton, add 1 point. And, as the "opener-becomes-responder," if your hand contains defécts, you will subtract 1 point for each defect: (a) only three trumps; (b) a 4-3-3-3 distribution; and (c) a short suit containing an insufficiently guarded picture card.*

Reverting to the three hands just presented:

Hand (1) is worth 15 points in support of spades: 13 in high cards, 1 for the four supporting trumps and the doubleton, and 1 for the promotion of the queen of trumps.

Hand (2) is worth 15 points in support of spades: 12 in high cards plus 3 points for a singleton with four supporting trumps.

Hand (3) is worth 14 points in support of spades: 12 in high cards, 3 for the singleton, less 1 point for the deduction of the defect of having but three supporting trumps. Had you rebid two clubs, the hand would also be worth 14 points: 12 in high cards plus two distributional points for the possession of a singleton.

Raising Partner's One-over-One Response to Three When

---

* The subject of defects is discussed in greater detail in Lesson 3, page 40.

the opening bidder raises his partner's new-suit response to three, he will always have a "good hand," that is, 16-18 points plus four or more supporting trumps.

This jump in partner's suit is *never* made on only three supporting trumps. To illustrate:

(1)	(2)
♠ A x x x	♠ K Q x
♡ A K x x	♡ J x x x
◇ x	◇ A K x x x
♣ A x x x	♣ x

Opener	*Responder*	*Opener*	*Responder*
1 club	1 spade	1 diamond	1 heart
?		?	

(3)
♠ K x x
♡ x x
◇ A Q x x
♣ A Q x x

Opener	*Responder*
1 diamond	1 spade
?	

(1) Raise to three spades. In support of spades, your hand is worth 18 points: 15 in high cards plus 3 for the singleton with four of partner's suit.

(2) Raise to three hearts. In support of hearts, your hand is worth 17 points: 13 in high cards, 3 for the singleton, and 1 for the promotion of the jack of trumps.

(3) Bid two clubs. Although your hand is valued at 16 points in support of spades, you cannot jump to three spades without at least four trumps. Two clubs is the recommended bid, with the hope that partner can bid again, in which case you will show your spade support.

The jump to three of responder's suit is not forcing: it can be passed by responder. However, since responder knows that opener has 16-18 points for his jump raise, responder will bid again whenever he has 9 or 10 points.

Raising Partner's One-over-One Major Response to Four
A raise by opener from one to four in partner's major suit

logically shows more than would be the raise from one to three. The reason? The raise from one to three can be passed by responder. So, when opener raises from one to four in a major suit, it is because he can see that the partnership belongs in a game, and is taking no chances of responder passing below the game level. As should be apparent, the raise from one to four is made on a "very good" hand: 19, 20, or 21 points, plus a minimum of four supporting trumps. Here are two examples:

	(1)		(2)
♠	K Q x x	♠	x
♡	x x	♡	Q x x x
◇	A K x	◇	A Q x x x
♣	A K x x	♣	A K x

You	Partner	You	Partner
1 club	1 spade	1 diamond	1 heart
4 spades		4 hearts	

(1) You have 20 points: 19 in high cards plus 1 for the doubleton heart. Partner, of course, has a minimum of 6 points.

(2) You have 19 points upon revaluation in support of hearts: in high cards, 15 points; plus 3 for the singleton spade, and 1 for the promotion of the queen of trumps.

Jump Rebid to Two No Trumps This bid portrays a hand that contains 19 or 20 points in high cards and is well suited for no-trump play (the partnership is assured that all unbid suits are protected). This jump bid is forcing to game, provided partner has the minimum of 6 points promised by his first response.

To illustrate:

	(1)		(2)
♠	A K J	♠	A Q x
♡	x x	♡	A Q x
◇	A Q x x	◇	K x x
♣	A Q x x	♣	K J x x

You	Partner	You	Partner
1 diamond	1 heart	1 club	1 spade
2 no trumps		2 no trumps	

(1) Your jump to two no trumps shows a balanced hand containing 19-20 points and protection in each of the unbid suits.

(2) You have the type of hand too good for an original one no trump opening (16-18) and not quite good enough for a two no trumps opening bid (22-24). Your scheme of bidding is to open with one of a suit, and to follow up with the planned jump rebid of two no trumps.

Jump Rebid to Three No Trumps Like the jump rebid to two no trumps, the jump rebid to three no trumps shows a balanced hand containing protection in each of the unbid suits. The point-count required for this bid is 21-22 in high cards. To illustrate:

(1)	(2)
♠ K x x x	♠ A K x
♡ K Q x	♡ x x x
◇ A Q	◇ A K J
♣ A K x x	♣ A K x x

You	Partner	You	Partner
1 club	1 diamond	1 club	1 heart
3 no trumps		3 no trumps	

(1) Your 21 points plus partner's 6 points guarantee 27 points. Even if your partner has but 5 points (it's "legal" to occasionally "cheat" by just 1 point) the requisite 26 points for game will be there.

(2) You hold 22 points, but couldn't open with two no trumps because you didn't have all suits protected. After partner's one-heart response, everything is perfect for no-trump play.

Jump Rebid to Three of Opener's Suit When the opening bidder has a good six-card (or longer) suit, he may make a jump rebid to three of that suit if his hand contains 19-21 points in "rebid valuation."

A few words on "rebid valuation" are in order at this point. You will recall that after partner has supported your suit, you add 1 point for the fifth trump, 2 for the sixth and each subsequent trump. The assumption is that, when partner has supported your suit, it tends to become a consolidated trump suit.

Where the opening bidder himself holds a consolidated (or self-sufficient) suit, he treats it as though partner has supported

104

it. With a long and powerful suit, he will therefore add "rebid valuation" points at once.

In illustration of the above:

	(1)		(2)
♠	A K J x x x	♠	x x
♡	K x x	♡	A K 10 9 x x
◇	A J x	◇	A Q x
♣	x	♣	K x

You	Partner	You	Partner
1 spade	1 no trump	1 heart	1 spade
3 spades		3 hearts	

(1) Your hand was worth 18 points at the outset: 16 in high cards plus 2 for the singleton club. For rebidding purposes, your spade suit is self-sufficient, requiring no support from partner. Therefore you add 1 for the fifth spade and 2 for the sixth spade, bringing the total rebid valuation to 21 points. Hence the three-spade rebid.

(2) The original valuation was also 18 points: 16 in high cards and 1 for each of the doubletons. In revaluating your self-sustaining heart suit, add 3 points. The 21 points justify a three-heart rebid.

This jump rebid to three of opener's suit is *not forcing* upon responder if the response has been made in the one-level. If partner has made a one-spade response on a hand which may not be helpful at a heart contract, he is at liberty to pass. However, responder should make every effort to respond again to this "pleading" rebid. If he holds more than his bare minimum (8 points, or even 7 points with reasonable support for opener's suit) he should bid again. This subject will be discussed further under RESPONDER'S REBIDS.

As to what determines whether a suit is self-sufficient, or self-sustaining, the following criteria are used as yardsticks:

(a) If a five-card suit, it must be A-K-Q-J-x, K-Q-J-10-x, or A-K-Q-10-9.

(b) If a six-card suit, the suit must contain either 7 points in high cards in addition to three of the five top cards, or three of the top four cards (A-K-10-x-x-x, A-Q-J-x-x-x, K-Q-J-x-x-x).

(c) If a seven-card (or longer) suit, it must be headed by a minimum of 4 points, including at least two picture cards (A-Q-x-x-x-x-x, K-J-x-x-x-x-x, A-J-x-x-x-x-x). The one exception, with a seven-card suit, is Q-J-10-x-x-x-x, which suit for all practical purposes is considered to be self-sustaining.

Jump Rebid to Four of Opener's Suit This bid is like the jump rebid to three of opener's suit (as above), except that it shows 22-23 rebid points. Opener wants to be in game in his suit even if responder holds the barest of minimums. To illustrate, suppose you hold:

♠ A K Q x x x ♡ K Q x ◇ A x ♣ x x

You open with one spade, and partner responds with one no trump. Your rebid is the leap to game at four spades. Originally, the hand was valued at 20 points: 18 in high cards and 2 in distribution. It is now worth 23 points, adding 1 for the fifth spade and 2 for the sixth.

Of course, if responder has a good hand, rather than a mere minimum, he may try for slam. Slam bidding is discussed in Lesson 6.

Jump-Shift by Opener The following rebids by opener are called "jump-shifts."

	(1)		(2)
Opener	*Responder*	*Opener*	*Responder*
1 diamond	1 heart	1 diamond	1 heart
3 clubs		2 spades	

	(3)
Opener	*Responder*
1 spade	2 clubs
3 diamonds	

. The jump-shift is one of the most powerful rebids that opener can make. It says: "Partner, game is guaranteed, and quite possibly we have a slam. Don't you dare pass until we get to at least a game!" The bid is absolutely forcing to game even if responder has a rock-bottom minimum hand.

Opener makes this bid in either of the following situations:

(a) The points for game are assured, but opener doesn't know in what suit to play the hand and is looking for direction from responder.

(b) Opener knows the right suit for game, but fears that, if he bids the game directly, a slam might be missed.

	(1)		(2)
♠ x x		♠ A x x x	
♡ A K Q x x		♡ A K J x x	
◇ K x		◇ A K J	
♣ A K J x		♣ x	

You	Partner	You	Partner
1 heart	1 spade	1 heart	1 spade
3 clubs		3 diamonds	

(1) You have 20 points in high cards and 2 points in distribution. Game is certain, but you don't know where to play the hand. The jump-shift three-club bid forces responder to bid again. And, as you'll see in the section on RESPONDER'S REBIDS, he'll help you set the proper final contract.

(2) You have 23 points in support of partner's spades. Game is a cinch. A jump to four spades would not do full justice to your hand—partner needs very little to make a slam. No matter what responder rebids, you will put him into a spade contract, at no less than a game-level.

Rebids by Opener over a Two-over-One Response It is most important to remember that, when partner names a new suit at the two-level, he is showing a minimum of 10 points. Logically, therefore, opener's approach to his rebid differs from his approach when responder names a new suit at the one-level, which promises but 6 points. Also, the opener will bear in mind that, when responder has 11-12 points, he will bid again, while with only 10 he will tend to pass next.

Whenever opener has a minimum-range opening bid, he will rebid as economically as possible, without offering any encouragement to his partner. To illustrate:

	(1)		(2)
♠ J x		♠ A Q J x x	
♡ A Q x x x		♡ x x	
◇ A Q x x		◇ K J x	
♣ x x		♣ Q x x	

You	Partner	You	Partner
1 heart	2 clubs	1 spade	2 diamonds
2 diamonds		2 spades	

(3)
♠ A Q x x x
♡ x x
◇ A Q x x
♣ x x

You	Partner
1 spade	2 clubs
2 diamonds	

With the above three hands, your rebids are made without any enthusiasm, as it were. If partner cannot bid again (he needs at least 11 points to bid again), no game can be made. On hand (2), you have the option of raising partner to three diamonds, instead of bidding two spades, but with your minimum hand, the raise, which would encourage partner, should properly not be made. On hand (3), if partner responds two hearts (instead of two clubs), your rebid is two spades, not three diamonds. With a minimum hand, economy should always be the watchword.

The thoughts may be flashing through your mind: "What is an *encouraging* rebid? When shall I make an encouraging rebid? When shall my rebid be made to sound unenthusiastic?"

The answers are found in the following principles:

(a) With a minimum-range opening, you should make one of these *unencouraging* rebids:

—A non-jump rebid of your original suit.

—A suit rebid that permits partner to return to your first suit at the two-level.

(b) With a good hand (usually 16 or more points), you should make one of these *encouraging* rebids:

—A rebid of two no trumps.

—A raise of partner's suit to three.

—A rebid of three in a new suit.

—Any rebid that compels partner to return to your first suit at the three-level.

Let us look at some illustrations:

(1)	(2)
♠ A Q x x x	♠ A K x x
♡ x x	♡ A K x x
◇ A Q x x	◇ x x
♣ x x	♣ x x x

You	Partner	You	Partner
1 spade	2 hearts	1 spade	2 clubs
2 spades		2 hearts	

(3)

♠ A K x x
♡ A Q x x
◇ K 10 x
♣ x x

(4)

♠ A K x x x
♡ K J x
◇ A J x
♣ x x

You	Partner	You	Partner
1 spade	2 clubs	1 spade	2 hearts
2 no trumps		3 hearts	

(5)

♠ A K x x x
♡ x x
◇ A Q x x
♣ K x

(6)

♠ A Q J x
♡ A Q J x x
◇ K x
♣ x x

You	Partner	You	Partner
1 spade	2 hearts	1 heart	2 diamonds
3 diamonds		2 spades	

(1) Don't bid three diamonds, a new suit, at the three-level. If you do, partner will count on you for at least 16 points.

(2) There is no choice but to bid two hearts.

(3) Bid two no trumps rather than two hearts. It is always more important to describe the strength of your hand as a whole than to describe a particular suit. A rebid of two hearts would depict a minimum hand. Actually, you have 16 high-card points, which the encouraging two no trumps rebid announces.

(4) Three hearts is the proper bid, as opposed to two spades. In support of hearts, your hand is worth 16 points: 16 in high cards, plus 1 for a doubleton, less 1 for the defect of having only three supporting trumps. A two-spade rebid would sound too discouraging.

(5) Three diamonds as opposed to a simple rebid of two spades, for the same reasons as in (4) above.

(6) Two spades, not the unencouraging two-heart rebid. On your very good hand (17 high-card points plus 2 points for distribution) it should be your desire to climb high. This

bidding sequence—one of a suit, then two of a higher-ranking suit at the two-level—is known as "reverse bidding." It always shows a very good hand, since it drives partner to the three-level if he prefers the first suit.

Raising a Minor-Suit Response When the responder's two-over-one response is in clubs or diamonds, opener sometimes has the problem of what to bid when he has four supporting trumps. When the response is a *major,* and opener has four cards of the suit, there is no problem: opener would promptly raise. But, bearing in mind that minor-suit game contracts should be avoided whenever possible, opener will strive to direct the contract into more fruitful channels. To illustrate:

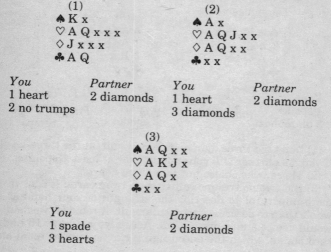

(1)
♠ K x
♡ A Q x x x
♢ J x x x
♣ A Q

You	*Partner*
1 heart	2 diamonds
2 no trumps	

(2)
♠ A x
♡ A Q J x x
♢ A Q x x
♣ x x

You	*Partner*
1 heart	2 diamonds
3 diamonds	

(3)
♠ A Q x x
♡ A K J x
♢ A Q x
♣ x x

You	*Partner*
1 spade	2 diamonds
3 hearts	

(1) If you bid three diamonds, partner will probably find himself hard-pressed to bid three no trumps, since he would have to have both of the unbid suits protected (spades and clubs). Your two no trumps rebid, while concealing the diamond support, indicates the desire and ability to play the hand at no trump. Remember, too, that partner also "hates" minor-suit game contracts; he'll be delighted to hear you bid two no trumps and will not be offended when he later sees your diamond support.

(2) Although your hand, with 19 points in support of dia-

monds, is worth a jump raise, such raise would preclude a three no trumps contract. So you take a calculated risk by bidding only three diamonds; conceivably, partner might pass, but much more often he'll be able to bid a game at three no trumps, or support you in hearts.

(3) The jump-shift rebid is forcing to game. Although you have excellent diamond support, to rebid any number of diamonds would be bad, since it would tend to preclude a three no trumps contract.

Rebids by Opener after a Forcing Jump Response Whenever your partner responds by jumping over your one of a suit opening, game is assured. Your rebid should concentrate on finding the proper suit.

Suppose you hold the following hands and the bidding has proceeded as indicated:

(1)	(2)
♠ A Q x x	♠ A K x x x
♡ A K x x	♡ A Q x x
◇ x	◇ x x
♣ J x x x	♣ x x

You	Partner	You	Partner
1 spade	3 spades	1 spade	2 no trumps
?		?	

(3)
♠ x x
♡ x x
◇ A K x x x
♣ A Q x x

You	Partner
1 diamond	2 no trumps
?	

(1) Bid four spades. Although you have but a four-card suit, you do not care for no-trump play with your singleton diamond.

(2) Bid three hearts. With your worthless doubletons in the minor suits, you would prefer a major suit to no trump. The three-heart bid will express an "unhappiness" at no trump, while at the same time showing at least four hearts. Responder will then set the final contract by rebidding either three no

111

trumps, four hearts, or three spades (which you will carry to four spades).

(3) Bid three no trumps. Although your hand has the same pattern as hand (2), you should not desire to get to an eleven-trick minor-suit contract. Since partner's two no trumps response indicates both spade and heart protection, the better gamble is to bid three no trumps for nine tricks.

PART TWO: REBIDS BY RESPONDER

At the outset of this lesson, in introducing opener's rebids, we said that opener's rebid is perhaps the most significant single bid in the partner's interchange of information. The opening bid of one in a suit covers a wide range of hands— anywhere from 13 to 22 or even 23 points. It is opener's second bid that narrows down the range, and places the hand in a more precise category, both point-wise and with regard to distribution.

In the same sense, it is responder's second bid that is *his* most important one. His first non-jump response may be of temporizing nature, with intent of defining the hand more precisely in subsequent bids. This response may be made on hands ranging all the way from 6 to 18 points; a rebid may be essential to clarify it.

General Strategy of Responder The following table is the responder's "bible"; his approach to bidding:

With 6-10 points, plan to bid only once.

With 11-12 points, plan to bid twice.

With 13 or more points, plan to make as many or as few bids as may be required to arrive at a game. Bear in mind that the bid of a new suit *by responder* is forcing and may not be passed.

Every bridge player should become thoroughly familiar with the above table. Let us examine its precise functioning.

I. When You Plan to Bid Only Once (6-10 points) Your hand is in the minimum responding range, and you should make a mild response. With 6 or 7 points, do not bid again unless your partner forces you to do so. With 8 or 9 points, you should bid again if your partner makes a strong bid that "pleads" with you to do so. With 10 points, you will tend to pass if your partner's rebid seems to indicate a minimum-range opening bid (13-15).

To illustrate:

(1)	(2)
♠ A K x x	♠ A K x x
♡ x x	♡ x x
◇ x x x	◇ J x x x
♣ x x x x	♣ x x x

Partner	*You*	*Partner*	*You*
1 heart	1 spade	1 heart	1 spade
2 hearts	Pass	3 hearts	4 hearts

(3)	(4)
♠ A Q x x	♠ A Q x x
♡ x x	♡ x x
◇ J x x	◇ J x x x
♣ K x x x	♣ K x x

Partner	*You*	*Partner*	*You*
1 heart	1 spade	1 heart	1 spade
1 no trump	Pass	2 hearts	Pass

(5)
♠ A Q x x
♡ x x
◇ J x x x
♣ K x x

Partner	*You*
1 heart	1 spade
2 diamonds	2 hearts or
	2 no trumps

(1) You have made your one allowable forward-going bid.

(2) Partner's three-heart bid shows a six-card suit, a good hand, well above minimum, and begs you to bid again if you have more than 7 points. Your doubleton is sufficient support.

(3) Your partner's one no trump rebid indicates a minimum holding of roughly 13-15 points. Opposite your 10 points, no game can be made.

(4) As in (3) above, your partner's simple rebid of his original suit denotes a minimum hand. You are not going anywhere, so stay where you are.

(5) Although you have but 10 points, your partner's rebid of a new suit at the two-level may well indicate a hand that

is above minimum. Give him another opportunity to bid, either by two hearts (the "corrective" bid, which is discussed a few pages hence) or two no trumps, announcing stoppers in each of the unbid suits.

II. When You Plan to Bid Twice (11-12 points) You have a good hand (opposite a partner who has just announced at least 13 points). It is worth two bids. In order to be sure of opportunity to make your second bid, your first bid should never be of the type that opener has the option of passing— that is, do not single-raise him (showing 7-10 points) and do not respond with one no trump (showing 6-10 points). With 11 or 12 points, name a new suit, to which opener must provide his guaranteed rebid, thereby giving you a second opportunity to bid.

To illustrate:

	(1)		(2)
♠ K Q x x		♠ A Q x x	
♡ x x		♡ K Q x	
◇ A J x		◇ J x x	
♣ Q x x x		♣ x x x	

Partner	*You*	*Partner*	*You*
1 heart	1 spade	1 heart	1 spade
1 no trump	2 no trumps	2 hearts	3 hearts

(3)
♠ A Q x x
♡ x x
◇ Q x x x
♣ A x x

Partner	*You*
1 heart	1 spade
2 hearts	2 no trumps

(1) Do not make the mistake of responding with one no trump over partner's opening one-heart bid. This erroneous bid will indicate 6-10 points, and opener might well pass, thereby depriving you of your second bid.

(2) Do not immediately raise partner's one-heart opening to two. If you do, he will assume that you have but 7-10 points, and he might pass.

(3) When you named a new suit, opener was forced to bid again. Your two no trumps rebid now informs him that you have 11-12 points, plus stoppers in both diamonds and clubs.

Since these 11-12-point responding hands occur with reasonable frequency, and often present a problem on responder's second bid, it might be well to examine a few more illustrations.

(1)	(2)
♠ A K x x x	♠ A K x x x
♡ x x	♡ J x x x
◇ K x x	◇ x x x
♣ x x x	♣ x

Partner	You	Partner	You
1 heart	1 spade	1 heart	1 spade
2 hearts	2 spades	2 hearts	3 hearts

(3)
♠ Q J x x
♡ x x
◇ A x x x
♣ A x x

Partner	You
1 heart	1 spade
2 clubs	2 no trumps

(1) It was your intention to bid spades again on the second round, showing five spades and 11-12 points. Whether your partner's rebid is one no trump, or two of a suit other than spades, rebid two spades. Had opener, instead of rebidding two hearts, raised you to two spades, you should bid three spades, informing him that you hold 11-12 points.

(2) You make a temporizing bid of one spade, intending to raise your partner in hearts on the next round. In support of hearts, your hand is worth 12 points: 9 in hearts, 2 for the singleton, and 1 for the promotion of the jack of trumps. To raise directly to two hearts is wrong, for that would show but 7-10 points; to bid three hearts directly is incorrect (as will be discussed soon) since this jump rebid shows at least 13 points and is a guarantee of game; to bid two-and-a-half hearts is illegal. Hence the temporizing bid of one spade, with intention

of raising hearts on the next round to show (a) your heart support and (b) 11-12 points.

(3) Open one spade originally, with the intention of bidding again as per plan with 11-12 points. If opener rebids two hearts or clubs, rebid two no trumps; if he rebids two diamonds, raise to three diamonds; if he rebids two spades (raising your suit), rebid two no trumps rather than three spades. (Opener knows you have four spades, and if the final contract belongs in spades, he'll put you back in your spade suit.)

III. When You Plan to Get to at Least a Game (13-15 points)
You have a very good hand: an opening bid facing an opening bid is like money in the bank. The only issue remaining to be resolved is where the game should be played. Either you will go to game yourself, in a suit or no trump, or continue to make forcing responses until the partnership arrives at a game. To illustrate:

(1)	(2)
♠ x	♠ x
♡ x x	♡ K J x x
◇ A Q J x x	◇ J x x
♣ A Q J x x	♣ A K J x x

Partner	You	Partner	You
1 spade	2 diamonds	1 spade	2 clubs
2 hearts	3 clubs	2 hearts	4 hearts
3 no trumps			

(3)
♠ A J 10 9 x
♡ A Q 10 x
◇ A 10 9 x
♣ x

Partner	You
1 club	1 spade
2 clubs	2 hearts
3 clubs	3 diamonds
?	

(1) After your partner opens the bidding, you know the combined hands have sufficient points to yield a game. Neither

116

your two-diamond nor three-club responses can be passed—
and, as it turns out, partner bids the game at three no trumps.

(2) You temporize with two clubs, knowing you have a game
somewhere. When partner bids two hearts, you know that
hearts is the right trump suit, and you promptly contract for
the game at four hearts.

(3) Each time you named a new suit, opener had to bid
again. He'll probably bid three no trumps now, and you will
then know that he doesn't like any of your suits—and you
don't like his suit.

*IV. When You Have an Even Chance for a Small Slam (16-
18 points)* When your partner opens the bidding, you know
the partnership holds 29, 30, or 31 points (with 33 required
for a small slam). You have a tremendously strong hand,
much more than a mere opening bid. To indicate your enormous
strength to partner, either you will jump in no trump immediately, or name a new suit first and follow up by making
a jump on your rebid. The specific types of jumps which responder may make are discussed later in this lesson and in
Lesson 6.

V. When You Hold 19 Points and Up With these responding
hands, a small slam will be made unless opener has an absolute
minimum (19 + 13 = 32). You will give an immediate slam
signal by jumping in a new suit (the jump-shift bid, see p.
114).

Corrective Bids In previous discussion of the responder's
approach, we have spoken of positive, forward-going bids.
There is one other type of bid which the responder makes,
known as the *corrective* or *preference* bid.

There is quite a difference between the corrective and the
positive bid. If the reader does not understand this difference,
he will continually find himself in hot water.

Let us look at a few illustrations. Your partner opens the
bidding with one heart, and you respond with one spade on
each of the following hands:

(1)	(2)	(3)
♠ A K x x x	♠ A K x x x	♠ A K x x x
♡ K x x	♡ x x	♡ x x
◇ x x	◇ x x x	◇ x x
♣ x x x	♣ K x x	♣ x x x x

(1) If opener rebids two hearts, you will raise him to three

117

hearts as your second positive bid (11-12 points). If, over your one-spade response, opener raises you to two spades, your second positive bid will be three spades.

(2) If opener rebids two hearts, you now rebid two spades as your second positive bid. If, over your one spade, opener bids two diamonds, you will bid either two spades or 2 no trumps. Both of these latter bids are positive, showing 11-12 points. The former bid indicates five spades, and the latter shows protection in the unbid suit, clubs.

(3) If opener rebids two hearts, you will pass, having made your one allowable positive bid (6-10). You have no more forward-going bids coming to you.

As should be evident from the above, a positive bid is one that expresses a desire to move higher, toward a game. And, of course, this desire is always backed up by the points required to sustain such a voluntary, aggressive attitude.

In hand (3) we come to the corrective or preference bid. To repeat the bidding sequence: partner has opened with one heart, and you have responded with one spade. Suppose that he now rebids two diamonds. Your 8 points suffice for just one positive bid. Do you pass because of the lack of values required to make a second positive bid? The answer is: No!

Let me emphasize categorically that a pass by you is out of the question. To leave your partner stranded in his second-bid suit when you have greater length in his first-bid suit is losing bridge. Since opener bids his longest suit first, it is nearly certain that your partnership has more hearts than diamonds. To pass with your two little diamonds would be to leave your partner in the worst possible trump suit.

Admittedly, you have but 8 points, with which you've already made one "allowable" positive bid. But, over partner's two-diamond rebid, you simply make the preference bid of two hearts. You thereby inform partner that you prefer hearts to diamonds—and nothing more. He will not expect you to have 11-12 points, for he will understand that your return to his first-bid suit is simply a preference for that suit.

The reader may ask: How can opener tell whether my second response was a positive or a corrective response? The answer is found in this definition:

A positive (forward-going) rebid is one in which you raise your partner's suit to the next-higher level, or else bid a suit of your own or bid no trump. A corrective (preference) bid is one by which you express your preference for one of the suits your partner has bid, without raising that suit to the next-higher level.

A corrective bid is "lateral"—you don't increase the level of the bidding (but there is one exception, which is discussed a few paragraphs hence).

Let us revert to hand (3).

♠ A K x x x   ♥ x x   ♦ x x   ♣ x x x x

Partner	You
1 heart	1 spade
2 diamonds	2 hearts

When you took your partner back to two hearts, this was the corrective bid, for you moved laterally from two diamonds to two hearts. Your preference bid showed no more strength than a pass would have shown had you held:

♠ A K x x x   ♥ x x   ♦ x x x   ♣ x x x

With the above hand you would pass partner's two-diamond rebid, since you would not prefer hearts to diamonds—in fact, you would have a mild preference for diamonds.

As can be seen from the above, a preference is sometimes indicated by passing, and sometimes by returning to the first suit. In making a choice, length is far more important than quality in the trump suit. As a rule, it is the duty of the responder to select that suit in which the partnership has the greatest number of cards.

With equal length in each of partner's suits, the practice is to prefer the suit he bid first. This has the twofold advantage of (a) giving partner one more chance to bid, if that is your desire and (b) returning to the suit in which the partnership will, more often than not, have the most trumps.

For example:

(1)	(2)
♠ J x	♠ x x x
♥ Q x	♥ A J x x
♦ x x x x x	♦ J x x
♣ A Q x x	♣ J x x

Partner	You	Partner	You
1 spade	1 no trump	1 diamond	1 heart
2 hearts	?	2 clubs	?

(1) Return to two spades, partner's first-bid suit. You actually have no preference, since the queen of hearts versus the jack of spades does not make hearts the better trump suit. Since partner has bid spades first, he figures either to have more spades than hearts or the same number, so that your reversion to spades will tend to put the partnership in the suit with the greater combined length. In addition, you have a "good" one no trump response (6-10 points), and you certainly want to give your partner another chance to go on to game.

(2) Bid two diamonds, the corrective bid, knowing that between you the partnership has either more diamonds than clubs, or, at worst, the same number. Partner will recognize this as a preference bid possibly made on just 6 points.

The one exception to the rule that a corrective must be "lateral" is as follows. Suppose the bidding has proceeded:

Partner	You
1 heart	2 clubs
2 spades	?

If you now bid three hearts, that is a corrective bid. You are stating merely: "Partner, you have bid two suits, hearts and spades. I prefer your first suit, hearts." Suppose that your hand is:

♠ x x x   ♡ J x x   ◇ J x x   ♣ A K Q x

To indicate your preference for hearts, you have no choice but to bid three. Partner, by bidding hearts first, then spades, has forced you to the three-level in order to express a preference for hearts. As a matter of fact, in this case you know that partner has at least five hearts, for with four spades and four hearts he would have bid one spade first. You also know that he has a strong hand. As remarked previously, his reverse bidding is justified only when his hand is strong enough to force you to the three-level.

One final illustration of the corrective bid. You hold, as the responding hand:

♠ Q x x x   ♡ x x x   ◇ x x   ♣ A x x x

To partner's opening one spade you respond two spades (7-10 points). Suppose that partner now bids any suit except spades. You are not permitted to pass, since spades have been agreed upon as the trump suit. Partner is bidding at the three-level in the full realization that you cannot possibly hold more than 10 points; and he is asking you whether your raise was based on a minimum holding (7 or 8 points) or a maximum holding (9 or 10 points). On the above hand you "correct" to three spades, since you have a minimum hand. Were your queen of spades the ace of spades, over partner's rebid (say, three diamonds) you would jump to four spades.

Test your understanding of the situations just discussed. In the following quiz, is the bid marked (?) positive or corrective?

	(1)		(2)
You	*Partner*	*You*	*Partner*
1 diamond	1 heart	1 club	1 heart
2 clubs	2 diamonds(?)	2 clubs	2 hearts(?)

	(3)		(4)
You	*Partner*	*You*	*Partner*
1 spade	2 diamonds	1 spade	2 hearts
3 clubs	3 diamonds(?)	3 clubs	3 spades(?)

	(5)		(6)
You	*Partner*	*You*	*Partner*
1 heart	1 spade	1 heart	1 spade
2 hearts	2 no trumps(?)	2 clubs	2 diamonds(?)

	(7)
Partner	*You*
1 diamond	2 clubs
2 hearts	3 diamonds(?)

(1) Corrective. Partner has merely expressed a preference for the first of your two suits.

(2) Positive. This forward-going bid shows five hearts and 11-12 points.

(3) Positive. A return to three spades would have been a corrective bid. The three-diamond bid shows 11-12 points and five diamonds.

(4) Corrective. Partner prefers your first-bid suit, spades, to your second-bid suit, clubs.

(5) Positive. Had partner held just 6-10 points, he would automatically have passed two hearts, since there is no need for a corrective bid (opener has bid but one suit). The two no trumps bid, therefore shows 11-12 points, and expresses a desire to play the hand at no trump.

(6) Positive. Partner refuses to accept either clubs or hearts and chooses instead to name a new suit voluntarily. He shows at least 11 points, compels you to bid again, since he names a new suit.

(7) Corrective. This is the exceptional "non-lateral" bid. Partner shows merely a preference for diamonds, your first suit, over hearts, your second suit.

There is just one exceptional situation where responder may make a second positive bid without the 11-12 points usually necessary to support such action:

Whenever the responder makes two bids *within the one-level*, the second bid may be made on 8, 9, or 10 points.

To illustrate:

	(1)		(2)
	♠ K J x x		♠ x x
	♡ x x x		♡ K Q x
	◊ K Q x x		◊ K x x x x
	♣ x x		♣ x x x

Partner	You	Partner	You
1 club	1 diamond	1 club	1 diamond
1 heart	1 spade	1 spade	1 no trump

(1) Your one-spade bid, a second bid made within the one-level, will not be construed as showing 11 points. Of course, you are going to pass on the next round, since you have bid your hand to the hilt (and then some!).

(2) Your one no-trump rebid promises no more than 8 points. It says merely "I don't like your suits, partner." If partner's rebid had been one heart instead of the actual one spade, your proper rebid would have been to pass, since you would have been quite satisfied to have found a playable trump suit.

Rebids by Responder after a Prior Minimum Response
Whenever responder either directly single-raises opener, or responds with one no trump, opener knows responder has a

poor hand, containing a maximum of 10 points. Opener, of course, has the action of passing either of these limit responses. If he nevertheless chooses to move again towards a game, he is asking responder to clarify the nature of his original response: was it based on a minimum or on a maximum? Let us see how responder clarifies his bid.

You hold the following hand and the bidding has proceeded as shown:

♠ x x   ♡ Q x x x   ◇ A Q x x   ♣ x x x

Partner	*You*
1 heart	2 hearts
3 hearts	?

Your correct course is to raise to four hearts. Opener knows you cannot have more than 10 points, yet he is trying to get to game (he had the option of dropping two hearts). You have the best "bad" hand you could be expected to have, 10 points. When you bid four hearts, partner will be most happy when he sees your hand as the dummy. Remember, you would have raised to two hearts with a queen less.

An analogous situation develops when you have made a one no trump response (6-10 points) to partner's opening bid and he either raises to two no trumps or jumps to three of his original suit. He is asking you to break down your 6-10 range—to pass with the minimum (6 or 7) or to carry on with 8, 9, or 10 points. To illustrate:

(1)
♠ Q J x
♡ x x
◇ K x x x
♣ K x x x

(2)
♠ Q J x
♡ x x
◇ K x x x
♣ K x x x

Partner	*You*	*Partner*	*You*
1 heart	1 no trump	1 heart	1 no trump
2 no trumps	?	3 hearts	?

(3)
♠ Q J x
♡ x x
◇ K x x x x
♣ K x x

123

Partner	*You*
1 heart	1 no trump
3 hearts	?

(1) Bid three no trumps.
(2) Bid three no trumps.
(3) Bid three no trumps.

QUIZ

Rebids by Opener and Responder   You are the opening **bidder** in each of the following hands. The bidding has pro**ceeded** as indicated. What do you rebid?

(1)
♠ x x x
♡ Q x x
◇ K J x
♣ A K x x

You	*Partner*
1 club	1 heart
?	

(2)
♠ x x
♡ x x x x
◇ A Q x
♣ A K x x

You	*Partner*
1 club	1 heart
?	

(3)
♠ Q J x x
♡ A Q x
◇ x x
♣ A x x x

You	*Partner*
1 club	1 heart
?	

(4)
♠ A J x
♡ A K Q x
◇ x x
♣ A K x x

You	*Partner*
1 club	1 diamond
?	

(5)
♠ A J x
♡ A K Q
◇ x x x
♣ A K x x

(6)
♠ A Q J 10 x x
♡ A x x
◇ A Q x
♣ x

You	Partner	You	Partner
1 club	1 diamond	1 spade	1 no trump
?		?	

(7)
♠ Q J x x
♡ A K x x x
◇ A Q x
♣ x

(8)
♠ x x
♡ A Q x x x
◇ A Q J
♣ A K J

You	Partner	You	Partner
1 heart	1 spade	1 heart	1 spade
?		?	

(9)
♠ K Q J x x
♡ x x
◇ A K x x
♣ A x

(10)
♠ A K J 10 x
♡ K Q x
◇ K Q x
♣ x x

You	Partner	You	Partner
1 spade	2 clubs	1 spade	4 spades
?		?	

(11)
♠ A K x x x
♡ A J x
◇ x x x
♣ x x

(12)
♠ A Q x
♡ A K x x x x
◇ x x
♣ x x

You	Partner	You	Partner
1 spade	2 spades	1 heart	1 spade
?		?	

(13)
♠ A Q J
♡ A J x
◇ A x x
♣ K Q x x

(14)
♠ A Q x x x
♡ A K x
◇ A J x
♣ x x

You	Partner	You	Partner
1 club	2 clubs	1 spade	2 spades
?		?	

(15)	(16)
♠ K x x	♠ x x
♡ K x	♡ A K x x x
◇ A K x x x	◇ A K x
♣ x x x	♣ x x x

You	*Partner*	*You*	*Partner*
1 diamond	1 no trump	1 heart	1 no trump
?		?	

(17)	(18)
♠ A K J x x	♠ Q J x x
♡ A K x x	♡ K x x
◇ x x	◇ K x x
♣ x x	♣ A Q x

You	*Partner*	*You*	*Partner*
1 spade	1 no trump	1 club	1 diamond
?		?	

(19)	(20)
♠ K J x	♠ K x
♡ A Q 10 x x	♡ K J x
◇ A K x	◇ A K 10 x x
♣ x x	♣ A Q x

You	*Partner*	*You*	*Partner*
1 heart	1 no trump	1 diamond	1 no trump
?		?	

(21)	(22)
♠ x x	♠ K Q x x
♡ A K x x x	♡ A Q x x
◇ A J x x x	◇ x
♣ x	♣ A x x x

You	*Partner*	*You*	*Partner*
1 heart	1 spade	1 club	1 spade
?		?	

(23)
♠ A x x
♡ x x
◇ K Q x x
♣ A J x x

You	Partner
1 diamond	1 spade
?	

(24)
♠ Q x x x
♡ x
◇ A Q x
♣ A K x x x

You	Partner
1 club	1 spade
?	

(25)
♠ x x x
♡ A K J 10 x x
◇ A K J
♣ x

You	Partner
1 heart	1 no trump
?	

(26)
♠ A J x x x
♡ x x
◇ A K x x
♣ x x

You	Partner
1 spade	2 clubs
?	

(27)
♠ A Q x x x
♡ A K 10 x
◇ x x
♣ K x

You	Partner
1 spade	2 diamonds
?	

(28)
♠ K Q J x x
♡ x x
◇ A K x x
♣ K x

You	Partner
1 spade	2 hearts
?	

(29)
♠ A K J x
♡ A K Q x x
◇ x x x
♣ x

You	Partner
1 heart	2 diamonds
?	

(30)
♠ A Q
♡ K x
◇ A Q x x x
♣ J x x x

You	Partner
1 diamond	2 clubs
?	

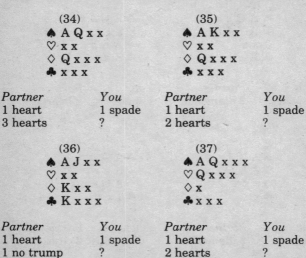

(31)

♠ A K x x x
♡ A Q x x
◇ x
♣ x x x

You	Partner
1 spade	3 spades
?	

(32)

♠ A Q x x x
♡ A K x x
◇ x x x
♣ x

You	Partner
1 spade	2 no trumps
?	

(33)

♠ K J x
♡ A Q x x
◇ x x
♣ A K x x

You	Partner
1 club	3 no trumps
?	

You are *the responder* on each of the following hands. The bidding has proceeded as indicated. What do you rebid?

(34)

♠ A Q x x
♡ x x
◇ Q x x x
♣ x x x

Partner	You
1 heart	1 spade
3 hearts	?

(35)

♠ A K x x
♡ x x
◇ Q x x x
♣ x x x

Partner	You
1 heart	1 spade
2 hearts	?

(36)

♠ A J x x
♡ x x
◇ K x x
♣ K x x x

Partner	You
1 heart	1 spade
1 no trump	?

(37)

♠ A Q x x x
♡ Q x x x
◇ x
♣ x x x

Partner	You
1 heart	1 spade
2 hearts	?

128

(38)		(39)	
♠ K J x x x		♠ K Q J x x	
♡ K Q x		♡ x x	
◇ A J x x		◇ x x	
♣ x		♣ x x x x	

Partner	You	Partner	You
1 club	1 spade	1 heart	1 spade
2 clubs	2 hearts	2 diamonds	?
3 clubs	?		

(40)		(41)	
♠ J x		♠ x x	
♡ J x		♡ x x	
◇ A K x x		◇ x x x x	
♣ x x x x x		♣ A K Q x x	

Partner	You	Partner	You
1 spade	1 no trump	1 heart	2 clubs
2 hearts	?	2 hearts	?

(42)		(43)	
♠ K x x x		♠ Q J x x	
♡ x x		♡ x x	
◇ A J x		◇ A Q x x	
♣ x x x x		♣ x x x	

Partner	You	Partner	You
1 spade	2 spades	1 club	1 diamond
2 no trumps	?	1 heart	?

(44)		(45)	
♠ K J x		♠ A x x	
♡ J x		♡ x x	
◇ Q x x x		◇ K J x x x	
♣ Q x x x		♣ x x x	

Partner	You	Partner	You
1 heart	1 no trump	1 heart	1 no trump
2 no trumps	?	3 hearts	?

(1) One no trump. You do not hold enough to raise to two hearts. In support of hearts, your hand is worth but 12 points: 13 in high cards plus 1 for the promotion of the queen of trumps, less 1 point for the defect of a 4-3-3-3 distribution, less 1 point for having only three supporting trumps.

(2) Two hearts. With a guaranteed minimum of 8 hearts between you, hearts is the proper trump suit.

(3) One spade, showing your second suit. Holding only three cards in partner's bid suit, a raise of his suit should be deferred if you have another biddable suit. Of course, should he rebid hearts, you will automatically raise him.

(4) Two hearts, the jump-shift rebid showing 22 or more points and guaranteeing a game. Responder must carry on to game.

(5) Three no trumps, showing 21-22 points and protection in each of the unbid suits.

(6) Four spades. With your self-sustaining suit, game in your suit is assured. Your hand is valued at 22 points: 17 in high cards, 2 for the singleton, plus 1 for the fifth card of a self-sustaining suit, plus 2 for the sixth card of a self-sustaining suit.

(7) Four spades. In support of partner's spades, your hand is valued at 20 points.

(8) Three no trumps. You have 21 high-card points and protection in each of the unbid suits.

(9) Three diamonds, a jump shift. You have only 19 points: 17 in high cards plus 2 for distribution. However, partner's two-over-one response has guaranteed 10 points, thereby assuring a game. If you rebid two diamonds, responder might pass.

(10) Pass. Partner has 9 points as a maximum.

(11) Pass. Game should not be bid opposite partner's announced 7-10 points.

(12) Two hearts. You have an excellent six-card suit, which should be rebid before raising partner on but three trumps.

(13) Three no trumps. The alternative is to try for a game at five clubs for 11 tricks. As we have seen, five-club and five-diamond contracts are to be avoided whenever possible. When you have all suits protected and the requisite points, 9 tricks

at no trump will invariably prove to be the more easily makable game.

(14) Four spades. Your hand is currently valued at 20 points: 18 in high cards, 1 for the doubleton, and 1 more for the fifth card of a supported suit.

(15) Pass. You have a minimum hand, and partner possesses 6-10 points. The best place to play mediocre hands is at one no trump.

(16) Pass. You have a balanced, minimum hand, and game is out of the question.

(17) Two hearts. You don't wish to play in no trump, and can conveniently show your second suit.

(18) One spade, not one no trump. Don't ever conceal biddable four-card major suits. If you do, you'll too often fail to arrive at the proper trump suit. You can always bid no trump later.

(19) Two no trumps, asking partner to bid three no trumps if he has a maximum one no trump bid (9 or 10).

(20) Three no trumps. Your 20 plus partner's 6 adds to 26, and all suits are protected.

(21) Two diamonds. Give partner a choice of your two suits. If he rebids his own suit, then bid three diamonds, informing partner that you have five diamonds and five hearts.

(22) Three spades. In support of spades your hand is valued at 18 points. If partner has more than a minimum response, he will carry on to four spades.

(23) One no trump. If partner can't bid again, you're in the right parking place.

(24) Three spades. This double raise shows 17, 18, or 19 points and four or more trumps. In support of spades your hand is valued at 19 points.

(25) Four hearts. You have a self-sustaining suit and 21 points: 16 in high cards, 2 for the singleton, plus 1 for the fifth card of a supported suit, plus 2 for the sixth card of a supported suit.

(26) Two diamonds. This will inform partner that you have five spades, since with four diamonds and four spades (non-touching suits) you would have bid one diamond originally.

(27) Two no trumps. It is more important to let your partner know that you have each of the unbid suits protected than to let him know that you have a four-card heart suit.

(28) Three diamonds, rather than two spades. You're perfectly willing to move aggressively towards a game since you have 18 points and partner's two-over-one response has denoted a minimum of 10 points.

(29) Two spades, the "reverse" bid showing a strong hand, since it compels partner, if he prefers hearts to spades, to go to the three-level to express that preference. (You have 19 points opposite partner's 10 points.)

(30) Two no trumps, rather than three clubs. This bid will announce protection in each of the unbid suits. Partner will not be offended because you "forgot" to show him your support for his minor suit.

(31) Four spades. Partner's response has announced four or more trumps and 13-15 points. Game is guaranteed.

(32) Three hearts. With your unbalanced hand, an effort should be made to play the game contract in one of your major suits. If partner doesn't like either of your suits, then he'll go on to three no trumps.

(33) Six no trumps, by addition. Partner has 16-18 high-card points. You have 17, which adds up to at least 33 points, which is the goal for a small slam.

(34) Four hearts. Opener's rebid announces 19-21 points, and is requesting you to continue if you have above the bare minimum needed to respond originally.

(35) Pass. Partner's rebid denotes a minimum hand, and your 9 points entitle you to only one positive bid.

(36) Two no trumps, showing 11-12 points. If partner has more than a minimum one no trump rebid, he will contract for game at three no trumps.

(37) Three hearts, showing 11-12 points as your second positive bid. Your hand, in support of hearts, is worth 12 points: 8 in high cards, 3 for the singleton, and 1 for the promotion of the queen of trumps.

(38) Three diamonds, "on the house." Opener cannot pass whenever you, as responder, name a new suit. Let him pick the spot to play the game.

(39) Two hearts, the preference bid at the two-level. Had you held three diamonds and two hearts, you would have passed two diamonds.

(40) Two spades, a preference for partner's first-bid suit, since he might have more spades than hearts, or the same number of each; but he couldn't have more hearts than spades.

(41) Pass. You have bid your hand to the hilt, and your

partner knows you have at least 10 points. If he couldn't bid more than just two hearts, no game can be made.

(42) Four spades. Opener could have passed your two-spade response. He knows you have 7-10 points. His two no–trumps rebid expresses a desire to get to game, and he is trying to ascertain whether you have a "bad" raise (7-8) or a "good" raise (9-10). You have a *real good* raise: 10 points (8 in high cards, 1 for the doubleton, and 1 for the promotion of the king of trumps).

(43) One spade. A second positive bid *within the one-level* can be made on 9-10 points, and partner will not interpret it as showing 11-12. Furthermore, you don't like hearts; to pass one heart would be to leave the partnership in the worst possible contract.

(44) Three no trumps. Partner knows you have 6-10 points, and he had the right to pass your response. His two no–trumps rebid asks you to go on to game if you have a "good" one no trump response. Your 9 points are real good—you could have had 6 or 7.

(45) Four hearts. Partner has 19-21 points and at least six hearts. You have 8 points, so game should be bid, and you cannot bid three no trumps with no stopper in the unbid club suit.

Lesson 6

POWERHOUSE HANDS AND SLAM BIDDING

THE OPENING BID OF TWO IN A SUIT

About nine out of every ten hands are normally opened with one of a suit, with the fond hope that responder holds enough points to bring the joint assets to 26, to make a game.

Occasionally, however, a player will hold a hand that is so powerful that he can make a game all by himself even if partner has virtually nothing. On these hands, he cannot afford to open with just one of a suit, lest partner pass. Nor can he afford to open with a game bid, because he may need partner's cooperation in exploring the possibilities of making a slam, and by opening with a game bid, opener would eliminate the room necessary for such exploration.

An opening bid of two in a suit tells partner you have this kind of powerhouse hand. It is often called a "two-demand" bid because it demands that partner respond and keep on responding until game has been reached; the responder may not pass at a lower level, with three rare exceptions:

1. He may pass if an opponent's bid or double has assured the opener of another chance to bid.

2. He may pass if the opener has doubled an adverse contract for penalties.

3. He may pass if, having been warned of weakness by a conventional response of two no trumps, opener's rebid is a repeat of the *same suit* at the *lowest possible level*, i.e.:

Opener	Responder
2 ♡	2 no trumps
3 ♡	

This third exception is a recent change in the Goren (Standard American) method. Hitherto, the rule was that the responder had to keep on bidding until game or a satisfactory double of the opponents had been reached. Undoubtedly that rule was easy to remember, but it had two great disadvantages. Either you could not open with a forcing bid of two in a suit on certain strong one-suited hands that could not ever be adequately described later, or you sometimes reached too high a contract with this kind of hand if you opened with a two-bid and partner turned out to have absolutely no help. Obviously, it was embarrassing when a player whose opening bid announced "game in hand" could not actually make the game. But it was equally embarrassing if he opened the bidding with a one-bid and his partner passed with very little strength, but that little was enough to produce a game.

This change in the opening two-bid rule is a great improvement, but it is not yet universally known. Therefore, when you play with a new partner be sure to discuss it and make certain that he too is aware of the change.

Needless to say, this situation will not come up very often. It is important to remember that *any other* rebid by the opener is forcing and compels responder to bid again if game has not been reached. It is also important to realize that opener needs very little from responder, even if his rebid is a minimum in the same suit. The "escape clause" operates only when the responder has a hopeless hand. Remember, if partner needed as much as 6 points to make game he would have opened with a one-bid, knowing that with 6 or more points you would keep the bidding open. Therefore, a hand with 3 or 4 points— even fewer high-card points with good trump support and a ruffing value—should carry on to game.

Conversely, if opener has a hand with which he can reasonably expect to make game even opposite a bust, he should avoid a simple repeat of the same suit at the lowest level. Of course, if partner makes any first response other than two no trumps—the warning of weakness—opener can rebid in the way that will best describe his hand, knowing that a positive response from partner guarantees that the bidding will reach at least a game contract.

Before presenting the requirements for an opening two-bid, let us take a quick glance at a few illustrations.

(1)	(2)	(3)
♠ A x	♠ A K	♠ A Q J x x
♡ A K Q J x x x	♡ x	♡ A K Q x x
◊ A x	◊ A K Q J x x x x	◊ A Q
♣ A x	♣ A x	♣ x
Bid 2 hearts	Bid 2 diamonds	Bid 2 spades

(1) You can make ten tricks in hearts or no trump even if partner throws his cards out of the window.

(2) Eleven tricks in diamonds are there for the taking. And, if your partner happens to have the ace of hearts or the king of clubs, you will make a small slam. If he has both of these cards, you will make a grand slam.

(3) You cannot absolutely guarantee a game, but your partner has thirteen cards and a game will be made if they happen to be a reasonable facsimile of:

♠ x x x   ♡ x x x   ◊ x x x   ♣ x x x x

The reader will concede that to assume that partner has the above is asking very little of life. Yet even with this "nothing" hand, you figure to lose, at a four-heart or four-spade contract, one spade, one diamond and one club.

The point-count requirements for the opening bid of two in a suit are as follows:

——With a good four-* or five-card suit, 25 points.

——With a good six-card suit, 23 points.

——With a good seven-card suit, 21 points.

With a second good five-card suit, 1 point less is needed. If both suits are minors, 2 points more will be needed.

Note: In valuing your hand for the purpose of making an opening two bid in a suit, you should assume that your partner's hand is worthless. Unguarded picture cards should therefore be assigned *no* value.

Here are some illustrations:

---

* It is undesirable to open with a two-bid on a four-card suit. However, if you hold 25 or more points, and you cannot bid three no trumps originally because you don't have all suits protected or have an unbalanced hand (4-4-4-1) then you have no alternative but to open with two of your best minor suit.

(1)	(2)	(3)
♠ A K J 10	♠ K Q J 10 x	♠ K Q x
♡ A K Q 10	♡ x	♡ A Q J 10 x x
◇ A K J	◇ A K Q x	◇ x
♣ x x	♣ A K J	♣ A K Q

(4)	(5)	(6)
♠ A K J 10 x x x	♠ A K J x x	♠ A K J
♡ A K	♡ A K Q x x	♡ K Q x
◇ A x	◇ A x	◇ A K Q J x x
♣ x x	♣ x	♣ x

(1) Bid two spades. You have the required 25 high-card points to bid two in a four-card suit. (When you have two strong four-card major suits, you may make an exception to the five-card major rule.)

(2) Bid two spades. With a good five-card suit, 25 points are necessary. You have 23 in high cards and 2 in distribution.

(3) Bid two hearts. With a good six-card suit, 23 points are needed. You hold 21 points in high cards and 2 in distribution.

(4) Bid two spades. With a good seven-card suit, 21 points are necessary. You have 19 in high cards and 3 in distribution (1 point apiece for each of the doubletons).

(5) Bid two spades. With two good five-card suits, 24 points are required. You have 21 in high cards and 3 in distribution (2 points for the singleton and 1 point for the doubleton).

(6) Bid two diamonds. If the good suit is a minor suit, 2 points more will be needed, since the minor-suit game needs eleven tricks. With your good six-card diamond suit, therefore, 25 points are required. You have 25 points: 23 in high cards and 2 in distribution.

The reader may feel that some of these examples do not guarantee that the opener can make a game all by himself. On hand (3), if responder has absolutely nothing, then opener may well lose two spades, one heart, and one diamond.

Actually, there are two criteria in judging whether a given hand should be opened with a two-bid in a suit. The major criterion has just been presented: The Point-Count. The other criterion is *the number of winning tricks* in the hand. The rule is that your winning tricks should total *within one trick of game*. To open with two hearts or spades, in addition to the requisite points, you must be able to win at least nine tricks all by yourself; to open with two clubs or diamonds, besides the points, you need ten tricks.

The reason for this one-trick "deviation" will be explained by an illustration:

♠ A K Q J 10 x   ♡ A K   ◇ A J x   ♣ x x

Suppose you open the above hand with only one spade. Your partner holds:

(1)	(2)	(3)	(4)
♠ x x	♠ x x	♠ x	♠ x x
♡ x x x x	♡ x x x x	♡ x x x x	♡ x x x x
◇ Q x x	◇ K x x	◇ x x x x	◇ x x x x
♣ x x x x	♣ x x x x	♣ A x x x	♣ K x x

On each of the above hands your partner will pass, since he does not have 6 points. Yet, if he holds hands (1), (2), or (3), a game is absolutely guaranteed, for his picture card adds a trick to your hand. With hand (4), there is a 50-50 chance of making four spades, depending on which of the opponents holds the ace of clubs. Further, hand (4) is a laydown for three no trumps, if opener is the declarer.

The rationale of the one-trick deviation thus is: if your partner has a "stray" ace, king or queen—nothing else—with which he would be unable to respond to your opening one-bid, that stray card will almost always make up your deficit. On probability, your partner will usually have that one hoped-for card.

RESPONSES TO OPENING TWO-BIDS

With the three exceptions noted earlier, the opening bid of two in a suit is forcing to game. It is often referred to as a "demand" bid—it demands that the responder keep on bidding even with a blank hand.

When the responder has a weak hand, he makes the standard, conventional, artificial, and negative response of *two no trumps*. This artificial response is a necessity, since responder is not permitted to pass.

Before discussing what a "weak" hand is, let us look at a typical bidding sequence. In experience, when partner opens with a two-bid in a suit, you will make the two no-trump response more often than any other single bid:

Opener	Responder
2 diamonds	2 no trumps (a)

(a) "I have a weak hand, as my two no–trumps response indicates."

Should the bidding then continue:

Opener	Responder
2 diamonds	2 no trumps
3 hearts	?

Responder is again forced to bid. Just as the two no–trumps response is used to indicate a weak hand, so the three no trumps response in the following sequence denotes a "weaker-than-weak" hand.

Opener	Responder
2 diamonds	2 no trumps
3 hearts	3 no trumps (b)

(b) "I have a weaker-than-weak hand, but I must keep the bidding open because you have rebid in a different suit."

Responder's hand might be:

♠ x x x x   ♡ x x x   ◇ x x   ♣ x x x x

If responder has definite values, he makes a positive, forward-going response. For an immediate positive response, he must hold at least an ace or king.

In support of an opening two-bid of a suit, count your winning tricks (or "quick tricks") by the following table:

Ace	1 trick
K-Q-x	1 trick
K-x	½ trick
K-x and K-x	1 trick (½ and ½)

What does responder need to make a positive response? Here are the requirements:

——A minimum of 7 points if the hand contains 1 quick trick.

——A minimum of 8 points if the hand contains only ½ quick trick.

——If responder does not hold at least ½ quick trick, his first response must be two no trumps. On the next round of bidding, responder may show his "decent" suit, if he finds it expedient to do so. A decent suit, for purposes of responding to a two-bid, is one headed by at least the Q-J or K.

With adequate trump support of opener's suit, responder should usually elect to raise opener's suit, rather than bid a shaky suit of his own. This will establish the trump suit, set opener's mind at ease, and will become the signal for the showing of aces and kings.

However, a five-card or longer major suit should be showed in preference to raising a minor. Also, a hand clearly worth two bids should show an establishable long suit (headed by ace, king, or queen-jack) prior to giving a raise. With a fit in responder's suit, opener may be able to move toward slam.

Now let us look at the specific positive responses that responder may make. There are three possible types.

   I. A response in a new suit.

  II. A single raise of opener's suit.

 III. A jump to three no trumps.

*I. New-Suit Responses** As was stated, this will show either (a) a minimum of 7 points with 1 quick trick, or (b) a minimum of 8 points with ½ quick trick. Also, responder's suit must be headed by at least the Q-J or K. To illustrate, you hold the following hands, and partner opens with two hearts:

(1)	(2)	(3)	(4)
♠ K x x x x	♠ A J 10 x	♠ Q J x	♠ Q J x
♡ x x x	♡ x	♡ x x	♡ x x
◇ K J x	◇ Q x x x	◇ x x x	◇ Q x x
♣ x x	♣ x x x x	♣ K Q x x x	♣ Q J x x x

(1) Bid two spades. You have 7 points in high cards and 1 in distribution, with 1 quick trick.

---

* Some play ace-showing responses, but we prefer natural responses. It is usually possible to locate an ace in responder's hand at a later stage, should opener wish to do so.

(2) Bid two spades, with your 7 high-card points, 1 quick trick.

(3) Bid three clubs. You have 8 points in high cards, more than ½ quick trick.

(4) Bid two no trumps. You have 8 points, but no quick tricks. To make a positive response, you must always have at least ½ quick trick.

II. The Single Raise of Opener's Suit Responder counts his distributional points as usual: that is, voids, singletons, and doubletons will be assigned their regular value. Also, subtractions for defects are made as usual.

The single raise should be made when responder holds normal trump support for opener, plus the minimum of 7 points and required quick tricks. For example, you hold the following hands and partner opens with two spades:

(1)	(2)	(3)	(4)
♠ Q x x	♠ x x x x	♠ A x x x	♠ J x x x
♡ K J x x	♡ x x	♡ x	♡ x x
◇ x x x x x	◇ A Q x	◇ x x x x	◇ Q x x x
♣ x	♣ x x x x	♣ x x x x	♣ x x x

(1) Bid three spades. You have adequate trump support, ½ quick trick, and 9 points in support of spades: 6 in high cards, 3 for the singleton, plus 1 for the promotion of the queen of trumps, less 1 for the defect of having only 3 trumps.

(2) Bid three spades. You have 7 points and 1 quick trick.

(3) Bid three spades. Your hand in support of spades is worth 7 points (3 for your singleton) and 1 quick trick.

(4) Bid two no trumps. In support of spades you have but 5 points, with no quick tricks.

III. The Jump to Three No Trumps This bid is made on a hand of 8 or 9 high-card points (including at least an ace or king), no biddable five-card suit, and no void or singleton; nor will it contain four or more cards of partner's suit. With the following hands, a jump to three no trumps is the prescribed response to partner's opening bid of two diamonds:

(1)	(2)	(3)
♠ A Q x	♠ K x x	♠ Q x x x
♡ Q x x	♡ K x x	♡ Q x x
◇ x x	◇ x x x	◇ J x
♣ J x x x x	♣ Q x x x	♣ K x x x

Having an apparent option of jumping to three no trumps or of bidding a new suit, elect to jump to three no trumps if your suit is minimum in high cards and/or length; elect to bid the suit if it is "good" in high cards. To illustrate, partner opens two hearts and you hold:

(1)	(2)	(3)
♠ Q x x x	♠ K Q x x x	♠ K x x
♡ x x	♡ x x	♡ x x
◇ K x x	◇ K x x	◇ K x x
♣ K 10 x x	♣ x x x	♣ Q J x x x

(1) Bid three no trumps.
(2) Bid two spades.
(3) Bid three no trumps. Any new suit headed by just the Q-J is definitely too weak to go to the three-level.

The Double Raise of a Major-Suit Two-Bid This bid has not previously been mentioned. It is neither positive nor negative, but a specialized, purely artificial bid that denies a strong hand. It describes a hand of 6 or fewer points, with good trump support (at least the Q-x-x-x or x-x-x-x-x), and *no ace, no king, no void,* and *no singleton.* It warns partner not to bid a slam unless all he needs is plenty of trump support. To illustrate, partner opens with two hearts, and you hold:

(1)	(2)	(3)
♠ Q x x	♠ x x	♠ x x x
♡ Q x x x x	♡ x x x x x	♡ Q x x x x
◇ x x	◇ x x	◇ x x x
♣ x x x	♣ Q x x x	♣ x x
Bid 4 hearts	Bid 4 hearts	Bid 4 hearts

In the minor suits, with hands such as the above, two no trumps is the preferred bid, since this negative bid will give partner the chance to contract for three no trumps, which opportunity would be precluded if you jumped to four of his minor suit. If opener doesn't rebid three no trumps, you will then support his original suit.

Over partner's two-diamond opening bid, two no trumps is proper on each of the following hands:

(1)	(2)	(3)
♠ Q x x	♠ x x	♠ x x x
♡ x x x	♡ x x	♡ x x x
◇ Q x x x x	◇ x x x x x	◇ Q x x x x
♣ x x	♣ Q x x x	♣ x x

Over your two no trumps response, should opener rebid three diamonds, you will raise to four diamonds with each of the above hands. Since you might have passed three diamonds, this bid is encouraging.

SUBSEQUENT BIDDING: THE DIRECT SHOWING OF ACES

After agreement in a suit has been reached, aces and kings will be shown either in natural fashion (by bidding the suit of an ace), or via the Blackwood Slam Convention, which is discussed later in this lesson. Let us observe how aces and kings are shown in natural, or direct, fashion.

First example. You, as responder, hold the following hand. The proper partnership bidding, and its interpretation, is indicated:

♠ A x x   ♡ x x x   ◇ x x x x   ♣ x x

Opener	Responder
2 hearts	2 no trumps
3 clubs	3 hearts (a)
4 diamonds (b)	4 spades (c)

(a) "Partner, I prefer hearts to clubs."
(b) "I have the ace of diamonds and I am interested in a possible slam!"
(c) "I have the ace of spades."

If you think you've done too much bidding with the above hand, please remember first, that your partner said he could make a game all by himself and that, therefore, your spade ace is excess; and, second, that your partner asked you to name an ace, if you had one. Don't start worrying—when you bid two no trumps, you told him you had a bad hand. How nice it would be if he held (and he might):

143

♠ K Q x   ♡ A K Q J x   ◇ A   ♣ A K Q x

Second example. You, as responder, hold the following hand. The correct partnership bidding, and its interpretation, is indicated:

♠ Q x x x   ♡ x x   ◇ A x x x   ♣ x x x

Opener	Responder
2 spades	3 spades (a)
4 clubs (b)	4 diamonds (c)

(a) "Partner, I have positive spade support—7 points and 1 quick trick."

(b) "I have the ace of clubs. What ace, if any, do you have?"

(c) "I have the ace of diamonds."

Third example. You, as responder, hold the following hand. The correct partnership bidding and its interpretation, is indicated:

♠ Q 10 x x   ♡ x x x   ◇ Q J x   ♣ K x x

Opener	Responder
2 spades	3 spades (a)
4 clubs (b)	5 clubs (c)

(a) "Spades is the trump suit."

(b) "I have the ace of clubs."

(c) "I have the king of clubs."

Had opener rebid four diamonds (instead of four clubs), then responder, having no ace to show, would merely have returned to four spades.

Fourth example. You, as responder, hold the following hand:

♠ Q J x x x   ♡ x x   ◇ K x x   ♣ A x x

Opener	Responder
2 hearts	2 spades (a)
3 spades (b)	4 clubs (c)
4 diamonds (d)	5 diamonds (e)

(a) "I have a positive bid. My suit is headed by the ace, king, or queen-jack."

144

(b) "Spades is our trump suit."
(c) "I have the ace of clubs. Respond in kind."
(d) "I have the ace of diamonds."
(e) "I have the king of diamonds."

Opener now knows enough about responder's hand to decide whether to settle for a small slam or a grand slam. Obviously, at least a small slam will be makable, since opener's two-bid stated that he could make a game with virtually nothing in opener's hand.

Fifth example.

Opener	Responder
♠ A Q J	♠ K x x x x
♡ A K Q J 10 x x	♡ x x x
◇ A x	◇ J x
♣ x	♣ A x x
2 hearts	2 spades (a)
3 hearts (b)	4 clubs (c)
7 no trumps (d)	

(a) "I have a positive bid—at least 7 points with 1 quick trick, or 8 or more points with at least ½ quick trick. Also my spade suit is headed by A, K, or Q-J."

(b) "Hearts is our trump suit, as my rebid indicates. Tell me more."

(c) "I have the ace of clubs."

(d) "Thank you! I can count thirteen tricks."

Sixth example.

Opener	Responder
♠ A x	♠ x x
♡ A K x	♡ Q J x x x x
◇ A K Q J x x x	◇ x x
♣ K	♣ A J x
2 diamonds	2 hearts (a)
3 hearts (b)	4 clubs (c)
7 no trumps (d)	

(a) A positive bid, showing a heart suit headed by A, K, or Q-J.

(b) In the full knowledge that partner's suit is headed by precisely the Q-J.

(c) Showing the ace of clubs, agreement in a trump suit having been reached.

(d) Opener can count more than thirteen tricks: seven diamonds, two clubs, a spade and at least four hearts.

Seventh example.

Opener	Responder
♠ A	♠ x x x x x
♡ K Q J 10 x x	♡ x x x
◇ A K Q J	◇ x x
♣ A x	♣ K x x
2 hearts	2 no trumps (a)
3 diamonds (b)	3 hearts (c)
4 clubs (d)	5 clubs (e)
6 hearts (f)	

(a) The conventional negative bid.

(b) Showing a secondary suit.

(c) Indicating a preference for hearts. Hearts have now become established as the trump suit.

(d) "I know you have a weak hand, but I'm still in quest of a slam. I have the ace of clubs. Do you have the king of clubs?"

(e) "I do."

(f) The small slam is now assured.

A PREFERRED APPROACH:
STRONG TWO-CLUB BIDS

Quite a few modern bridge players prefer to play that all hands worthy of a strong two-bid in a suit are opened with two clubs. This artificial opening bid is forcing, of course, and partner shows a weak hand by bidding two diamonds (also conventional), giving opener as much room as possible to show his suit. The two no trumps response is now positive, showing 8-9 points.

This strong two-club opening has many advantages. You may use opening two-bids in the other suits to show weak (Lesson 7) or less powerful hands. The bidding is kept at a lower level, making it possible to exchange information below game. Finally, if the hand is to be played at no trumps, the lead will come up to the strong hand instead of the weak hand shown by a two no trump response to other forcing two-bids.

To illustrate, refer again to the sixth example cited above:

Opener	Responder
♠ A	♠ x x x x x
♡ K Q J 10 x x	♡ x x x
◇ A K Q J	◇ x x
♣ A x	♣ K x x

2 clubs (a)	
2 hearts (c)	2 diamonds (b)
3 diamonds	2 spades (d)
4 clubs	3 hearts
6 hearts	5 clubs

(a) Conventional and forcing; showing a strong two-bid with the suit as yet undefined.

(b) Conventional, showing a hand that would have responded two no trumps to a strong two-bid using standard methods.

(c) Opener's real suit—and still forcing.

(d) Having already shown a weak hand, responder can mention the spade suit without fear that partner will expect too much.

If you elect to use this method, be sure to discuss it in advance with your partner.

SLAM BIDDING

In the preceding material on opening two-bids and responses thereto, the broad subject under discussion was, in part, slam bidding. The opening two-bid proposes a game, and the ensuing bidding is for the purpose of determining whether a slam can be made. We also discussed slam bidding in Lesson 4, where it was illustrated that 33 points in high cards will yield a small slam, and that 37 points in high cards will yield a grand slam. In no-trump bidding, the determination of whether a slam could be made necessitates nothing more than routine addition, since opener's bid is precise (16-18; 22-24; 25-27); and responder has to do nothing more than to add his points to opener's ($17 + 16 = 33$; $11 + 22 = 33$; $12 + 25 = 37$; etc.). If the total adds to 33 or 37, responder bids either a small slam or a grand slam, respectively.

Obviously, there is much more to slam bidding than was presented in the foregoing lessons. Most slams are arrived at after an opening bid of one in a suit, since nine out of ten deals are so opened. In the realm of suit bidding, slams cannot be determined exclusively by point-count. The point-count must be supplemented by location of the "key" cards—that is, aces and kings, or equivalent voids or singletons. A glimpse into the meaning of key cards was revealed in Part One of this lesson, where specific aces and kings were shown after agreement in a trump suit was reached. Let us examine further this matter of key cards. Suppose you hold the following hand:

♠ x   ♡ A K Q x x x x x x   ◇ A   ♣ x

Your partner opens with one spade. Can you make a small slam? Or a grand slam?

The answer is: you don't know. If your partner holds hand (1) below, you *cannot* make a slam. If he holds hand (2), you *can* make a small slam. And if he has hand (3) a grand slam is guaranteed.

(1)	(2)	(3)
♠ K Q J x x	♠ A Q J x x	♠ A Q x x x
♡ x	♡ x	♡ x
◇ K Q J x	◇ K Q x x	◇ x x x
♣ K Q x	♣ x x x	♣ A J x x

(1) Despite opener's 19 points, you cannot make any slam, since the opponents will cash two aces.

(2) Although opener has but 14 points, a small slam is assured, since your only loser will be the ace of clubs.

(3) Although opener has a minimum hand of 13 points, a grand slam is guaranteed, since his ace of spades and ace of clubs will take care of your two losers in spades and clubs.

With freak distributions, it is evident that "points" have nothing to do with the determination of whether a slam can be made. The sole issue, from responder's point of view is: HOW MANY ACES DOES OPENER HAVE? If no aces, no slam; if one ace, a small slam; if two aces, a grand slam. Putting it another way, 8 points in opener's hand, if they consist of two aces, are worth infinitely more than 19 points, consisting of no aces. On this deal, then, aces become the key cards.

Let us look at another example of key cards, in terms of reinforcing the point-count in slam bidding. You hold the following opening hand (1) and partner holds either of the other two hands (2) and (3).

(1)
♠ A Q x x x x
♡ A K J
◇ Q x
♣ A x

(2)   (3)
♠ K J x x   ♠ K J x x x
♡ Q x x   ♡ x x x
◇ x x   ◇ x
♣ K Q J x   ♣ K Q J x

You open hand (1) with one spade, and on both hands (2) and (3), responder will jump to three spades, showing 13-15 points, and four or more trumps. In terms of point-count you know you have at least 33 between you. Yet, as the reader can see, if responder holds hand (2), a slam cannot be made, since the opponents will cash the ace and king of diamonds. If responder holds hand (3), a small slam will be made, for responder's singleton diamond—a key card—will effectively prevent the opponents from cashing two diamond tricks.

The natural question at this point, is, of course, how does one find out about these key cards? Let us examine the process, step by step.

The Blackwood Slam Convention This convention will enable you to determine with accuracy, exactly *how many* aces and kings your partner holds. The Blackwood Convention is used universally, and is a precision instrument without which most slams cannot be bid with any degree of assurance. Here it is.

When the preliminary rounds of bidding have indicated that a slam is probable, and a suit has been established as the trump suit, either player may employ the convention by bidding FOUR NO TRUMPS. No special holding is required for this bid, but the player making it must be quite convinced that the hand will play safely for eleven tricks.

Partner cannot pass this four no trumps bid, which is a request for him to show his aces.

The artificial responses to four no trumps are as follows:

——With no aces, bid five clubs.

——With one ace, bid five diamonds.

——With two aces, bid five hearts.

——With three aces, bid five spades.

——With four aces, bid five clubs.

After aces have been shown, the originator of the four no trumps bid may ask for kings by bidding FIVE NO TRUMPS, to which partner will respond (artificially) in the same fashion as he did to four no trumps:

——With no kings, bid six clubs.

——With one king, bid six diamonds.

——With two kings, bid six hearts.

——With three kings, bid six spades.

——With four kings, bid six no trumps.

As the reader can see, the responses to this convention are given according to the rank of suits, from the lowest to the highest (clubs, diamonds, hearts, spades, no trumps). And, of course, the originator will then know exactly how many aces and kings partner holds.

Let us apply this convention to a hand previously discussed. Partner opens with one spade, and you hold:

♠ x
♡ A K Q x x x x x x x
♦ A
♣ x

Partner's possible hands are:

(1)	(2)	(3)
♠ K Q J x x	♠ A Q J x x	♠ A Q x x x
♡ x	♡ x	♡ x
♦ K Q J x	♦ K Q x x	♦ x x x
♣ K Q x	♣ x x x	♣ A J x x

The bidding:

	(1)		(2)
Partner	*You*	*Partner*	*You*
1 spade	4 no trumps	1 spade	4 no trumps
5 clubs	5 hearts	5 diamonds	6 hearts

	(3)
Partner	*You*
1 spade	4 no trumps
5 hearts	7 hearts

(1) Partner's response of five clubs shows no aces. You know a slam cannot be made, hence you stop at five hearts. Whenever responder shows his ace-count, and originator then signs off at the five-level, responder *must pass*.*

(2) Partner's response of five diamonds shows one ace. Whichever ace it is, twelve tricks are now guaranteed.

(3) Partner's response of five hearts shows two aces. You can now count thirteen sure tricks.

The five no trumps bid is never used by the Blackwood originator unless the partnership has all four aces. The bid is known as a "grand slam try," since responder is forced to the six-level in any event. If responder has the right number of kings, opener will bid a grand slam.

Before the Blackwood Convention can be initiated, a suit must be established as the trump suit. In the foregoing example, your ten hearts firmly established that suit in your mind as trumps. But, in many cases, you will not have a self-sustaining trump suit, and partnership exploration in the early rounds will be necessary before the proper trump suit can be established. Let us look at an example of how this is arrived at prior to the initiation of the Blackwood Slam Convention.

You are the responder, holding the following hand:

♠ A K x x x x   ♡ K Q x   ◇ A x   ♣ x x

The bidding has proceeded:

---

* If a suit has been agreed upon and originator bids a new suit at the five-level, it requests partner to bid five no trumps.

Partner	*You*
1 club	1 spade
3 spades (a)	4 no trumps (b)
5 hearts (c)	5 no trumps (d)
6 hearts (e)	7 spades or
	7 no trumps (f)

(a) Showing 17-19 points and four or more spades.

(b) The Blackwood Convention, asking for aces.

(c) Showing two aces.

(d) The Blackwood Convention, asking for kings.

(e) Showing two kings.

(f) You can now count thirteen tricks: six in spades, three in hearts, two in diamonds, and two in clubs.

Here is an illustration of the Blackwood Convention as employed by the opener:

Opener	*Responder*
♠ A x	♠ x x x
♡ A K x x x x	♡ Q J x x x
◇ K Q J x	◇ A x x
♣ x	♣ A x

1 heart	
4 no trumps (b)	3 hearts (a)
5 no trumps (d)	5 hearts (c)
6 hearts (f)	6 clubs (e)

(a) Showing 13-15 points and four or more trumps.

(b) Asking for aces.

(c) Showing two aces.

(d) Asking for kings.

(e) No kings.

(f) Opener knows that since responder has no kings, a spade trick will probably be lost to the opponents' king of spades. If, over five no trumps, responder had bid six diamonds, showing one king, opener would have bid seven hearts or no trumps, since in this case, he could count on thirteen winning tricks: six hearts, four diamonds, the ace of spades, the ace of clubs, and partner's king (spades or clubs).

The Blackwood Convention is also utilized after an opening bid of two in a suit. To illustrate:

152

	You		Partner
	♠ A K Q J 10 x x		♠ x
	♡ x		♡ K Q J x x x
	◇ A K		◇ Q J x x
	♣ K Q J		♣ x x

2 spades	3 hearts (a)
4 no trumps (b)	5 clubs (c)
5 spades (d)	

(a) The positive response showing a minimum of 7 points and a minimum of ½ quick trick.

(b) The Blackwood Convention.

(c) No aces.

(d) "Why can't you ever have an ace or two?"

The originator of the Blackwood bid decides whether or not a small slam can be made. His sign-off at the five level indicates a shortage of aces. However, if the originator next bids five no trumps, responder may proceed on the assurance that his side has all the aces.

Between partners playing the Blackwood Convention, a bid of four no trumps at any time is understood to be conventional, except as follows:

Whenever the immediately preceding bid by partner has been any number of no trumps, four no trumps is *NOT* the Blackwood Convention, and can be passed.

For example:

	(1)		(2)
Opener	Responder	Opener	Responder
1 no trump	4 no trumps	1 diamond	2 no trumps
		4 no trumps	

	(3)
Opener	Responder
1 club	1 heart
3 no trumps	4 no trumps

(1) The response is simply a raise in no trumps. It asks opener to bid a small slam if he has a maximum no trump bid (18 points). The response would be made on the following hand:

153

♠ K Q x   ♡ A x x   ◇ K J x x   ♣ Q x x

(2) The four no trumps bid states: "Partner, I have too much to bid merely three no trumps. If your jump was made on a maximum hand (15 points, rather than 13 or 14), bid six no trumps. Otherwise, pass." The four no trumps rebid by opener would be made on the following hand:

♠ x x   ♡ A K x   ◇ A K Q x   ♣ Q 10 x x

(3) The four no trumps bid tells opener to bid six no trumps if his jump to three was based on a maximum holding (22 or more points, as opposed to a minimum of 21). Responder's hand might be:

♠ Q x x   ♡ A K x x   ◇ J x x   ♣ J 10 x

Stated in negative fashion, whenever the immediately preceding bid has *not* been any number of no trumps, four no trumps is deemed to be the initiation of the Blackwood Convention. In the following examples, each four no trumps bid is conventional.

	(1)		(2)
Opener	*Responder*	*Opener*	*Responder*
1 heart	1 spade	1 spade	4 no trumps
3 hearts	4 no trumps		

	(3)		(4)
Opener	*Responder*	*Opener*	*Responder*
1 heart	1 spade	1 diamond	3 diamonds
2 clubs	3 hearts	4 no trumps	
4 no trumps			

	(5)		(6)
Opener	*Responder*	*Opener*	*Responder*
1 club	2 hearts	1 no trump	3 spades
3 clubs	4 no trumps	4 spades	4 no trumps

The Gerber Four-Club Convention The question arises: if the immediately preceding bid by partner has been either one, two, or three no trumps, how can I then find out about his aces? For example, partner opens the bidding with one no trump, and you hold:

♠ x   ♡ A K x x x x x x   ◇ A K   ♣ x x

You want to know how many aces and kings your partner holds, not how many points. If you bid four no trumps he will probably interpret this bid as a direct raise, and will pass with less than a maximum hand. Obviously, that is not the interpretation you want him to make.

In such situations, where the Blackwood Convention cannot be used, the solution is to jump to FOUR CLUBS, which is the initiation of the Gerber Four-Club Convention.

This bid requires responder to show his aces artificially, going up the ladder according to the rank of suits:
——With no aces, or all four aces, bid four diamonds.
——With one ace, bid four hearts.
——With two aces, bid four spades.
——With three aces, bid four no trumps.

The four-club bidder, after having learned about aces, may then ask for kings by bidding that suit (or no trump) *ranking directly over the last response,* e.g., if the response to four clubs is four hearts, the originator may now bid four spades to ask for kings. A response of four no trumps would now show no kings; five clubs = one king; five diamonds = two kings; five hearts = three kings; five spades = four kings.

Or, if the response to four clubs is four spades, four no trumps would now ask for kings. A response of five clubs would show none; five diamonds, one; etc. For example:

Opener	*Responder*
♠ Q x x x	♠ A x
♡ J x x	♡ A K x x x x x
◇ A K x	◇ x x
♣ A K x	♣ x
1 no trump	4 clubs (a)
4 spades (b)	4 no trumps (c)
5 hearts (d)	7 no trumps (e)

(a) The Gerber Convention
(b) The response showing two aces.
(c) The next-ranking "suit," asking for kings.

(d) The response showing two kings.

(e) Responder can now count thirteen tricks.

Showing Specific Aces and Kings The Blackwood and Gerber Slam Conventions are utilized whenever the originator desires to know the *number* of aces and kings his partner holds. But there are other situations where it becomes necessary for him, for slam purposes, to determine *which* ace or king partner holds. These cases illustrate the "direct" method of showing aces and kings:

♠ A K Q x   ♡ A Q x x x x   ◇ x x x   ♣ —

Opener	Responder
1 heart	3 hearts
3 spades (a)	4 diamonds (b)
6 hearts (c)	

(a) "I have the ace of spades or a void in spades and am interested in a slam." (If opener were not interested in a slam, he would simply bid four hearts.)

(b) "I have the ace of diamonds."

(c) "Thank you. Now I don't have to worry about the opponents winning the first two tricks in diamonds."

Responder's hand was:

♠ x x   ♡ K J x x   ◇ A J x   ♣ Q J x x

If responder's hand had been:

♠ x x   ♡ K J x x   ◇ Q J x x   ♣ A J x

a slam would have been defeated, since the opponents then would have been able to win the first two tricks with the ace and king of diamonds. But responder's bid of four clubs would avert this tragedy. In general, when cue-bidding the lowest ace is shown first.

On the actual hand, neither the Blackwood nor the Gerber Convention would have been able to provide the specific information needed: does responder have the ace of diamonds?

An ace-showing bid can be made and will be so interpreted according to the following principle:

Whenever a suit has been emphatically agreed upon (via a jump bid by either partner), a bid in a new suit by either partner shows the ace of that suit. And, of course, the showing of aces after emphatic agreement in a suit has been reached expresses a positive interest in a slam.

Here is an illustration of the showing of a specific king:

Opener	Responder
♠ K x	♠ x x
♡ A K x x x x	♡ Q J x x x
◇ —	◇ A J x x
♣ A Q x x x	♣ K x

1 heart	
4 clubs (a)	3 hearts
5 clubs (c)	4 diamonds (b)
6 hearts (e)	6 clubs (d)

(a) Showing the club ace, as a try for slam.

(b) The answer in kind, showing the ace of diamonds.

(c) A quest for the king of clubs.

(d) I have it!

(e) The ace of spades is the only trick the opponents will get.

The Singleton in Slam Bidding   Aces and kings, either in quantity or specific ones, do not alone make a slam. Many slams are dependent upon the possession of a singleton that effectively prevents the opponents from cashing two tricks in that suit.

For example, you hold:

♠ A K Q x x x   ♡ K x x   ◇ Q x   ♣ x x

The bidding has proceeded:

You	Partner
1 spade	2 hearts
2 spades	3 diamonds
3 hearts	4 spades
?	

What should you do? The immediate impulse would be to pass, but this would be incorrect.

You should recognize first that partner has a very strong hand. He could have bid four spades right over your two-

157

spade rebid, instead of introducing the diamond suit and later leaping to four spades. From his bidding, he should have just one club in his hand (in a moment, we'll analyze why), and his heart suit should be consolidated by your king.

Actually his hand was:

♠ J x x   ♡ A Q J x x   ◇ A K x x   ♣ x

The recognition by opener of the singleton in clubs in partner's hand is the important feature of this hand. How was opener to know this?

As a principle of bidding: whenever a player names three suits, and incorporates a jump in his sequence of bids, he shows that he has no more than a singleton in the fourth suit.

Splinter Bids Another means of reaching distributional slams is by use of *Splinter Bids*. (This is an advanced convention which should be used only if you and your partner have previously discussed the subject.) In response to a bid of one in a suit, a *double* jump in a new suit (one higher than necessary for a forcing jump bid, i.e. 1 ♡ − 4 ◇, or 1 ♡ − 3 ♠) shows strong support for opener's suit—the strength equivalent to a game-forcing double raise—AND no more than a singleton in the suit of the response. This bid may also be used with a void, which may be shown by repeating the splinter suit after opener's rebid. For example:

Opener	Responder
1 ♠	4 ♣
4 ◇	?

Responder may hold:

(1)	(2)	(3)
♠ A Q 10 x	♠ A Q 10 x x	♠ A J 10 x x
♡ K J 10	♡ A x x	♡ K Q x
◇ Q J 10 x x	◇ K J x x	◇ Q J 10 x x
♣ 2	♣ 2	♣ —
Rebid four spades	Rebid four hearts	Rebid five clubs

(1) You have already described your hand. Assuming partner to be cue-bidding, your diamond "support" does not include the king so you should not raise.

158

(2) It is convenient to show your side-suit ace. If partner rebids only four spades, you will nevertheless bid five diamonds, showing your second-round control of that suit.

(3) The repeat of your splinter bid shows a void or singleton ace. You are interested in a small slam or possibly a grand slam. By inference, you are denying the ace of hearts, since you would bid four hearts before bidding five clubs. Should partner bid five hearts after your repeat of the splinter suit, you should now bid six hearts to show second-round control of that suit, NOT six diamonds in which you lack second-round control. Remember that your first bid has positively agreed the trump suit will be spades and partner's rebids are cue-bids and do not necessarily show real suits.

QUIZ

The bidding has proceeded as indicated. What do you bid with each of the following hands?

	(1)		(2)
♠	x x x	♠	A K x x x
♡	K Q x	♡	A x x
◇	A J x	◇	K x x
♣	A K x x	♣	x x

You	Partner	You	Partner
1 club	3 no trumps	1 spade	3 spades
?		?	

	(3)		(4)
♠	A Q x x x x	♠	A K x x x
♡	A K J	♡	K Q x
◇	K x x	◇	x x
♣	x	♣	K x x

You	Partner	You	Partner
1 spade	3 spades	1 spade	4 no trumps
4 no trumps	5 diamonds	5 diamonds	5 spades
?		?	

	(5)		(6)
	♠ x		♠ A K x x x
	♡ A K x x x x		♡ A J x x
	◊ K Q J 10		◊ A x
	♣ K Q		♣ x x

You	*Partner*	*You*	*Partner*
1 heart	4 hearts	1 spade	2 diamonds
?		2 hearts	4 hearts
		?	

	(7)		(8)
	♠ x		♠ A Q x x x
	♡ x		♡ x x
	◊ K Q x x x x x x x x		◊ —
	♣ A		♣ A K J x x x

Partner	*You*	*You*	*Partner*
1 no trump	?	1 club	1 spade
		?	

	(9)		(10)
	♠ K Q x x x		♠ K x x x
	♡ A J 10 x x		♡ x x x x
	◊ x x		◊ A x x
	♣ x		♣ x x

You	*Partner*	*Partner*	*You*
1 spade	3 spades	1 spade	2 spades
?		4 clubs	?

	(11)		(12)
	♠ x x		♠ K
	♡ A K J		♡ A K Q 10 x
	◊ Q J x x		◊ A J x
	♣ Q x x x		♣ A x x x

Partner	*You*	*You*	*Partner*
1 diamond	3 diamonds	1 heart	3 no trumps
4 clubs	4 hearts	?	
5 diamonds	?		

ANSWERS

(1) Six no trumps. You have 17 high-card points and partner has 16-18. 33 high-card points are guaranteed.

(2) Four spades. There can be no slam with partner's 13-15 points opposite your 16 points (15 points originally, plus 1 for the fifth card of a suit which has been supported).

(3) Six spades. You have 22 points (1 point was added for the fifth spade and 2 for the sixth spade). Partner has 13-15 points—and the opponents don't have two aces to cash. Whenever the partnership holds three aces, a good trump suit, and 33 points, a small slam should be bid.

(4) Pass. If your partner thought a slam was makable with your one ace, he would have bid it. Obviously, one ace wasn't enough, so don't let your 16 points move you to bid a slam.

(5) Pass. Partner's bidding shows 9 or fewer high-card points. It's most unlikely that he has two aces—as a matter of fact, good players have learned never to make a direct leap to game with two quick tricks.

(6) Five diamonds. You have 18 points, and partner has at least 13. To bid four no trumps is futile if partner lacks the club ace; slam might be cold with just the king or a singleton club. Your overbid of a game requests him to bid a slam if he holds second-round control of the unbid suit, clubs.

(7) Four clubs, the Gerber Convention. If your partner has three aces, you will bid a grand slam; two aces, a small slam; one ace, you'll bid five diamonds, as the final contract.

(8) Six spades. You can't get scientific on this one—partner can have any one of thousands of combinations and you can never find out which "key" cards he holds: the king of spades, the ace or king of hearts, etc. It's conceivable that you might go overboard at six spades, and equally conceivable that you might be missing a lay-down grand slam contract. On experience, I would guess that—four times out of five—you'll make your six-spade contract.

(9) Four spades. You have strictly a minimum hand and if partner can't bid a slam, neither can you. With a minimum hand, one should never get aggressive.

(10) Four diamonds. You told your partner you had a bad hand, and he knows it. Obviously he could have bid at least four spades, since you can't pass four clubs. Show him your ace of diamonds—it's on the house.

(11) Pass. You've bid your hand to the hilt, showing 13-15 points on your first bid, plus four or more diamonds. On the second bid, you've shown the ace of hearts. Partner is probably looking for a spade control (hoping you have the king or ace of spades). But, whatever he's looking for, you haven't got it.

(12) Seven no trumps, with absolute assurance. He has 16-18 high-card points; you have 21 high-card points, which adds to 37 points, a grand slam. In addition, partner's jump to three no trumps shows a 4-3-3-3 distribution and with eight hearts between you, you should win five heart tricks. I'll wager partner will be able to win fifteen tricks with your dummy. (If only he could save the two extra tricks for the next deal!)

Lesson 7

PRE-EMPTIVE BIDDING

THIS LESSON will concern itself with the various specialized jump bids that proclaim weakness. The purpose of these bids is to pre-empt bidding space away from the opponents, to make it as difficult as possible for them to get together and find their optimum contract. Pre-emptive bids will be discussed from the viewpoint of the opening bidder, the responder, and the defending opponents.

OPENING PRE-EMPTS

An opening bid of three, four, or five in a suit is a pre-emptive or shut-out bid. Its primary purpose is to deprive the opponents of the rounds of bidding they require in order to arrive at a game or a slam contract.

There are always two distinguishing features of the pre-emptive opening bid: (a) the hand will be lacking in high cards, and (b) the hand will always contain a long suit. But there is one additional element to be considered in all pre-emptive bidding, the *safety factor*. When you make a "weakness" bid, you should stay on a relatively safe level.

Let me put it this way. The purpose of a shut-out bid is to prevent the adversaries from reaching a game or slam contract. The bid is losing strategy, however, if by doubling you for penalties they can collect more than the game or slam would be worth.

A game is worth, on the average, 500 points. Therefore, a pre-emptive bid is never made if the danger exists of going down more than 500 points. Conversely, going down 500 points is deemed to be a fair sacrifice for the game that the opponents could have made. Consequently, every pre-emptive bid against a game contract, is geared to an expected loss of 500 points.

How does one determine whether he'll go down no more than 500 points?

Whenever you open with three, four, or five of a suit, you must expect to be doubled for penalites; you should assume your partner has absolutely nothing and that you will win only those tricks you can see in your own hand. Of course, it won't always be as bad as anticipated: your partner sometimes will have a trick or two. Nevertheless, when you open with a pre-emptive bid, your appraisal of the result will be based exclusively on what your own hand will produce in the way of winning tricks. Partner's hand will be assumed to be devoid of values.

According to the present scoring table, if you are not vulnerable and go down three tricks doubled, you lose 500 points. If you are vulnerable, and go down two tricks doubled, you lose 500 points.

So, whenever you open with a bid of three, four, or five in a suit, you will be three tricks short of your contract if not vulnerable, and two tricks short of your contract if vulnerable. For example, if you open four spades not vulnerable, you will have at least seven winning tricks; if you open four spades vulnerable, you will have at least eight winning tricks. To summarize:

| | Number of winning tricks | |
Opening bid of	Not vulnerable	Vulnerable
3 in a suit	6	7
4 in a suit	7	8
5 in a suit	8	9

These are the requirements for an opening bid of three, four, or five in a suit:

——The hand should contain no more than 9 points in high cards if not vulnerable, and not more than 10 points in high cards if vulnerable.

——The suit should be of at least six-card length, preferably longer. The suit should be of such quality that it alone will win a minimum of four tricks.

Here are some illustrations of pre-emptive type hands:

(1)	(2)	(3)
♠ K Q J 10 x x x x	♠ x	♠ x x
♡ x x	♡ Q J 10 9	♡ A Q J 10 x x x
◇ x x	◇ Q J 10 9 x x x	◇ x x x
♣ x	♣ x	♣ x

(4)	(5)	(6)
♠ —	♠ x x	♠ A x x
♡ J 10 9 x	♡ A K Q 10 x x x	♡ K Q J x x x
◇ K Q J x x x x x	◇ x x	◇ J x x
♣ x	♣ x x	♣ x

(1) You can win seven tricks all by yourself. If not vulnerable, open four spades; if vulnerable, open three spades. Even if your partner has absolutely nothing, you cannot go down more than 500 points.

(2) You can win five diamond tricks and two heart tricks. Open four diamonds if not vulnerable, or three diamonds if vulnerable.

(3) You have six winning heart tricks. If not vulnerable, open three hearts; if vulnerable, pass.

(4) You can win seven diamond tricks and one heart trick. If not vulnerable open five diamonds; if vulnerable, open four diamonds.

(5) Holding seven winning heart tricks, open four hearts if not vulnerable, or three hearts if vulnerable.

(6) Open one heart. Do not pre-empt when you have a legitimate, sound opening bid of one in a suit, with 13 or more points.

Do not be afraid to make these pre-emptive bids because the contemplated loss of 500 points seems excessively high. Admittedly, it is a natural human trait to refuse to yield anything which conceivably might not have to be yielded (after all, the opponents might not get to game). To deliberately sacrifice 500 points naturally goes against the grain—but, in the long run, it will prove cheaper to make a pre-emptive bid whenever your hand calls for it.

Also, don't try to "economize" on pre-emptive bids; that is, don't open with three when your hand calls for an opening bid of four. To illustrate, you hold the following hand, not vulnerable, and you are the dealer:

♠ K Q J 10 x x x x　　♡ x　　◇ x x　　♣ x x

Do NOT open with three spades, figuring that if you get doubled and go down you'll lose only 300 points instead of 500 points. Bid four spades. The purpose of your bid is to prevent the opponents from getting together, and from making a game or a slam. If you bid only three spades, they'll have more room to find their proper contract, conceivably a small or grand slam in hearts. If you properly open with four spades, they will have to start their exploration at the five-level. So don't skimp—it will turn out to be false economy.

The Weak Two-Bid Many players use this "weak two-bid" as a pre-emptive measure. An opening bid of two spades, hearts, or diamonds indicates a hand that is not quite an opening one-bid; an opening bid of two clubs, however, is reserved for the "rock-crusher," the hand with which we would make our strong two-bid.

An opening bid of two clubs is an artificial bid embracing all kinds of hands that would normally qualify as a "legitimate" game-forcing bid of two in a suit. The negative response by partner is two diamonds (instead of two no trumps), after which the opener shows his real suit. The bidding then proceeds in normal fashion.

The "weak" two-bid is made on a fairly good suit, usually of six-card length, and 6 to 12 points. Here are two examples:

    ♠ K Q 10 9 x x   ♠ x x
    ♡ x x   ♡ Q x x
    ◇ A x   ◇ A K J 10 x x
    ♣ x x x   ♣ x x

The users of this weak two-bid have enjoyed considerable success. The primary reason for the success is due to the fact that many opponents hate to be "shut-out" of something, and they develop the feeling that the "weak" two-bidder is trying to steal something from them. These opponents are then goaded into taking forward action which they would not have taken otherwise—that is, they assume that since the opening bidder has shown "weakness," their side is necessarily strong. Of course, this assumption is precarious—the opening bidder's partner is often the strong one, and the defenders get clipped.

RESPONDING TO AN OPENING PRE-EMPT

What should you do if your partner opens with a pre-emptive suit bid and the next hand passes? The answer is simple, provided that you forget about your points. You know *exactly* how many winning tricks he holds: he is overbidding by two tricks vulnerable or three tricks not vulnerable. It therefore is a routine proposition to count your winning tricks, and correctly appraise your joint assets.

For example, suppose that you are my partner, and I have opened the bidding vulnerable, with a bid of three hearts. You hold:

♠ A K x x   ♡ x x   ◇ x x x x   ♣ x x x

What do you do? The answer is PASS! My bid showed seven winning tricks. You provide two winning tricks, so if you pass, I'll fulfill my contract. Suppose you held:

♠ A x x x   ♡ x x   ◇ A K x x   ♣ x x x

and again I opened vulnerable with three hearts. This time you would raise to four hearts, since you would provide three winning tricks, which, added to my seven winning tricks, would produce game. Note that two little trumps are sufficient for a raise, since I have promised that I have at least a six-card suit.

Now let's view your responses in non-vulnerable situations. I am your partner and open the bidding with three hearts, non-vulnerable. You hold the following hands:

(1)	(2)	(3)
♠ x x x x	♠ A x x x	♠ A x x x
♡ x x	♡ x x	♡ K x
◇ A K x x	◇ A K x x	◇ A K x x
♣ x x x	♣ x x x	♣ x x x

(1) Pass. I have six winning tricks, you have two. So we'll go down a trick or so at three hearts.

(2) Pass. I have six winning tricks; you have three. We'll make our nine-trick contract.

(3) Bid four hearts. I have six tricks; you provide four tricks. That adds to ten, and a game.

PRE-EMPTS BY THE OPENING BIDDER'S PARTNER

There are two situations in which the responder makes a pre-emptive bid:

I. The direct raise of partner's opening one of a suit to a game in his suit.

II. The direct raise of partner's suit from one to three or higher over a take-out double.

I. The Triple Major-Suit Raise   This jump raise was discussed in Lesson 3. It describes a hand very rich in trump support and distribution (containing either a void or a singleton), but with a maximum of 10 points in high cards. Although this bid is pre-emptive in nature—to crowd the opponents—the responder will nevertheless feel that there will be a fair chance of fulfilling the contract. The following is the type of hand with which responder would raise partner's opening one-spade bid to four spades:

♠ Q x x x x   ♡ x   ♢ K x x x x   ♣ x x

The reader will remember that when the responder has previously passed, a jump to game in opener's suit shows a good hand, a hand that has been transformed into the equivalent of an opening bid by virtue of opener's bid. For example, you as South hold the following hand and the bidding has proceeded as indicated:

♠ K x x x   ♡ A J x x   ♢ Q x x x   ♣ x

South	West	North	East
Pass	Pass	1 spade	Pass
4 spades			

In support of spades, you have 14 points: 10 in high cards, 3 for the singleton with four supporting trumps, 1 for the promotion of the king of spades.

The Jump Raise over a Take-out Double   Suppose you as North hold the following hand:

♠ K x x x x   ♡ x x x   ♢ J x x x   ♣ x

South	West	North
1 spade	Double	3 spades

Without the double, your three-spade response would have denoted 13-15 points, and four or more trumps—a good hand. But with the double, the meaning of the bid is changed, since if you had 11 or more points, you would have redoubled. So, by logic, partner knows you have a bad hand point-wise, with lots of trump support. The three-spade bid is a pre-empt, designed to create a barricade against the doubler's partner, thereby making it more difficult for him to enter the auction. Of course, your partner is at perfect liberty to pass your jump response.

As opener, then, when your partner jumps to three of your suit over a take-out double, bear in mind that he has a bad hand. Don't bid game on a hand of this type:

♠ A Q J x x   ♡ Q x   ◇ A x x   ♣ x x x

South	West	North	East
1 spade	Double	3 spades	Pass
?			

As South in the above situation, pass, since your partner figures to have a hand like the one just presented:

♠ K x x x x   ♡ x x x   ◇ J x x x   ♣ x

Note: Any jump bid made by opener's partner over a take-out double will indicate a hand containing no more than 10 points, since, with 11 points or more, he would redouble. So, when your partner makes a jump bid over a take-out double: beware!

QUIZ

You are the dealer, holding each of the following hands. What do you bid if (a) non-vulnerable? (b) vulnerable?

(1)	(2)	(3)
♠ A Q J 10 x x	♠ A Q J 10 x x	♠ A Q J 10 x x
♡ K J x	♡ x x x	♡ x x
◇ x x x	◇ x x x	◇ J 10 9 x
♣ x	♣ x	♣ x

169

(4)	(5)	(6)
♠ x x x x	♠ A Q J 10 x x x x x	♠ A K x
♡ x	♡ x	♡ x
◊ Q J 10 x x x x x	◊ x x	◊ J 10 9 x x x x
♣ —	♣ x	♣ x x

Your partner opens the bidding with three hearts, and the next hand passes. What do you bid if (a) non-vulnerable? (b) vulnerable?

(7)	(8)	(9)
♠ K J x x x	♠ Q J x	♠ x
♡ A x x	♡ A K x	♡ x x x x x
◊ A x	◊ A x x x	◊ J x x x
♣ x x x	♣ Q J x	♣ x x

Your partner opens with one spade, next hand passes. What do you bid, holding:

| (10) |
| ♠ K x x x x |
| ♡ — |
| ◊ K x x x x |
| ♣ x x x |

ANSWERS

(1) One spade. You have a solid opening bid. Never make a pre-emptive bid on a hand that contains more than 10 points in high cards.

(2) Pass. You have but five winning tricks. If you open with three spades, you'll expect to go down four tricks, which is 700 points not vulnerable, and 1100 points vulnerable. (Using weak two-bids, you may open two spades, not vulnerable.)

(3) You have six winning tricks. If not vulnerable, open three spades; if vulnerable, pass, or open with two spades, weak.

(4) You have six winning tricks. If not vulnerable, open three diamonds; if vulnerable, pass.

(5) Four spades, vulnerable or not vulnerable. You have eight winning tricks, and by yourself you'll go down no more than two tricks.

(6) Pass. When you open with a pre-emptive bid, the preponderance of your high-card strength should be concentrated in the suit bid.

(7) If not vulnerable, pass; if vulnerable, gamble four hearts, since partner has seven winning tricks and you have two or three.

(8) Three no trumps, whether vulnerable or not. Your partner has at least six hearts headed by Q J 10 with at least six winning tricks. Nine tricks at no trump should prove to be easier than ten tricks at hearts.

(9) Four hearts, and start praying! Your partner has a bad hand defensively, and you have a horrible hand. In all probability the opponents can make either a small slam or a grand slam. If they allow you to play the hand at four hearts doubled, you'll be lucky, no matter how many tricks you go down, for your loss will be less than the profit they could have made in their proper contract. (Not vulnerable, you might even bid six hearts.)

(10) Four spades, a pre-emptive bid to jam up the opponents. You have a fair chance to make your contract—especially if your partner has three or more hearts which you'll be able to trump.

Lesson 8

DEFENSIVE BIDDING AND DOUBLES

ALL OF the bidding up to this point has been that of the opening bidder and his partner, the responder. Their opponents have not yet intruded into the auction, and this exclusion has been deliberate. Now, having learned the weapons available to the offense and how they should be used, you are ready to learn what can be done to defend against them.

The bidding by the opponents of the player who opens is called "defensive bidding," even though opener's opponents may actually take over the offensive and bid aggressively toward game, or even toward slam. It might also be described as "competitive" bidding, except that this term would include the further participation in the auction by the side that has opened, and for the moment we are concerned only with the opener's opponents.

In the past decade, defensive bidding is the one aspect of the game that has changed most. Change often means added complication, but in defensive bidding the opposite is true. Modern defensive bidding is easier to understand and use correctly. Indeed, in describing old-time defensive bidding a writer might properly have warned: *Beware of valuing your hand by point count.* Today, by learning how to revise its use, point count will serve almost as effectively in defensive bidding as it does in the bidding by opener's side.

WHY YOUR OBJECTIVES CHANGE

The player who opens announces a minimum of 13 points, suggests a trump suit or a hand suited to no trump play. He hopes his side will be able to bid and make game, anticipating that partner is likely to have the strength needed to bring the combined total to 26 or more points. If opener's partner holds only his average share of the outstanding available points, he will have 9 and their combined holding will provide a majority of strength in the majority of cases.

Opener's opponent does not have the same expectation. Opener has already announced 13 points at least. True, some of these points may be distributional, but it is also true that opener may have more than 13. And the more balanced his hand, the more likely that he will have at least 13 points in high cards. So, unless your hand or your partner's bidding provides positive evidence to the contrary, you should assume that opener has 13 of the 40 high-card points available. This leaves only 27 to be divided among the other three players. Therefore, unless distribution adds a great number of points to your hand AND nullifies some of the opener's points, your chances of making game are considerably less than the opener's chances. Furthermore, partner of the opener already knows a great deal about the strength of the opener's hand, whereas the first defender to enter the competitive auction does not have this advantage; in fact, he is warned that his partner is likely to hold less strength than the opener could have expected of his partner because there simply is that much less to be shared.

From this unpleasant fact of life at the card table, you must draw a basic conclusion: the defender usually must put hopes of game well down the list of his aims in getting into the act. First come:

(1) To indicate a good lead to partner by bidding a suit.

(2) To suggest a possible profitable sacrifice against the game or part-score the opponents may bid.

(3) To compete for a makable part score, or to push the opponents to a higher contract than they can make.

Unless your hand meets at least one of these objectives— or the less likely one that you might make a game in spite of the opponents' declared strength—you should *pass*. Furthermore, even if your hand does meet one or more of the requirements, you must weigh the danger of incurring a large set— a penalty that would be more than the opponents could otherwise score. Here is where a warning against point count must be given. Some of the most costly penalties have been incurred by a player who offered as an alibi: "But partner, I had enough points for an opening bid!"

For example, suppose that East, the dealer, opens with one spade and South holds:

♠ Q J x x   ♡ A Q x x x   ◊ K J x   ♣ x

This hand counts 13 points in high cards alone; you could also add 2 points for the singleton club if you were considering making the opening bid. You have better than a minimum opening bid, so it looks as though you have a good overcall. But your suit is full of holes; you have too many cards in opener's suit (the 3 points in spades must be discounted because they are minor honors in a suit bid against you); and you must make your overcall at the two-level. If your left-hand opponent has a respectable hand, you could be set from 700 to 1100 points. Therefore, the risk of disaster is far greater than the possible advantage from bidding.

Now suppose instead that East opens with one diamond. This time you can overcall at the one level; your diamond king is favorably placed behind the opponent who has bid this suit so only the diamond jack need be discounted; and your side could conceivably find a good spot in either major suit. Therefore, your proper course is to bid one heart. You would like to have a stronger suit, but the fates weren't that kind. It is much safer to act now than to pass and back in later. However, you would pass one diamond if you held the following hand:

♠ Q J x x   ♡ Q x x x x   ◊ K J x   ♣ x

Your suit and your overall values are too meager to justify any action.

When an opponent opens, your distribution and the solidity of your suit become more important than your high-card points, especially when some of your points are minor honors in the suit your opponent has bid. The more balanced your hand, the more points you need, or the better your suit must be, to warrant venturing into the auction.

In fact, the closer your hand is to the minimum values for an opening bid—12, 13, 14-point hands especially—the more compelling your reason must be for getting into the bidding at all. Putting this another way, *defensive bidding* is less attractive when your hand includes *defensive* strength. Length in the opponent's suit, especially three or four small cards, is another strong deterrent. The more cards you hold in his suit, the more likely it is that your left hand opponent—the partner of the opening bidder—will be anxious to play against you for penalties.

The 500-point guide Everything you have learned thus far is based on the estimate that a game is worth about 500 points. If you are set 500 points or less, you will show a profit over having the opponents bid and make game against you. If you are set more, you will show a loss, and the loss may be even greater if it turns out that they couldn't make a game at all. Therefore, any bid you make should not expose you to a penalty of more than 500 points: two tricks doubled if you are vulnerable; three tricks if you are not vulnerable.

You will not always be able to estimate this with complete accuracy. You are entitled to assume that your partner will not always have a worthless hand, and a misfit at that. For your first bid, at least, you are entitled to expect that you will not lose more than the losers that are reasonably apparent. For example:

♠ K Q J 9 6 5   ♡ 2   ◇ Q J 10 7   ♣ 4 3

It is reasonable to assume that you will lose one spade, one heart, two diamonds and two clubs. If your right-hand opponent opens with one heart, a spade overcall is justified by the rule of 500, by the fact that you would like to have a spade lead from partner if your left-hand opponent becomes declarer, and by the possibility that you may have a good sacrifice against four hearts if your partner has the right hand.

Counting Losers You may lose more than six tricks with the foregoing hand if you run into a very bad break in spades, or a ruff in diamonds. But as a general rule of thumb, in any suit of four or more cards you should count one loser for each missing ace, king or queen. In shorter suits, the number of losers will be self-evident.

We are agreed, therefore, that you should overcall in spades. The question is, how many spades should you bid. Here is where we meet one of the big changes from old-style defensive bidding. Let us return to this hand after we have considered the seven options at the disposal of the player who is considering a defensive bid: simple overcall; jump overcall; pre-emptive overcall; no trump overcall; unusual no trump; takeout double; and, finally, the strongest available action, a cue-bid in the opponent's suit.

THE OVERCALL

About 50 per cent of all game contracts are won or lost by the opening lead. When your partner overcalls, he makes it easy for you to find the right lead. Suppose that the bidding has gone:

South	West	North	East
1 heart	Pass	1 no trump	Pass
4 hearts	Pass	Pass	Pass

As West, you hold this hand:

    ♠ K x   ♡ Q x x   ◇ Q x x x   ♣ Q x x x

What should you lead? All you know is that the opponents have 26 points or more between them, and that South has a self-sufficient heart suit. The best player in the world will pick the "killing" lead only by luck. But suppose East, instead of passing, bid two spades over one no trump. Your opening lead has been made easy. You bang down the king of spades. The guesswork has been eliminated.

Requirements for an Overcall Simple (non-jump) overcalls fall into two classes: (a) the overcall at the one-level, and (b) the overcall at the two-level. While the expressed purpose of the overcall is to tell partner what he should lead, there will be days when you will be left to play the hand in your over-calling suit. It stands to reason, then, that when you overcall at the two-level, you had better have a hand that can win more tricks than when you overcall at the one-level.

I. Overcalls at the One-Level The suit requirement is a suit of at least five cards headed by a minimum of two of the top four picture cards (A-K, A-Q, K-Q, K-J, or Q-J).

The point-count requirement is, if not vulnerable, 9 to 14; if vulnerable, 10 to 14.

Let us look at some illustrations of the overcall at the one-level.

You are sitting East, non-vulnerable, and North has opened the bidding with one diamond.

(1)	(2)	(3)
♠ A K x x x	♠ x x x	♠ K Q x
♡ K x x	♡ K Q J x x	♡ Q x x x x
◇ x x	◇ A x	◇ x x
♣ x x x	♣ x x x	♣ Q J x

(1) Overcall with one spade, showing 9-14 points, and at least a five-card suit headed by no fewer than two of the top four cards.

(2) Overcall with one heart, to direct the heart lead from partner.

(3) Pass, because your long suit is too weak. If you overcall with one heart you will be asking your partner to lead a heart; whereas if you don't overcall, partner will lead *his* best suit—either spades or clubs; and, whichever he leads, your high cards in that suit will either win tricks directly, or help partner establish his suit.

You are vulnerable, sitting East, and North has opened the bidding with one diamond.

(4)	(5)	(6)
♠ A J x x x	♠ K Q J x x	♠ x x
♡ x x	♡ x x	♡ A K Q x x x
◇ J x x	◇ x x	◇ x x
♣ x x x	♣ A x x x	♣ x x x

(4) Pass. You are far too weak to overcall.

(5) Bid one spade. Your hand is perfect for an overcall at the one-level: a good suit and 2 points more than the required 10 points.

(6) Bid one heart. A "solid" overcall—hearts must be the best lead from your point of view. So you tell your partner to lead the suit.

Now let us examine the reasons for the requirements.

At least a five-card suit. This is primarily for self-preservation. Bear in mind that if you are left to play the contract in your overcalling suit, the presence of the fifth card of that suit will cushion the impact of whatever loss may develop. For example, you hold the following hand, and the bidding has proceeded as indicated:

♠ x x x	♡ A K Q x x	◇ x x x	♣ x x

Opponent	You	Opponent	Partner
1 club	1 heart	Pass	Pass
Pass			

Exactly what will happen cannot be predicted: you don't know what your partner holds. Obviously you will win three tricks with your A-K-Q of trumps. Whether you'll win a trick with the fourth trump is problematical. But after four rounds of hearts have been played, your fifth heart will almost surely win a trick.

As a consequence of the five-card guarantee, overcaller's partner has a permanent guide if he chooses to bid. He knows that three small cards of that suit are adequate support.

An Exceptional Case As a general rule, overcalls are never made on four-card suits. However, the tactical overcall on a four-card suit can occasionally be made with good results. The purpose is to direct the opening lead. The bid is analogous to the "light" third-position opening bid.

To overcall on a four-card suit, you should hold at least three of the top four cards (A K Q, A Q J, K Q J), and a minimum of 13 points. Typically, the hand is unsuitable for a take-out double, because your partner may bid a suit for which you have no support, and you have no suit to fall back upon. Here are two examples with which you might well overcall an opening bid of one diamond with your four-card suit:

♠ x x	♠ A K Q x
♡ A Q J 10	♡ A x x
◇ A Q x x	◇ x x x
♣ x x x	♣ x x x

At least two of the top four cards within the suit. Since the purpose of the overcall is to tell partner what to lead, you should hold high-card strength. Lacking that strength, don't overcall—let your partner pick his own lead.

On the point-count requirements.

The requirements of 10-14 points for a non-vulnerable overcall at the one-level, 11-14 points for a vulnerable, have been determined by experience. The reason for the higher minimum if vulnerable is simple: if you go down, vulnerable, it will be more expensive. Hence when you make a vulnerable overcall you should expect to be able to win more tricks.

Note that when you overcall at the one-level, you will never have more than 14 points. What to do if you have more than 14 points, and your right-hand opponent opens the bidding, will be discussed later in this lesson.

II. Overcalls at the Two-Level Your hand should contain 13-15 points,* that is, an opening bid or a little better. But the most important requirement is that you have a very good suit, a suit that figures to lose no more than two tricks if it becomes trumps. Suits like the following are treacherous:

A Q x x x   K J x x x   Q J x x x

The above suits may produce very few tricks against a bad trump break, whereas the combinations that follow—no richer in point count—are protected against a bad break of the remaining outstanding trumps.

K Q J 9 x x   Q J 10 9 8 x   Q J 10 x x x

A "very good" suit is defined as:

(a) A five-card suit containing at least three of the top four picture cards (A K J, A Q J, or K Q J).

(b) A six-card suit, containing either at least 6 points in high cards (A K, A Q, or K Q J); or at least three of the top five cards (A J 10 x x x, K J 10 x x x, or Q J 10 x x x).

There is no breakdown for vulnerability at the two-level; that is, 13-15 points and a very good suit constitute a satisfactory two-level overcall regardless of vulnerability. But the reader should be most careful about making "light" vulnerable overcalls at the two-level, such as a 12-point overcall, or a 13-15 overcall on an inadequate suit. When you are vulnerable, you cannot afford to "stick your neck out" and defy the opponents to do something to you. They will do something.

Let us clarify this matter of vulnerability. When you are either the opening bidder or the responder, vulnerability does not affect your bidding: you bid according to your points,

---

* If you have a "very good" six-card suit, a minimum of 12 points is sufficient. The sixth trump will more than compensate for the point deficiency. The subject of what constitutes a "very good" suit is discussed in the succeeding paragraphs.

toward either a game or a slam. But when you are overcalling—bidding in the face of announced strength—you are treading on dangerous ground, and you might get caught between two strong hands. When you go down to defeat, your loss is greater when you are vulnerable than when you are not. The opponents are also aware of this, and they are much more apt to double you when you are vulnerable than when you are not. Consequently, stay in line when you make overcalls, especially if you are vulnerable.

Here are some two-level overcall situations. The opening bid in front of you is one spade and you hold each of the following hands:

(1)	(2)	(3)
♠ x x x x	♠ Q x x	♠ A x
♡ A Q x x x	♡ A K Q x x	♡ A K Q 10 9
◊ A Q x	◊ x x	◊ J 10 x
♣ x	♣ x x x	♣ x x x

(4)	(5)	(6)
♠ x x	♠ x	♠ x x x x
♡ x x	♡ x x x	♡ A K Q x
◊ A J 10 9 x x	◊ A x x	◊ x x
♣ A Q x	♣ K Q J 9 x x	♣ A x x

(1) Pass. Your five-card suit is not good enough for a two-level overcall. Furthermore, beware of overcalling on hands where you have length in the opener's suit. Opener's partner figures to be short in that suit, and if he happens to have a good hand in high cards, you might be hurt seriously by his penalty double.

(2) Pass. Your suit is a "very good" one, but the hand lacks 13-15 points.

(3) Bid two hearts. A solid overcall; the suit is there and the points are there.

(4) Bid two diamonds. The points are there (13-15 counting distribution), and the six-card suit is "very good."

(5) Bid two clubs. Although the hand contains but 12 points, the sixth card of the "very good" suit compensates for the deficiency.

(6) Pass. Avoid an overcall at any level on a four-card suit.

(What to do with good hands lacking a long suit is discussed later in this lesson.)

Responses to Overcall at the One-Level Whenever your partner overcalls at the one-level, you know he has 9-14 points (not vulnerable) or 10-14 points (vulnerable). Hence, you will never freely raise your overcalling partner unless you have at least 11 points, since you can entertain no hopes of being even near the 26 points required for a game.

The following is your guide to responding to a partner who has overcalled at the one-level.

——With 10 or fewer points, pass.

——With 11 or 12 points, make one constructive bid either by raising your partner's suit (with three or more supporting trumps), or by bidding a suit (or no trump) of your own.

——With 13-14 points, strongly invite a game by jumping either in partner's suit or in no trump. He will then know that you have a minimum opening bid, and he can decide whether to go on to game or to pass.

——With 15 or more points, promptly bid a game in his suit, no trump, or in your own suit; else, jump in your own suit, which is forcing.

Let us look at some illustrations of how to respond to a partner who has made an overcall at the one-level.

You are East, not vulnerable. You hold the following hands, and the bidding proceeds:

South	West	North	East
1 heart	1 spade	Pass	?

(1)	(2)	(3)	(4)
♠ x x	♠ J x x	♠ x x x	♠ x x
♡ x x x	♡ A x x	♡ x x	♡ x x x
◇ A Q x x x	◇ A Q x x x	◇ A Q x x x x	◇ A Q J x x
♣ Q x x	♣ x x	♣ x x	♣ A x x

(1) Pass. You have 9 points opposite partner's maximum of 14; game is impossible.

(2) Bid two spades. Your raise of partner's overcall shows 11-12 points (you have 11 in high cards, plus 1 for distribution, plus 1 for the promotion of the jack of trumps, less 1 for the deficiency of three trumps). If partner has a maximum overcall, he will carry on to game.

(3) Pass. Your hands cannot produce a game. If somebody

pointed a gun at you and said "BID!" you would bid two spades, since you know partner has at least five spades.

(4) Bid two diamonds, a constructive bid on 11-12 points. If partner has a maximum hand, he will bid again. Partner will know, also, that you don't have three spades, else you would have raised him.

You are East, vulnerable. You hold each of the following hands, and the bidding proceeds as indicated:

South	West	North	East
1 heart	1 spade	Pass	?

(5)
♠ x x x x
♡ x
◇ A Q x x x
♣ K J x

(6)
♠ x x
♡ Q 10 x x
◇ K x x
♣ A Q x x

(7)
♠ K x x
♡ x x
◇ A Q x x
♣ A Q x x

(8)
♠ x x
♡ A Q x
◇ A x x x
♣ K Q x x

(9)
♠ x x x
♡ x x
◇ A K Q J x x
♣ A J

(5) Bid three spades, announcing 13-14 points. If partner has more than a minimum, he will bid four.

(6) Bid one no trump, showing 11-12 points, and protection in hearts, the adversely-bid suit.

(7) Bid four spades. You have 15 points, partner has at least 11 points and a minimum of five spades.

(8) Bid three no trumps, on your 15 points, and the adversely-bid heart suit twice protected.

(9) Bid three diamonds, showing 15 or more points and forcing to game. If partner bids three no trumps, pass. If partner bids three spades, bid four.

Responses to Two-Level Overcalls Whenever your partner overcalls at the two-level, his hand will contain 13-15 points.

——With 10 or fewer points, pass.

——With 11 or 12 points, raise your partner to the three-level, or bid two no trumps, or bid your own good suit, according to the composition of your hand.

——With 13 or more points, game should be bid if your side has a fit, since partner's overcall shows at least 13 points.

Either bid a game directly in partner's suit, in your suit, or in no trump; or jump in your own suit, which is forcing to game; or bid the opponents' suit, which is forcing to game.

As East, you hold each of the following hands and the bidding has proceeded:

South	West	North	East
1 spade	2 hearts	Pass	?

(1)	(2)	(3)
♠ x x x	♠ x x	♠ x x
♡ x x	♡ 10 9 x	♡ J x x x
◇ K J x x	◇ K Q x x	◇ A Q x x
♣ A J x x	♣ A Q x x	♣ x x x

(4)	(5)	(6)
♠ A J x	♠ x x x	♠ Q J 10 x
♡ Q x x x	♡ x x	♡ x x
◇ x	◇ A K J x x	◇ A Q x x
♣ K x x x x	♣ Q x x	♣ A Q x

(1) Pass. You have 9 points opposite partner's 13-15. Do not count distributional points for shortage.

(2) Bid three hearts, showing 11-12 points, and establishing hearts as the trump suit. Partner will bid a game if he has more than just 13 points.

(3) Pass. You have only 9 points, so game is out of the question.

(4) Bid four hearts. Your hand contains 14 points (10 in high cards, 1 for the promotion of the queen of trumps and 3 for the singleton).

(5) Pass. You have only 10 points, and you can tolerate playing in hearts. (Remember, partner's overcall promises a respectable suit.)

(6) Bid three no trumps. You have 15 points, partner has at least 13, and the adversely-bid spades are well protected.

Overcalls at the Three-Level and Higher When your first opportunity to overcall occurs at the three-or-higher level, your bid is for the purpose of demanding a specific lead; it should always be based on a self-sustaining suit of at least six-card length (preferably longer). To illustrate, the bidding has proceeded as indicated, and you (East) hold the following hands:

South	West	North	East
1 spade	Pass	2 diamonds	?

(1)	(2)	(3)
♠ x x	♠ x x	♠ K x x
♡ x x	♡ K Q x	♡ x x
◇ x x	◇ Q x	◇ x x x
♣ A K Q J x x x	♣ A J x x x x	♣ A K Q x x

(1) Bid three clubs, to direct the lead. Even if the opponents double you, you won't go down more than two tricks, which is a cheap sacrifice against a game.

(2) Pass. Your side can't make a game, and you can get hurt badly should the missing clubs be stacked against you. Incidentally, your partner figures to have virtually nothing, since South has at least 13 points, North has at least 10 points for his response in a new suit at the two-level, and you have 12 high-card points.

(3) Pass. Your hand is not strong enough to warrant your stepping out at the three-level in the face of the strength displayed by the enemy.

The Jump Overcall Originally, the jump overcall was used to describe a hand of considerable strength. Unfortunately, it showed a too-specific type of hand, and the occasions for its use did not arise frequently enough. So this bid was discarded. As currently utilized, the jump overcall shows a weakish hand with a long suit. The primary purpose of the "new" jump bid is to interfere with the enemy when it appears that they have the preponderance of strength. Further, it has the merit of pointing out to partner that the jump bidder has very little in the way of defensive values. And, finally, it indicates to partner where a profitable sacrifice may be taken if partner is convinced that the opening side can make a game.

The requirements for the "weak" jump overcall are as follows:

——The bid should be based on a good suit, of at least six-card length.

——The hand should contain no more than 9 points in high cards.

——The high-card strength of the hand should be concentrated in the bid suit, with never more than 1 quick trick in the other three suits.

——The jump bidder should have a reasonable expectation

184

of winning within three tricks of his contract if not vulnerable, or within two tricks of his contract if vulnerable.

Here are some illustrations. You are East; the previous bidding is indicated in each example:

(1)

♠ K Q J 10 x x x
♡ x x
♢ x x
♣ x x

North	East
1 diamond	2 spades

(2)

♠ x
♡ x x
♢ J 10 9 8
♣ A Q J 10 x x

North	East
1 heart	3 clubs

(3)

♠ x
♡ K Q J 9 8 x x
♢ Q J 10
♣ x x

North
1 spade

East
3 hearts

(4)

♠ x
♡ x x
♢ K Q 10 9 x x x
♣ K x x

South	West	North	East
1 heart	Pass	1 N.T.	3 diamonds

(5)

♠ x x
♡ x x
♢ K Q J 10 x x
♣ A J x

North	East
1 spade	2 diamonds

(6)

♠ A J 10 x x x
♡ x x x
♢ K Q
♣ x x

North	East
1 club	1 spade

Hand (5) is too good for a jump overcall. You should make a simple two-level overcall denoting a reasonable hand and a very good suit.

Hand (6), like (5), is too good for a jump overcall.

Double- and Triple-Jump Overcall This bid is virtually the same as the single-jump overcall. It shows a weak hand, containing no more than 9 points in high cards, and very little defensive strength. This jump of one more than necessary

185

should have one additional winner, usually in trump length, compared to the single-jump overcall.

With each of the following hands, a double-jump bid of three spades should be made, over opponent's one diamond.

(1)	(2)	(3)
♠ Q J 10 9 x x x	♠ A K Q 10 x x x	♠ A Q 10 9 x x x
♡ x x	♡ x	♡ —
♣ Q J 10 9	◇ x x x x	◇ Q J 10
◇ —	♣ x	♣ x x x

(If you are not vulnerable, a bid of four spades is recommended, since you do not figure to go down more than three tricks even if your partner has nothing.)

Not vulnerable, you hold the following hands, and the bidding has proceeded as indicated:

(1)	(2)
♠ K Q J 10 x x x	♠ K Q J 10 x x x x
♡ x	♡ x
◇ x x x	◇ x x x
♣ x x	♣ x

Opener	*You*
1 heart	?

(1) Bid three spades, having six sure winning tricks.
(2) Bid four spades, having seven sure winning tricks.

Your criteria for making a pre-emptive overcall of three or four are the same as above even if *both* the opponents have bid. In this situation, however, your bid will lose some of its effectiveness, since the opening bidder and partner will have already exchanged some information.

To illustrate, you are East with the following hand, not vulnerable:

♠ Q J 10 9 x x x   ♡ Q J 10   ◇ x x   ♣ x

South	*West*	*North*	*East*
1 diamond	Pass	2 clubs	3 spades

Safety is yours when you jump to three spades, since you can win six tricks in your own hand. But opener knows his

186

partner has at least 10 points for having named a new suit at the two-level; and responder knows opener has at least 13 points. Nevertheless, your pre-emptive bid is fully justified: you are depriving them of valuable bidding space, which they will certainly require if they think that a slam might be in their cards.

One No Trump Overcalls This bid is the equivalent of an opening bid of one no trump—that is, it is the type of hand with which, had you been first, you would have opened one no trump: 16-18 high-card points, a balanced hand, and protection in the opponent's suit. Partner will then take over just as though you had opened with one no trump. To illustrate, you hold:

(1)	(2)
♠ A J x	♠ A x
♡ K Q x	♡ K x x
◇ A J x	◇ A K Q x x
♣ Q x x x	♣ J x x

Opponent	You	Opponent	You
1 spade	1 no trump	1 heart	1 no trump

Two No Trumps Overcalls This bid indicates a hand worth an opening two no trumps bid: 22-24 points, a balanced hand, and all suits protected. In responding, partner will take the position that you have opened the bidding with two no trumps.* To illustrate, you hold:

♠ A Q x
♡ K J x
◇ A K Q x x
♣ K x

Opponent	You
1 heart	2 no trumps

On occasion, this overcall is made on an unbalanced hand, with fewer than 22 points. Typically, the hand contains a long, solid, minor suit, and the bidder expects to win seven or eight tricks in his own hand. To illustrate, you hold:

---

* But see Unusual No Trump Overcall (page 188).

$$\spadesuit \text{ K x}$$
$$\heartsuit \text{ Q J x}$$
$$\diamondsuit \text{ A x}$$
$$\clubsuit \text{ A K Q J x x}$$

Opponent	*You*
1 spade	2 no trumps

The Unusual No-Trump Overcall   Among the more recent developments in contract bridge, perhaps one of the most colorful is the "Unusual No-Trump Convention," which provides that, when a player makes a bid of any number of no trumps that cannot possibly mean what it says, the bid is to be construed as asking partner to bid his *longest minor suit.* To illustrate:

(1)	*West*	*North*	*East*	*South*
	1 spade	Pass	2 hearts	2 no trumps

Obviously, South's two no trumps bid could not be construed as showing 22-24 points. There aren't that many points in the deck, what with West having at least 13 and East at least 10. Even if there were that many points left, South would know that North had zero points—and would keep quiet, waiting for East-West to get themselves in a jam.

(2)	*West*	*North*	*East*	*South*
	1 heart	Pass	2 spades	2 no trumps

Again, South's bid could not show a legitimate two no trumps opening. West has 13 points and East has at least 19 for his jump-shift response. South's bid is a command to North to bid his longest minor suit, in order that North-South may take a sacrifice save against East-West's game or slam.

The types of hands South might have:

(1)	(a)		(b)
	$\spadesuit$ x		$\spadesuit$ —
	$\heartsuit$ x		$\heartsuit$ x
	$\diamondsuit$ K J 10 x x x		$\diamondsuit$ Q J 10 x x x
	$\clubsuit$ K Q 10 x x		$\clubsuit$ A J x x x x

(2)   (a)   (b)
♠ x   ♠ —
♡ —   ♡ —
◇ Q J x x x x   ◇ 10 x x x x x x
♣ Q J x x x x   ♣ K x x x x x

Obviously, since East-West have shown tremendous
strength, North cannot be expected to have much in the way
of high-card strength. But whichever minor suit North bids,
South will be able to furnish at least five-card support; usually
the bid is for purposes of finding a profitable sacrifice, but
sometimes it is in hopes of making game.

Warning: The unusual no trump conveys considerable information to the opponents. Its use should therefore be re-
stricted to hands where you expect to buy the contract. Otherwise, you simply warn the opponents to expect bad breaks
in the major suits and you guide them to playing accordingly.

It is most important to emphasize that the normal overcalls
in no trump do not lose their obvious and natural significance.
For example:

North	*East*
1 heart	1 no trump

Here East's bid is a normal overcall, showing 16-18 points
(possibly 19), a balanced hand, and the requisite stoppers in
the four suits (including positive protection in hearts, the
adversely-bid suit).

So much for the overcall. Now let us examine what the
opponent of the opening bidder does when (a) he has a good
hand of 13 or more points, but his suit does not qualify as an
overcalling suit; or (b) his hand contains more than 15 points
and thus is too strong for a simple suit overcall.

THE TAKE-OUT DOUBLE

Whenever an opponent has made a bid to win a specified
number of tricks, and you think you can prevent him from
winning those tricks, you utter the word "double," which,
roughly speaking, doubles the amount of the penalty he will
sustain if he is defeated. This is known as a "penalty double"
(sometimes called "business double") and is a punitive weapon.

But there is another kind of double, known as the "take-out" or "informative" double. This double serves as a signal to your partner, a signal which commands him to name his best suit. Used in this context, "double" does not state that you expect to defeat the opponents but that you are desirous of purchasing the contract, and require partner's assistance in selecting the best suit.

When partner utters the word "double," how can you tell whether he means it as a penalty double or a take-out double? The next few paragraphs will answer this question.

A double is for "take-out": if made at the doubler's first opportunity to bid over an opponent's *suit* declaration; and provided that the doubler's partner has not previously made a contractual bid. For example:

(1)	*South*	*West*	*North*	*East*
	1 diamond	Double	Pass	?

(2)	*South*	*West*	*North*	*East*
	Pass	Pass	1 heart	Double
	Pass	?		

(3)	*South*	*West*	*North*	*East*
	1 diamond	Pass	1 heart	Double

In each of the three above illustrations, the double is a take-out double. Note the difference between the foregoing and the following two illustrations.

(4)	*North*	*East*	*South*	*West*
	1 spade	2 hearts	3 diamonds	Double

This is a penalty double, stating that West can defeat South's contract. It is a penalty double because East, the doubler's partner, had previously bid.

(5)	*North*	*East*	*South*	*West*
	1 heart	Pass	1 no trump	Pass
	2 hearts	Double		

This is a penalty double, since East did not double at his first opportunity. If East had wanted his partner to bid, he would have doubled North's opening bid.

(6)	West	North	East	South
	1 heart	*Pass*	*2 hearts*	*Double*

This double is for a take-out. It says: "Partner, you have not yet made a bid, and although the contracting has reached the two-level, it is my first opportunity to assert myself. I *demand* that you bid."

A take-out double is an absolute command for partner to bid. With one rare exception mentioned later, partner cannot pass. Even if partner doesn't have a picture-card, and his best suit consists of 5 4 3 2, he must name that suit.

Since partner of the doubler is expected to bid no matter how hopeless his hand, the doubler must hold a good hand. Usually this means a hand as strong as an opening bid, but the take-out double may rely a bit more heavily upon distributional strength. The opener may value a singleton at only 2 points and a void at 3 because there is great likelihood that the suit in which he is short may be his partner's best suit. When supporting partner, however, the responder increases these values to 3 and 5. The opener, therefore, may pass a border-line hand, either because his distributional values actually leave him short of 13, or because if partner is long in opener's short suit the bidding may become awkward.

When the opening bid is in your short suit, however, a double requests your partner to bid some other suit; he is warned against bidding the suit in which you are short because an opponent has already bid it. The doubler is therefore entitled to lend a little added weight to a singleton or void in the opponent's suit. This is not only because his ruffing values are increased. (As you will see later, there is no guarantee that partner will not hold length only in the opponent's suit, and he may be compelled to bid a three-card suit.) There is the additional consideration that the player who is short in the suit the opponent has bid is apt to nullify a considerable part of the high-card strength of opener's hand. In modern bidding, therefore, the take-out double may not be much stronger than an overcall except in its distributional strength, which in most cases will include ability to support any suit that partner may bid in response to the double. (An exception occurs when the doubler has a powerful trump suit of his own.)

To summarize the requirements for the take-out double:

(a) The doubler must hold the equivalent of an opening bid, that is 13 or more points.

(b) The doubler must hold either

——support for any suit partner bids, or

——an excellent suit of his own to fall back upon, should partner name a suit for which the doubler has no support.

Let us examine the two types of hands with which a take-out double is made.

Your right-hand opponent opens the bidding with one spade and you hold:

♠ x   ♡ K J x x   ◇ A J x x   ♣ K J x x

You should double. Your hand is worth 13 points in high cards. Whenever partner responds in hearts, diamonds or clubs, you will furnish four supporting trumps and a singleton, giving you 3 more points in dummy valuation. And, more important, whichever of the three unbid suits your partner names, you will arrive at the proper trump suit.

Your right-hand opponent opens the bidding with one spade and you hold:

♠ x x   ♡ A K J x x x   ◇ K x   ♣ A x x

Again, your correct call is double. Although you can't stand clubs or diamonds if partner names either of those suits, you have an excellent heart suit to fall back upon.

As to overcalling directly, with two hearts, the answer is NO! Whenever you overcall at the two-level, you will have no more than 15 points. The given hand is much too good, containing 17 points. If you overcall, you will mislead your partner into believing that you have no more than 15 points; as a consequence, your partnership might easily miss a game. How you will get around to showing the great strength of your hand (over and above the minimum of 13 points required for a take-out double) will be explained shortly. But to overcall may never give you the chance to show the full strength of your hand.

Be careful not to deviate from the requirements for a take-out double, or you'll find yourself in a mess on too many occasions. For example, suppose that you are South and hold:

♠ A J x x   ♡ x   ◇ K J x x   ♣ K J x x

East	South	West	North
1 spade	Double ?	Pass	2 hearts

Suppose that your partner, North, happens to hold:

♠ x x   ♡ J x x x x   ◇ x x x   ♣ x x x

As can be observed, the result will be a catastrophe, whether you pass or whether you bid. And the blame will be exclusively yours; you doubled when you were unable to support hearts or to fall back upon a suit of your own if North responded in hearts.

So, with the above hand, don't double. Simply sit back and wait for the opponents to get beyond their depth.

Let us now turn our attention to the partner of the take-out doubler, to see what action he takes with different types of hands.

Responses to a Take-Out Double The doubler's partner must always remember that he is being forced to bid, even with a worthless hand. The doubler knows that his partner may have nothing; consequently he is under *no obligation to rebid* after doubling. After partner has responded to a take-out double, the bidding is quite apt to die at that point. To illustrate:

North	East	South	West
1 heart	Double	Pass	2 clubs
Pass	Pass	Pass	

If West held hand (1) below, he would be delighted to hear East pass; but if he held hand (2) he would be most unhappy.

(1)	(2)
♠ x x x	♠ Q x x
♡ x x x	♡ x x
◇ x x	◇ A J x
♣ Q x x x x	♣ A Q x x x

The question naturally arises: how does the doubler's partner indicate that he has a fair hand or a good hand, as opposed to a weakish hand or a horrible hand?

First, you must count your points somewhat differently than usual. Except when you are considering bidding no trump in response to partner's double, do NOT count for low honors—queens and jacks—in the opponent's suit. The take-out double is almost always based on shortage in the opponent's suit, so these low cards are not likely to be worth much in a suit contract. Count a king as only 2 points, unless it is behind the bidder.

Count short suits as if you were raising partner, not as if you were opening the bidding. In a way, partner's double was a bid in all three suits other than that bid by the opponent, so if you have a shortage in some other suit count a void as 5 and a singleton as 3. (But do NOT promote your values for shortage in the opponent's suit; partner is probably counting these also.)

Count an extra point for every card over four in any suit except the opponent's, just as if you were revaluing your hand after your suit had been raised. Partner's double was—at least until he declares otherwise—the equivalent of a raise for any of these suits.

In choosing between suits in which to respond, generally prefer a major. Especially if partner has doubled one major, respond with four cards in the other major in preference to showing a five-card minor.

In general, you can show partner your approximate strength by observing the following table:

With 0-6 points make the cheapest response in your longest suit. (If your only long suit is the one opener has bid, you must respond in your cheapest three-card suit. Do NOT pass; requirements for a penalty pass are given later.)

With 6-8 points, plan to bid twice if given the opportunity.

With 8-10 points and a stopper in opponent's suit, bid one no trump. Never respond one no trump with a weak hand and length only in the opponent's suit.

With 9-12 points, jump in your best suit—even if it includes only four cards.

With 11-12 points and at least one firm stopper in opponent's suit (usually two), respond with two no trumps.

With 13 or more points respond with a cue bid—a bid in the opponent's suit. This is the only absolutely forcing response, although under certain circumstances it may stop short of game. It does not guarantee first-round control of the opponent's suit. It may, for example, be the initiation of showing a strong two-suiter. South holds:

♠ x   ♡ A Q x x x   ◇ A Q x x x   ♣ x x

West	North	East	South
1 club	Double	Pass	2 clubs
Pass	2 spades	Pass	3 hearts

South's cue-bid response is forcing; so is his bid of a new suit, three hearts over two spades. But if, with another hand, South had merely raised North's bid of two spades to three, North could pass. South should therefore bid another suit or raise directly to game, unless he is prepared to have North pass if he has doubled with a light hand.

Let us view some illustrations. You are South, and hold each of the following hands. The bidding has proceeded as indicated:

West	North	East	South
1 heart	Double	Pass	?

(1)
♠ x x x x x
♡ x x x
◇ x x x
♣ x x

(2)
♠ A Q x x x
♡ x x x
◇ K J x
♣ x x

(3)
♠ x x
♡ x x x
◇ x x x
♣ x x x x x

(4)
♠ x x
♡ x x x
◇ K J x
♣ A Q 10 x x

(5)
♠ x x x
♡ K J x x
◇ A 10 x
♣ K x x

(6)
♠ Q J 10 x x x
♡ x x x
◇ A J x
♣ x

(7)
♠ J x x
♡ K J x
◇ x x x
♣ K J x x

(8)
♠ x x
♡ J x x x x
◇ x x x
♣ J x x

(9)
♠ Q x
♡ K J x
◇ Q x x
♣ A x x x x

(1) Bid one spade. You have no choice. Of course, if your partner knew you held this hand, he would have "stood in bed" and awaited a better day.

(2) Bid two spades, showing 9-12 points and at least four spades.

(3) Bid two clubs; you aren't happy, but have no choice.

(4) Bid three clubs, the jump bid to show 9-12 points.

(5) Bid two no trumps. This bid shows 11-12 points with protection in the adversely-bid suit.

(6) Bid two spades. Your 10 points and six-card suit fully justify the jump response. When a player makes a take-out double over an opening major suit bid, he almost invariably has good support for the other major suit.

(7) Bid one no trump, not two clubs. You have a fair hand, considering that you would have had to bid even with zero points. If you bid two clubs, your partner may fear that you have zero points, and will probably pass, whereas if you bid one no trump he will know that you have 8-10 points.

(8) Bid two clubs. This will hurt. However, partner has forced you to bid one of the other three suits, and you have none of the four-card length. Since one no trump is out, you have no choice but to bid your "cheapest" three-card suit.

(9) Bid two no trumps, rather than three clubs. The no trump bid is more descriptive, since it announces a balanced hand, 11-12 points, and the desire to play for game at no trump.

The Penalty Pass of a Take-Out Double There is just one situation where you are permitted to pass partner's take-out double: when you are reasonably certain that the opponent's contract can be defeated. Responder's hand should contain at least four winning tricks of which no fewer than three are in the opponent's suit. To illustrate, you are South, holding the following hands, and the bidding has proceeded:

West	North	East	South
1 heart	Double	Pass	?

(1)	(2)
♠ x x	♠ x x
♡ Q J 10 9 x	♡ J x x x x
◇ A x	◇ x x
♣ x x x x	♣ x x x x

(1) Pass. You can win three trump tricks, and a fourth trick with the diamond ace. Your partner, having doubled, can reasonably be expected to provide at least three winning tricks.

(2) Bid two clubs. With this barren hand you would be lucky to win one trick against hearts. If you incorrectly pass, West

196

will play the contract at one heart doubled, and will probably make two or three overtricks.

Procedure by Doubler's Partner after an Intervening Bid
As yet we have discussed only the *forced* responses to a take-out double—forced because the intervening opponent has passed. But suppose the bidding has gone:

South	West	North	East
1 diamond	Double	1 heart	?

Now the situation is different. As East, you are not forced to bid. Your partner will have another opportunity to bid, if he wishes. Any bid made by you in these circumstances is a *voluntary* bid, and asserts some measure of strength.

It is not, however, to be viewed as a full free bid, which usually shows a minimum of 9 points. The requirements for a free bid in this situation are not as rigid as they are when your partner opens the bidding, second hand overcalls, and you freely step into the auction. By doubling, partner is trying to get you to send a message, and the opponents are usually trying to block your communication. If you have 7 or 8 points, you should regard it as a fair-to-middling holding, worth a voluntary bid.

For example, you are East with the following hand, and the bidding proceeds as shown:

♠ x x x   ♡ A Q 10 x x   ◇ x x x   ♣ x x

South	West	North	East
1 diamond	Double	2 diamonds	2 hearts

Your heart bid, while a slight stretch of the "voluntary" bid concept, is justified.
Another example:

♠ x x x   ♡ x x   ◇ Q x x   ♣ A J 10 x x

South	West	North	East
1 heart	Double	1 spade	2 clubs

The club bid, on your 8 points, is proper. If North had bid two hearts (instead of one spade), requiring you to go to the three-level to show your clubs, the decision would be a toss-up. Either a pass or a three-club bid could not be criticized.

If you have an opportunity to make a free bid in the above circumstances at the one-level, 6 points will suffice if you have a six-card major suit. Thus, you are East, holding:

♠ K J x x x x   ♡ x x x   ◇ x x x   ♣ x

South	West	North	East
1 club	Double	1 heart	1 spade

Your 6 points constitute just enough to eke out a one-spade bid.

Procedure by Doubler's Partner after an Intervening Redouble
The situation to be discussed is this:

South	West	North	East
1 heart	Double	Redouble	?

As will soon be illustrated, North's redouble shows 10 or more points. It is therefore obvious all around the table that you hold little or nothing—South has at least 13 points; West has at least 13; and North has at least 10. Out of the approximately 40 points in the deck, there are very few unaccounted for. What do you do with your "bad" hand?

Well, first, you have the option of passing, because the auction will revert to partner, and he can then name his best suit. The pass indicates that you have nothing worthwhile to say, and that whichever suit partner names you are more or less satisfied with. However, a bid by you at this point *does not* promise any strength, since it is obvious that you have no strength. Partner has asked you for your best suit and if you have a five-card or longer suit, you should bid it, points notwithstanding. For example, the bidding has proceeded as indicated, and as East you hold:

(1)	(2)
♠ x	♠ J x x x x
♡ K 10 x x	♡ x x
◇ x x x x	◇ x x x
♣ x x x x	♣ x x x

South	West	North	East
1 diamond	Double	Redouble	?

(1) Bid one heart. Partner has promised support for all suits, and you don't want to hear him bid spades.

(2) Bid one spade. Your five-card suit should find support in partner's hand, since partner's double has indicated support for the three other suits (unless he has an excellent suit of his own, in which case he'll bid it).

Admittedly, you are not overjoyed at bidding with either of the above hands, but remember this: when your partner doubled, he did so with the reasonable expectation that you had your fair share of the outstanding strength. The redouble kills that hope, and he may be in trouble, and will usually require your help to be extricated. So you bid your suit, in the hope that it will afford a refuge.

As the partner of the doubler, you should never forget these facts: that you are usually going to do your bidding with hands that range from fair to horrible; and that your partner realizes this fully, but is nevertheless seeking your cooperation. So don't be afraid to bid with a mediocre hand—your partner won't be expecting much.

The Doubler's Rebids   As the doubler, bear in mind that you have *forced* your partner to bid. He may have nothing— and his hand will usually be nearer to "nothing" than to "something"; if he has failed to jump, you know he doesn't have 9 points. When you raise his forced response be sure that you have very good trump support, for his suit might be x x x x.

When, after doubling, and hearing your partner's forced response, you contemplate raising him, use this table as your guide:

———With 16 points, you may go to the two-level.
———With 19 points, you may go to the three-level.
———With 22 points, you may go to the four-level.

To illustrate, you are West, holding these hands, and the bidding has proceeded as indicated:

(1)	(2)	(3)	(4)
♠ K x x x	♠ K 10 9 x	♠ A J 9 x	♠ A K x x x
♡ x x	♡ x	♡ x	♡ x
◊ A J x	◊ A x x x	◊ A J 10 x	◊ A Q J x
♣ A x x x	♣ A Q x x	♣ A Q x x	♣ A Q x

South	West	North	East
1 heart	Double	Pass	1 spade
Pass	?		

(1) Pass. You have 14 points in support of spades. Partner has from 0 to 8.

(2) Bid two spades. Your hand is worth 17 points in support of spades: 13 in high cards, 3 for the singleton, and 1 for the promotion of the king of trumps.

(3) Bid three spades. In support of spades, your hand is valued at 19 points. If partner has some positive values (6 to 10) he will bid four spades.

(4) Bid four spades. If partner has as much as

♠ Q x x x   ♡ x x x   ◇ 10 9 x x   ♣ x x

a game should be made easily. Your A-Q-J of diamonds and A-Q of clubs are fortunately located, for they lie over the opening bidder, who figures to have both minor suit kings. By repeated finesses, declarer may avoid the loss of any club or diamond tricks.

THE CUE-BID

If your right-hand opponent opens with one of a suit and you bid two of that same suit, this *cue-bid* announces a game-going hand with fine support for all three unbid suits—a sort of super-powerhouse take-out double. For example, suppose you are North with the following hand:

♠ A K J x x   ♡ —   ◇ K Q 10 x   ♣ A Q x x

West	North	East	South
1 heart	2 hearts (a)	Pass	3 diamonds (b)
Pass	3 spades (c)	Pass	3 no trumps (d)
Pass	4 diamonds (e)	Pass	5 diamonds (f)
Pass	Pass (g)	Pass	

(a) The cue-bid directly over opponent's opening bid announces a game-going hand.

(b) A forced response, since South cannot pass. All you know is that he has four diamonds.

(c) Showing the cue-bidder's suit.

(d) Showing some semblance of a stopper in hearts, the adversely-bid suit.

(e) Again, a safe bid, since it cannot be passed. You are looking for spade support, to play the contract for ten tricks at spades rather than eleven tricks at diamonds. Slam aspirations have now been discarded, in view of your partner's unenthusiastic bidding (his hearts are of no use to you, since you are void of that suit).

(f) Showing length or good diamond support.

(g) There can be no slam in the hand, and even the game may not be there, but it is worth a try. Your partner will recognize that you have bid a game virtually by yourself. If he has a quick trick (outside of the heart suit) he should bid the slam.

The partnership hands, in the above bidding sequence, might have been:

North	South
♠ A K J x x	♠ x x
♡ —	♡ Q x x
◊ A Q x x	◊ J x x x x
♣ K Q 10 x	♣ J x x

The five-diamond contract figures to make, there being one diamond loser and one club loser.

A final illustration of the cue-bid. You are North.

North	South
♠ A x	♠ x x x
♡ K J 10 x x x	♡ Q x
◊ A Q J 10 x	◊ x x
♣ —	♣ Q x x x x x

West	North	East	South
1 spade	2 spades (a)	Pass	3 clubs (b)
Pass	3 hearts (c)	Pass	4 clubs (d)
Pass	4 diamonds (e)	Pass	4 hearts (f)
Pass	Pass (g)	Pass	

(a) The cue-bid, insisting that at least a game be reached.
(b) The forced response.
(c) With no fear of being passed.

201

(d) Showing at least five clubs.

(e) You show your second suit, giving South a choice of your two suits.

(f) South shows his preference.

(g) End of the line. Your partner has expressed no enthusiasm for anything (except, perhaps, clubs).

The cue-bid of the opponents' suit is a most powerful weapon, but it is also a most dangerous weapon if not wielded properly. Use it when you have a hand on which a game seems certain and you wish to probe for a slam.

REOPENING THE BIDDING

Let's take this situation. You are South:

West	North	East	South
1 diamond	Pass	Pass	?

Whenever opener's partner passes, denying 6 points, it is highly improbable that his side can make a game. Therefore, you need have little fear in keeping the auction open when you sit in fourth position. Your partner may have a good hand with which he was yet unable to overcall or make a take-out double. Your side may be able to (a) make a game, (b) make a part-score, or (c) inflict defeat upon the opponents. In this position, then, you will reopen the bidding on a hand with which, in normal circumstances you would not be so aggressive—in other words, on a hand that isn't too good. The reason, again, is not that you have "stuff" but rather that "they" seem to have disclaimed having "stuff," and that your partner figures to have more than his pass indicated.

As South, in the above sequence, you should take the action indicated with the following hands:

(1)	(2)	(3)
♠ K J x x	♠ A x x	♠ x x
♡ A x x x	♡ K x x	♡ A Q J 10 x
◇ x x	◇ K 10 x x	◇ x x x
♣ Q J x	♣ A 10 x	♣ x x x

(1) Double, for a take-out. You don't have the 13 points you should normally have, but your partner will recognize that your double in this position can be light.

(2) Bid one no trump. The one no trump overcall is normally made on hands that contain 16-18 points. However, this is an abnormal situation; trust your partner to take that into account.

(3) Bid one heart. In normal circumstances, this is a pretty bad overcall, since a one-level overcall should be made on no fewer than 10 points. However, you are more or less bound to "protect" your partner, who may have passed a good hand.

DOUBLES OF PRE-EMPTIVE BIDS

I. Pre-empts Three-Level If an opponent opens with a pre-emptive bid of three in a suit, you need about 16 points to double. This double is intended for a take-out, but partner may pass if he feels that he can defeat the opponents' contract.

Over an opening three-heart bid, the following is a type hand with which you should double:

♠ A x x x   ♡ x   ◇ A J x   ♣ K Q x x x

Partner will now cooperate with you in this fashion: (a) he will bid his best suit, as he would in response to a take-out double at the one-level, or (b) he can pass for penalties, if he has at least 6 high-card points including one sure winning trick in the opponents' suit.

Here are three types of hands that your partner might hold in the above sequence, where you doubled the opening three-heart bid on the given hand:

(1)	(2)	(3)
♠ x x	♠ x x	♠ K Q x x x
♡ K Q x x	♡ x x x	♡ x x x
◇ x x x	◇ x x	◇ x x
♣ Q x x x	♣ Q x x x x x	♣ K Q x

(1) Pass.

(2) Bid four clubs.

(3) Bid four spades, showing real strength. The doubler must have strong support for spades or else a tremendous suit of his own.

II. Pre-empts Four-Level The double of any four-level opening bid shows at least 16 points. However, since doubler's partner has very little bidding space, and will usually tend to pass, the doubler should always have at least four defensive tricks, with which he can beat the doubled contract all by himself.

Here is the guide for doubler's partner when the double has been made at the four-level:

(a) A double of four spades is for penalties. Responder should pass unless he can foresee a slam for his side.

(b) A double of four hearts is also for penalties, but the doubler will be prepared for a spade response.

(c) A double of four clubs or diamonds is intended for take-out; doubler is prepared for either a heart or spade response from partner. However, if responder has no major suit, he may pass for penalties.

A double of a *four-spade* opening bid will be made on such hands as:

♠ A Q	♠ x x
♡ K x x x	♡ A K x x
◇ A J x x	◇ A K x x
♣ Q x x	♣ A x x

A double of a four-heart opening bid will be made on hands of this type:

♠ K Q x x	♠ A Q x
♡ x x	♡ A x x
◇ A Q x	◇ A K x
♣ A K x x	♣ x x x x

Over the doubled four-heart opening bid, partner of doubler will pass on hand (1) below; and he will bid four spades on hand (2).

(1)	(2)
♠ x x x	♠ K x x x x x
♡ x x x	♡ x
◇ K x x	◇ Q x x
♣ x x x x	♣ x x x

A double of an opening four-diamond bid will be made on:

♠ A J x x	♠ A J x x
♡ A J x x	♡ Q J x x
◇ x	◇ x x
♣ A J x x	♣ A K Q

Over the double of an opening four-diamond bid, partner will pass with hands (1) and (2) below; with hand (3) he will bid four hearts.

(1)	(2)	(3)
♠ x x x	♠ Q x	♠ K x x
♡ x x x	♡ x x x x	♡ K x x x x
◇ K J x x	◇ x x x	◇ x
♣ x x x	♣ x x x x	♣ x x x x

III. Weak Two-Bids A take-out double of a weak two-bid should be based on a hand that revalues to at least 16 points as dummy. It should contain either support for each of the unbid suits or a more-or-less self-sustaining suit that doubler can bid if partner names a "wrong" suit.

Here are some illustrations as to how to cope with the weak two-bid. Your right-hand opponent has opened the bidding with two hearts:

(1)	(2)	(3)
♠ A x x	♠ A J x x	♠ A Q J 9 x
♡ K x x	♡ x x	♡ x x
◇ J x x x	◇ A J 10 x x	◇ A Q 10 x
♣ A Q x	♣ A J	♣ x x

(1) Pass. This hand is not strong enough to step in. It barely qualifies for a take-out double over an opening one-bid.

(2) Double. Although there is a risk, man cannot live by bread alone. You have a good hand, and if partner bids spades or diamonds, or passes for penalties, you're in good shape. If partner happens to bid three clubs, you can then use your intuition to guide you whether to bid three diamonds or to pass.

(3) Bid two spades. You will need to find enough in partner's hand to justify his free bid or raise if you are to make game.

THE PENALTY DOUBLE

The penalty double is the call you make when you expect to defeat the opponents at their contract.

To review the question of how partner distinguishes the penalty double from the take-out double:

If you double after your partner has previously made a contractual bid, that is a penalty double. Even if your partner has not previously bid, your double is still a penalty double if the double was not made *at your first opportunity*.

As was stated at the end of the preceding section, a double of any opening no-trump bid is a penalty double.

Now to the prime question: "How much do I need to make a penalty double?" The answer to this cannot be given in a word; it depends on a number of factors: (a) how many tricks the opponents have contracted for; (b) how many tricks you can take; (c) how many tricks your partner can take.

In counting the tricks you think you can win on defense, the point-count valuation of your hand is superseded by the quick-trick valuation. The quick-trick table follows:

A K	2 quick tricks
A Q	1½ quick tricks
A	1 quick trick
K Q	1 quick trick
K x	½ quick trick

Quick-trick valuation is affected by what you can assume from the bidding. An A-Q is worth 2 quick tricks if your right-hand opponent has bid the suit, thereby indicating that he probably has the king. The K-x of the suit which your right-hand opponent has bid is promoted to 1 quick trick, since the ace figures to be in the hand of the enemy bidder. Conversely, an A-Q in a suit bid by your left-hand opponent is probably only 1 quick trick, and K-x in a suit bid by left-hand opponent must be discounted. For example:

(1)	(2)	(3)
♠ A K x	♠ K x x	♠ A x x x x
♡ A Q x x	♡ K Q x	♡ x x x x
◇ x x x x	◇ x x x x	◇ K x
♣ K x	♣ A x x	♣ x x

If the opponents have bid diamonds, hand (1) figures to produce 5 winning tricks against a diamond contract. If the opponents have bid clubs, hand (2) figures to produce 2½ tricks against an adverse club contract. If the opponents have bid hearts, hand (3) figures to produce 2½ winning tricks against a heart contract, counting 1 for four trumps.

Now to the question: "How can I tell how many tricks my partner can win?" Once this is known, there no longer is any problem as to how many tricks your partnership can take, and whether you can defeat the opponents. Here is your guide:

(a) If partner has opened the bidding with one of a suit, count on him to win three tricks.

(b) If partner has opened the bidding with one no trump, count on him to win four tricks.

(c) If partner has made a take-out double, count on him to win three tricks.

(d) If partner has overcalled at the one-level, count on him to win one trick; if partner has made an overcall at the two-level, count on him to win two tricks.

(e) If you have opened the bidding, and partner has made one positive response, count on him to win one trick; if he has made two positive responses, count on him to win two tricks; and if he has made three positive responses, count on him to win three tricks.

Let's now examine the application of the above. You are North and hold the given hands:

(1)
♠ x x
♡ Q J 10 x x
◇ A Q x x
♣ K x

South	West	North
1 spade	2 hearts	Double

You figure to win five tricks and your partner figures to win three tricks. Therefore the opponents, contracting for eight tricks, figure to take no more than five tricks, for a three-trick set. Business is good!

(2)

♠ x x
♡ A K x x x
♢ K 10 x x
♣ K Q

North	East	South	West
1 heart	Pass	1 spade	2 clubs
2 diamonds	3 clubs	3 spades	4 clubs
Double			

You figure to win at least three tricks and partner, who has made two positive bids, figures to win two tricks. Therefore, the opponents should make no more than eight tricks.

(3)

♠ Q J 10
♡ x x
♢ A x x x
♣ x x x x

South	West	North	East
1 heart	1 spade	Pass	2 spades
Pass	4 spades	Double	

Take note of the following cautions:

——Whenever you make a penalty double of a below-game contract, you should do so only if you expect to defeat the opponents *at least two tricks*. A one-trick margin is not sufficient, for if they make their contract, you will have doubled them into a game.

——Do not double a low-level overcall when your hand includes only length and non-immediate tricks in opponent's suit, e.g., Q J 9 x x. You may drive them into a better contract, against which you have no defense.

——Never count more than two defensive winners in a suit other than trumps. For example:

♠ x x   ♡ A K Q x   ♢ x x   ♣ A K Q x x

If you hold the above hand, and the opponents arrive at some spade contract, count just two winners in hearts: after you cash the ace and king, the queen will in all probability

208

be trumped. As a matter of fact, there will be days when your king of hearts will be trumped—but that's a calculated risk.

In the trump suit, you count as many defensive winners as your judgment indicates. With the K Q J 10 9 in the opponents' suit, nothing on earth can prevent you from making four tricks; with the K x of their trump suit, whether you make a trick or not will depend on which opponent has the ace.

The Double of One No Trump   The double of an opening one no trump bid is always construed as a business or penalty double. To double the opening one no trump bid, the doubler must hold the equivalent of an opening one no trump bid—that is, 16-18 points. The theory behind this high requirement is the same as for the double of an opening bid of one in a suit: the doubler is announcing that he is at least as strong as the opening bidder. If the partner of the doubler has 5 or 6 high-card points, he should pass, for the doubling side will have 21-24 high-card points against 16-19 points for the opening side. This edge, plus the advantage of the opening lead, should suffice to prevent declarer from fulfilling his contract.

Here are two hands with which you should double an opening one no trump bid:

	(1)		(2)
♠	K x	♠	A x x
♡	A J x	♡	A J x
◇	K Q J x x	◇	K x
♣	Q x x	♣	A K Q x x

When partner of the doubler has hands of the following types, he will take the indicated action:

	(1)		(2)
♠	Q x x	♠	x x
♡	Q x x	♡	x x x
◇	x x x	◇	Q J x x x x
♣	K x x x	♣	x x

(1) Pass. Defeat of the one no trump contract is assured.

(2) Two diamonds. He "can't stand" one no trump doubled and should take out, even though a double of any opening no trump bid is a penalty double.

The two number (1) hands above and, similarly, the two number (2) hands might be the partnership hands.

209

A double of an opening bid of two or three no trumps is always for penalty; you expect to beat the contract. Similarly any double of two or three no trumps arrived at in any fashion is a penalty double.

QUIZ

Your right-hand opponent has opened the bidding with one heart. What do you call on each of these hands?

(1)
♠ A x x
♡ x x x
◇ A K x x
♣ x x x

(2)
♠ A K x x
♡ x x x
◇ A x x
♣ K J x

(3)
♠ A K x x
♡ A x x
◇ K x x
♣ K x x

(4)
♠ A K Q x x
♡ x x
◇ Q x x
♣ x x x

(5)
♠ x
♡ A x x
◇ K J x
♣ A x x x x x

(6)
♠ x
♡ A x x
◇ x x x
♣ A K x x x x

(7)
♠ x
♡ A Q x x
◇ A J x x
♣ K x x x

(8)
♠ A Q J 10 x x
♡ x x
◇ Q x x
♣ x x

(9)
♠ x x x
♡ x
◇ A x x
♣ A Q J 10 x x

(10)
♠ Q J x x
♡ x x
◇ A Q x
♣ A Q x x

(11)
♠ A Q
♡ K Q J 10 x x
◇ x x
♣ x x x

You, South, hold each of the following hands, and the bidding has proceeded as indicated:

(12)

♠ Q J 10 x x   ♡ x x   ◇ x x x   ♣ x x x

North	*East*	*South*
1 diamond	1 spade	?

210

♠ A x x x x   ♡ A Q x   ◇ x x   ♣ x x x

West	North	East	South
1 heart	Double	Pass	?

♠ x x   ♡ x x   ◇ K Q J x x   ♣ A x x x

West	North	East	South
1 diamond	Double	Pass	?

♠ K J 9 x   ♡ x x   ◇ A x x x   ♣ K x x

North	East	South
1 heart	2 spades	?

♠ x x x   ♡ x x x   ◇ x x   ♣ A K Q J x

West	North	East	South
1 no trump	Double	Pass	?

♠ x x   ♡ Q x x   ◇ A K Q x x x   ♣ x x

West	North	East	South
1 spade	2 hearts	Pass	?

♠ A x   ♡ A x x   ◇ J x x x   ♣ J x x x

West	North	East	South
1 heart	1 spade	Pass	?

(19)

♠ A x x   ♥ Q x x x   ♦ A J x x   ♣ x x

West	North	East	South
1 heart	1 spade	Pass	?

(20)

♠ A x x   ♥ Q x x   ♦ Q x x x   ♣ x x x

West	North	East	South
1 no trump	2 hearts	Pass	?

(21)

♠ x x   ♥ A   ♦ K J x x x   ♣ Q J x x x

East	South	West	North
1 spade	Pass	2 spades	Pass
Pass	?		

(22)

♠ Q 10 x x   ♥ x x   ♦ K x x x   ♣ x x x

West	North	East	South
1 heart	Double	Pass	1 spade
Pass	3 spades	Pass	?

(23)

♠ A Q   ♥ Q x x   ♦ A K Q 10 x x   ♣ x x

East	South
1 spade	?

(24)

♠ x   ♥ A K J 10 x   ♦ A K Q x x   ♣ x x

East	South
1 spade	?

(25)

♠ A Q x x x   ♡ J x x   ◇ x x   ♣ x x x

West	North	East	South
1 heart	Pass	2 clubs	Pass
2 hearts	Double	Pass	?

(26)

♠ x   ♡ A J x x   ◇ A J x x   ♣ A J x x

East	South	West	North
1 spade	Double	Pass	2 no trumps
Pass	?		

(27)

♠ x x x   ♡ A x   ◇ Q J 10 9 x x x   ♣ x

East	South
1 spade	?

(28)

♠ A Q   ♡ A K 10 9 x x x   ◇ Q x   ♣ x x

East	South
1 diamond	?

(29)

♠ Q x x   ♡ Q x x x   ◇ K J x x   ♣ x x

West	North	East	South
1 diamond	Double	Pass	?

ANSWERS

(1) Pass. Two-level overcalls on four-card suits are always frowned upon.

(2) Double, for a take-out. You have at least mild support

213

for any suit partner may be forced to name. Whichever non-jump response he makes, you intend to pass.

(3) One no trump, showing 16-18 points, and the type of hand with which, had you been first, you would have opened with one no trump. This one no trump overcall is also permitted with 19 points.

(4) One spade. You have the requirements for an overcall at the one-level; a good suit and adequate points.

(5) Pass. Although you hold the requisite points for a two-level overcall, you do not have the "very good suit" required (a six-card suit must be headed by at least the A-K, K J 10, etc.).

(6) Two clubs. The points and the "very good" suit make this a proper two-level overcall.

(7) Pass, with the hope that the opponents climb too high. If you make a take-out double, partner will almost surely respond in spades, and you'll find yourself out on a limb.

(8) One spade. You are slightly too good for a weak two spade overcall.

(9) Two clubs, as a non-jump overcall, showing a very good suit and 13-15 points.

(10) Double for a take-out. You are prepared for any suit response partner might be forced to make.

(11) Pass. You have no place to go except the opponents' heart suit.

(12) Pass. To make a penalty double at the one-level, you need a minimum of four defensive tricks, including at least one outside of the trump suit.

(13) Two spades, a jump bid showing 9-12 points. If partner bids again but does not support spades, you will then bid no trump to indicate your fine protection in the adversely-bid heart suit.

(14) Pass, for penalties. Your hand figures to produce one trick in clubs, and at least three tricks in diamonds. Your partner's hand figures to produce at least three winners.

(15) Double, for penalties. You have three winning trump tricks behind the spade bidder, and you'll probably win two or more tricks with your diamond and club high cards. Declarer figures to take a bad beating.

(16) Pass. Your partner has 16-18 high-card points, you have 10 high-card points. Something is wrong somewhere, since there aren't 16 high-card points left for the opening one no trump bidder. Since your partner is always assumed to be

214

"honest"—until it's proven that he's not—the opening bidder must have miscounted his hand.

Do not bid two clubs, for that would be interpreted as a sign of weakness, showing fewer than 6 points.

(17) Four hearts. Your partner's two-level overcall shows a very good heart suit and 13-15 points. You yourself have an opening bid, and more than adequate trump support. Don't bid three diamonds—partner might pass.

(18) Pass. A game cannot be made, since partner has at most 14 points. Why drive him higher?

(19) Two spades, a raise of partner's overcall. This bid shows 11-12 points, and invites him to bid a game if his overcall was based on a maximum holding.

(20) Pass. Partner has at most 13-15 points. Your side cannot make a game. Against an opening one no trump a game will rarely, if ever, be made, and your partner's overcall was not designed to get you to a game. If partner had at least 16 points, he would have doubled the opening bid.

(21) Two no trumps. This is the perfect "set-up" for the "unusual" no trump overcall, requesting partner to select his best minor suit.

(22) Four spades. Partner, who has doubled and then jumped in your suit, has a minimum of 19 points. You have 6 points and a game is a worthwhile risk, considering that partner could have 20 or 21 points.

(23) Double for take-out. If partner responds in clubs, you will rebid two no trumps. If he bids hearts, your rebid should be three diamonds. (Remember, he may have only four small hearts.)

(24) Double for take-out. Whatever your partner responds, it is your intent to jump in hearts on the next round. This hand is much too good to make a mere overcall.

(25) Pass. Your partner's double was a penalty double; he figures to beat the two heart contract all by himself. Had he wanted to make a take-out double, he would have done so at his first opportunity to bid.

(26) Three no trumps. Partner has at least 11 points and the spade suit protected. Had he held a biddable heart suit, he would have jumped to three hearts instead of two no trumps. If you now bid three hearts, partner is entitled to assume that you have a five-card suit.

(27) Three diamonds, the weak jump overcall, showing a bad hand (no more than 9 points), and a long suit. The intent of the bid is to deprive the opponents of bidding space.

(28) Double for take-out. This hand is too good to make a mere overcall of one heart, and a jump to two hearts would denote weakness.

(29) One heart. When partner has made a take-out double, he is looking for a suit, especially a major suit. You will be able to bid no trump later, if the opportunity arises, to show the protection in the adversely-bid suit.

Lesson 9

DECLARER PLAY

THE READER will appreciate that, in this book, it is impossible to present a comprehensive treatise on the play of the cards. This is a vast subject and hundreds of pages would be needed to illustrate adequately the hundreds of situations that arise during the play.

Fortunately, many of these fall into certain definite patterns—ones that continually repeat themselves, and which are immediately recognized by the knowledgeable bridge player. It is these major patterns that will comprise the contents of the final two lessons. By mastering them, the reader will be well on the way towards becoming well qualified in the play of the cards.

THE FINESSE

Although the reader is undoubtedly familiar with the workings of the simple finesse, the importance of the subject is so great that, even at the risk of offending the reader by my naiveté, I feel that I must introduce it, as a prologue to declarer's play. On virtually every deal that you will ever encounter, there will exist the opportunity to create winning tricks by finessing.

The Single Finesse A *single finesse* is directed against a single outstanding high card, such as the king.

```
Q J                              Q x
  N                                N
W   E              or           W   E
  S                                S
A x                              A J
```

In each of the above situations, the queen is led out of the North hand. Whenever East has the king, declarer will win two tricks in the suit, regardless of whether East plays the king or doesn't.

Where the ace and queen are not in the same hand, and neither declarer nor the dummy holds the jack, leading the queen would simply throw it away. The correct play is to lead up to the queen. To illustrate:

```
            Q 7 5
              N
  J 9 8 3   W   E   K 10 4
              S
            A 6 2
```

If declarer leads the queen from the North hand, East will cover it with the king, forcing South to play his ace. South will now be unable to avoid the loss of two subsequent tricks in this suit. Nor is the situation changed if the East-West hands are interchanged:

```
            Q 7 5
              N
  K 10 4   W   E   J 9 8 3
              S
            A 6 2
```

If the queen is led from the North hand, the result will be the same as far as declarer is concerned: he will win just one trick, the ace.

The proper play is to lead the ace from the South hand first, and then lead the two-spot towards the queen. The queen will win a trick if West holds the king—a 50 per cent chance—as against the 100 per cent certainty that the queen will win nothing if led.

The finesse against a queen or a jack is a simple, straight-forward play. To illustrate:

```
        (1)                              (2)
      A K J                            K Q 10
        N                                N
      W   E                            W   E
        S                                S
        x                                x
```

(1) South leads the little card from the South hand, and if West plays small, North's jack is played; 50 per cent of the time the jack will win; 50 per cent of the time it will lose.

(2) Suppose that, on the previous round of this suit, North has led the ace and East has failed to follow. West is thus marked with the jack. South now leads the little one, and puts up dummy's ten, which must win the trick. This situation is called a "marked" finesse—that is, you *know* where the adverse high card you're looking for is located.

The Double Finesse The double finesse is necessary when two intervening key cards are outstanding. The first finesse has the effect of reducing the situation to a simple finesse. To illustrate:

```
            x x x
              N
     K x x  W   E  Q x x
              S
          A J 10 x
```

If South, holding the given seven cards of the suit, were to play his ace, he would not figure to catch either the king or queen, and eventually he would lose a trick to each of them.

For a double finesse, a small card is led from the North hand, and when East follows with a small one, South's ten-spot is played and captured by West's king. When North leads later, he plays another small card, East follows low, and South's jack is put up, winning that trick. South then plays his ace, dropping East's queen. By employing the double finesse, South's only loser in the suit is one trick, to West's king.

Here is another frequently occurring double-finesse situation:

```
              x x x
               N
      x x x   W   E   K J x
               S
            A Q 10 x
```

North leads small, East plays small, and South plays his ten-spot, which wins the trick. The North hand is then re-entered, via some side suit, and a second card of this suit is led. Whatever East then plays, he is trapped. South avoids the loss of any trick in the suit.

Of course, South is lucky to find both the jack and king in the East hand. Let's assume that the spades are divided in the following ways:

```
         (1)                          (2)
        x x x                        x x x
         N                            N
  J x x  W   E  K x x          K J x  W   E  x x x
         S                            S
      A Q 10 x                     A Q 10 x
```

(1) The first finesse, against the jack, loses; but the second finesse wins. South loses one trick in the suit.

(2) If West has both the king and jack protected, then South can't avoid the loss of two tricks no matter how he plays.

DECLARER'S PLAY AT SUIT CONTRACTS

Fundamentally, declarer creates tricks by (a) finessing, (b) ruffing out losers, and (c) establishing winners upon which losers can be discarded. Let us examine (b) and (c), while at the same time viewing (a), the finesse, in action:

```
              ♠ Q 8 7 3
              ♡ 6 5 3
              ◇ 9 4
              ♣ K 9 5 2

♠ 6 5                              ♠ A K
♡ Q 10 8 2        N               ♡ 9 7 4
◇ J 7 6 2      W     E            ◇ K 10 5 3
♣ Q 4 3           S               ♣ J 10 8 7

              ♠ J 10 9 4 2
              ♡ A K J
              ◇ A Q 8
              ♣ A 6
```

Against South's four-spade contract, West opens a spade, which is captured by East's king. East then leads a heart which South's ace wins. South leads another trump, East's ace winning, and East returns another heart. This time South plays the jack, finessing for the queen, but West wins the trick (the 50-50 finesse didn't work this time). West now plays a third round of hearts, taken by declarer's king.

Declarer then enters dummy via the king of clubs. He leads a small diamond, and when East follows small, South's queen is played. This time the finesse wins, the diamond king being favorably located.

Next declarer plays the ace of diamonds, followed by the eight of diamonds, which is trumped in dummy. The remainder of the tricks belong to declarer. Declarer's only losers are two trump tricks and a heart trick.

Let us briefly examine the major principles of suit play which were employed in the above hand. First, in most situations, as soon as declarer obtains the lead the first thing he does will be to take away the opponents' trumps. The exception to this will be illustrated in a moment; trumps will not be drawn if declarer has a better use for them than to merely use them as extractors. Secondly, declarer had two finesses to take, against the queen of hearts and the king of diamonds. One finesse lost (hearts) and one finesse won (diamonds), which is what figured to be, since each finesse is a 50-50 proposition. And, finally, declarer had a losing diamond, which he disposed of by trumping (ruffing) in dummy.

The reader will probably say that the above deal is absurdly simple. He is right. Yet on about 50 per cent of all deals at a suit contract, proper play necessitates nothing more than the application of the correct way of winning tricks, as demonstrated above.

On occasion, both declarer's hand and dummy will each have a void or a singleton, and in these situations trumps should *not* be drawn, since more tricks can otherwise be won by ruffing declarer's losing cards in dummy, and ruffing dummy's losing cards in declarer's hand. This ruffing back and forth is known as the "cross-ruff."

```
              ♠ A Q 10 8
              ♡ 4
              ◇ A 9 8 5 3
              ♣ Q 9 5

  ♠ 3                          ♠ 5 4 2
  ♡ J 9 8 3        N           ♡ K Q 10 5
  ◇ Q 10 7 4    W     E        ◇ K J 6
  ♣ A K 6 3        S           ♣ 10 8 4

              ♠ K J 9 7 6
              ♡ A 7 6 2
              ◇ 2
              ♣ J 7 2
```

South arrived at a four-spade contract, against which West opened the king of clubs and then played the ace of clubs, after which he led a third club, North's queen winning.

Declarer perceived that if he now played trumps—removing dummy's trumps in the process—he would be left with one or two losing hearts. South also saw that his nine trumps were all high, the opponents having only the 2, 3, 4, 5.

After winning the third trick, declarer cashed the heart ace and diamond ace, then led hearts and diamonds back and forth, trumping each lead. Thus he won the rest of the tricks, losing only the two clubs at the outset.

Another valuable technique is known as ruffing out a suit. Suppose you are South, playing the following hand at six hearts.

```
                    ♠ A K 7
                    ♡ K Q 10
                    ◇ A K 8 4 3
                    ♣ 8 2
♠ 10 8 4 3                              ♠ Q J 9
♡ 6 5              N                    ♡ 8 4
◇ Q 9 2         W     E                 ◇ J 6 5
♣ K Q 10 9         S                    ♣ J 7 6 5 3
                    ♠ 6 5 2
                    ♡ A J 9 7 3 2
                    ◇ 7 5
                    ♣ A 4
```

West opens the king of clubs, which you capture with the ace. You perceive that you have two losers, one in clubs and one in spades. If both tricks are lost, you go down.

Since you have no special use for dummy's trumps, you then play two rounds of trumps, which gather in all of the opponents' trumps. Then comes the ace of diamonds, followed by the king of diamonds, both opponents following suit. A third diamond is now led, and trumped in the closed hand. Since both opponents have followed suit to three rounds of diamonds, there are no diamonds left in their hands—both of dummy's little diamonds are now high! You go back to dummy with a high spade, cash the two diamonds and discard your club 4 and a spade. Then you claim the rest. The fortunate 3-3 division of the six outstanding diamonds has let you make all thirteen tricks. Had the diamonds been divided 4-2, you still could have made twelve tricks by establishing one winner in diamonds on which to discard a loser, thus:

```
              ♠ A K 7
              ♡ K Q 10
              ◇ A K 8 4 3
              ♣ 8 2

♠ 10 8 4 3              N              ♠ Q J 9
♡ 6 5 4           W         E          ♡ 8
◇ J 2                  S               ◇ Q 9 6 5
♣ K Q 10 9                             ♣ J 7 6 5 3

              ♠ 6 5 2
              ♡ A J 9 7 3 2
              ◇ 7 5
              ♣ A 4
```

Against South's six-heart contract, West opens the king of clubs which is captured by declarer's ace. Three rounds of trumps are drawn. Then follows the ace of diamonds, the king of diamonds, and a third diamond which declarer trumps. The queen of diamonds is still outstanding, as the sole surviving diamond in the opponents' hands.

Dummy is now re-entered via the spade ace, and a fourth round of diamonds is led, declarer ruffing. On this trick East's queen of diamonds falls, establishing dummy's fifth diamond as a winner. The North hand is then entered via the king of spades and the established diamond is led. Upon it declarer discards either his losing spade or his losing club. At the end declarer concedes a trick to his opponents, but that is his only losing trick.

DECLARER'S PLAY AT NO-TRUMP CONTRACTS

No-trump play differs appreciably from suit play. In a suit contract, you have both your high cards and your trumps to effectively prevent the opponents from cashing their suit: in a no-trump contract, you have only your high cards for this purpose. Generally speaking, the opponents have the initial advantage at no-trump contracts, since their lead is usually in their best suit, in which suit you figure not to be too strong.

In theory, the play of the cards at a no-trump contract is a race to establish as winners the small cards of long suits, the defenders being one step ahead. The time element is a most vital factor: you, as declarer, must establish and cash your long suit before the opponents can establish and cash theirs.

In no-trump contracts, tricks are won by: (a) high cards, (b) promotion of low cards into winners, and (c) finessing (as in a suit contract). At virtually every no-trump contract, all three of these ways of winning tricks will be utilized. Let us look at a few illustrations:

```
                    ♠ 7 2
                    ♡ K J 5
                    ◇ A J 10 8 5
                    ♣ K 6 3

  ♠ K 9 5 3                         ♠ Q J 10 8
  ♡ 8 7 4            N              ♡ Q 9 3 2
  ◇ 6            W       E          ◇ K 6 2
  ♣ Q J 10 9 2       S              ♣ 7 5

                    ♠ A 6 4
                    ♡ A 10 6
                    ◇ Q 9 7 3
                    ♣ A 8 4
```

Against South's three no-trumps contract, West opens the queen of clubs. Before playing to the first trick, declarer stops to take inventory. He perceives that he has one sure spade trick, two hearts, one diamond, and two clubs, a total of six tricks. Obviously diamonds is the suit to attack, since three additional tricks can be established by force.

Declarer wins the opening club lead with his ace, and promptly leads the queen of diamonds, finessing against the king. However, East has the king (the 50-50 proposition), and captures this trick, after which he returns a club, his partner's suit. Dummy's king of clubs wins the trick, and from here in declarer has smooth sailing, for the J 10 9 of diamonds have been promoted into winners.

```
              ♠ K 6 4
              ♡ A 8 3
              ◇ A K J 6
              ♣ 6 4 3

♠ J 8 3                        ♠ Q 10 9 2
♡ Q J 10 7 4      N           ♡ 9 5
◇ 9 5          W     E        ◇ Q 10 8 4
♣ K 10 5          S           ♣ 9 8 7

              ♠ A 7 5
              ♡ K 6 2
              ◇ 7 3 2
              ♣ A Q J 2
```

Against South's three no-trumps contract, West opens the queen of hearts. Once again, declarer stops to take inventory. He counts seven sure winners: two in spades, two in hearts, two in diamonds, and one in clubs. He needs two additional tricks.

Perceiving that if East has the king of clubs, South's queen and jack of clubs can provide the two additional tricks by finessing for the king, declarer wins the opening lead with the ace of hearts. A little club is then led, and South's queen is finessed, losing to the king. West leads the jack of hearts, which declarer captures with his king. Having started with seven sure tricks, declarer can now count eight, since the jack of clubs has been promoted to a winner.

But a real danger has now developed: declarer no longer has any protection in hearts; if the opponents again obtain the lead, they will cash the suit which they have established. Hence, to take the diamond finesse right now—the 50-50 hope that West has the diamond queen—is to run the risk of immediate defeat.

Declarer therefore cashes the ace and jack of clubs. Since all hands follow suit, the deuce of clubs is now the sole surviving club, it becomes declarer's ninth trick. The only skill required of declarer is the ability to count 4-8-12 to the three club leads.

If the clubs had not split 3-3, declarer would have finessed against the queen of diamonds as his sole remaining chance to make the contract.

The Hold-up Play There is one additional play, of a counter-attacking nature, which every declarer must learn and master, since the occasions for its practical employment will be quite frequent. This play, known as the "hold-up," is probably the most important single play available to declarer in no-trump contracts. It is also used occasionally in suit contracts.

This play consists of withholding a high card that could win a trick, to be used on a later trick. The hold-up is particularly essential when the lead against a no-trump contract is a suit in which declarer has only the ace (or other sure stopper). Declarer holds up his ace until he is compelled to play it; he may thereby break the line of communication between the defenders, and effectively prevent them from cashing their established suit.

Let us examine some illustrations of the hold-up play.

```
                    ♠ 7 2
                    ♡ K J 5
                    ◇ A J 10 8 5
                    ♣ K 6 3
  ♠ K J 9 5 3                        ♠ Q 10 8
  ♡ Q 8 2              N             ♡ 9 7 4 3
  ◇ 6 4            W       E         ◇ K 2
  ♣ Q 9 7              S             ♣ J 10 5 2
                    ♠ A 6 4
                    ♡ A 10 6
                    ◇ Q 9 7 3
                    ♣ A 8 4
```

Against South's three no-trumps contract, West opens the five of spades and East puts up the queen. Suppose that South (incorrectly) wins this trick with the ace. He must then attack the diamond suit, and when West takes his king of diamonds, the defenders will cash four spades. Declarer will go down.

But suppose that declarer holds up the ace of spades. East will then play the ten of spades, and again South will refuse to play his ace. A third round of the suit forces the ace. Note that East now has no spades left. Declarer will finesse the diamonds and lose to East's king. What can East now return that will hurt declarer? Nothing, for he has no more spades; whatever else he returns, declarer will win, to cash the three

227

established diamond tricks. By holding up his spade ace until the third round, declarer eliminated all the spades from the East hand, thereby "cutting the communication" between East and West in spades.

The logic behind the hold-up play is this: if declarer can void one defender of a dangerous suit before declarer loses command of it, he greatly reduces the chances that the danger suit will be run against him the moment he loses the lead. If the danger suit is evenly split, this hold-up is futile—but then the suit is less apt to be dangerous. In the foregoing example, if the adverse spades were divided, 4-4, then declarer couldn't lose more than three spade tricks and a diamond in any event.

Let us look at another example of the hold-up to "cut communication."

```
              ♠ K J 7 2
              ♡ K 3
              ◇ A K 6 5 2
              ♣ 9 6

  ♠ Q 5 3                        ♠ 8 6 4
  ♡ 8 7 2           N            ♡ J 10 9 4
  ◇ Q 9         W       E        ◇ J 10 7
  ♣ K Q J 7 4       S            ♣ 10 8 5

              ♠ A 10 9
              ♡ A Q 6 5
              ◇ 8 4 3
              ♣ A 3 2
```

Against South's three no trumps, West opens the king of clubs, which is permitted to win the trick. Then follows the club queen; declarer again holds up his ace. A third club is led, forcing the ace.

In spades, declarer has a "two-way" finesse against the queen. But now it has become "one-way," since he cannot risk letting West in the lead. Declarer leads the ace of spades, followed by the ten of spades, a small spade being played from dummy on the latter trick. Even if this finesse loses, the contract is assured. If East has a fourth club, the suit was originally divided 4-4, and declarer is safe.

SAFETY PLAYS

A safety play is one calculated to minimize the loss of tricks in a suit, in case the break of the adverse cards is unexpectedly bad.*

The safety plays discussed below are standard situations that arise frequently during the course of a single session of bridge. The reader should examine them closely, and earmark them for future reference.

The safety play will frequently sacrifice the possibility of winning an extra trick, the better to assure the contract. As you will learn from bitter experiences, danger frequently abounds, and it does not pay always to try for the maximum number of tricks. Use the safety play as insurance against a bad break. The number of 30-point overtricks lost by "safety-playing" will be more than offset by the number of games retrieved on the brink of disaster.

All of these safety plays assume that declarer has the side entries needed (if any) for the recommended play.

```
      Q 9 x x
        N
    W       E
        S
      A K 10 x x
```

Take the ace or king first (*not* the queen), to guard against either of the opponents holding the J x x x. You can then pick up the jack wherever it lies.

```
      Q 9 x x
        N
    W     E
        S
      A K 8 x x
```

Take the queen first, to guard against an East holding of J 10 x x (if West has the J 10 x x, he has a sure stopper). If East has the J 10 x x, declarer, by retaining the A K 8, will be able to pick up his entire holding without loss of a trick. If the suit

---

* The table of probabilities of suit divisions is presented on page 274.

is divided 2-2 or 3-1, South will win five tricks regardless of whether the ace, king or queen is played first.

```
        x x
         N
      W     E
         S
     A K J 10 x x
```

Lead from the North hand and finesse the jack. Do not lay down the ace first, and then get to the North hand to lead for a finesse of the jack.

```
       x x x
         N
      W     E
         S
      A K J x x
```

Lay down the ace first, then enter the North hand to lead for a finesse of the jack.

```
       x x x
         N
      W     E
         S
      A K J x
```

If you need *three* tricks, lay down the ace and king, then get to the North hand to lead up to the jack. This safety play will win a third trick whenever East has the queen, or whenever the queen is held singleton or doubleton by West.

```
       K 9 x x
         N
      W     E
         S
       A J x x
```

If you need *three* tricks, lay down the ace and play small towards the king, finessing the nine-spot if West follows small. This play will gain a trick whenever West has the Q 10 x x—

as opposed to leading the king originally, which will lose two tricks if West started with the Q 10 x x.

```
        K x
         N
       W   E
         S
      A 10 9 x x
```

Cash the king, then lead a small one, putting up the ace (as opposed to finessing the ten-spot).

```
        K x
         N
       W   E
         S
     A 10 9 x x x
```

Play the king first, then lead North's remaining card. If East plays small, put up the nine-spot. If West wins, then the ace will drop the last remaining card of the suit. This safety play is designed to guard against an East holding of the Q J x x, which would win two tricks if declarer directly cashed both the king and the ace.

```
       J x x x
         N
       W   E
         S
      A Q 9 x x x
```

Lead the jack, finessing against the king. If you lead low from the North hand, and finesse the queen, you will lose a trick if East has K 10 x.

```
       A 9 x x
         N
       W   E
         S
      K 10 x x x
```

If you cannot afford to lose more than one trick, lead low from either hand, putting up the nine or ten if the second-hand opponent plays low. This play will gain a trick whenever second hand has the Q J x x. If you cash the ace first, you will lose two tricks whenever West has the Q J x x; and if you cash the king first, you will lose two tricks if East has the Q J x x.

K J x

N

W   E

S

A 9 x x x

If you cannot afford to lose more than one trick, cash the king first, then enter the South hand via some other suit to lead a small one towards the jack. If either of the opponents has the Q 10 x x, you will lose only one trick by the indicated play. Should the ace be played first, you will lose two tricks if East has the Q 10 x x.

Q x x x

N

W   E

S

A 10 x x x x

To guarantee the loss of no more than one trick, lead a small card from the North hand, and if East plays small, put up the ten-spot.

A 10 x x

N

W   E

S

J x x x

To guarantee the winning of two tricks, cash the ace, then lead towards the jack. Do not double-finesse by leading the jack first, for this will lose three tricks if East has the K Q 9 x or K Q 9 x x.

232

Lesson 10

DEFENDERS' PLAY

DEFENSE is generally regarded as the most difficult aspect of bridge. But here again, there are important fundamental situations that occur repeatedly, and these will form the subject of our concluding lesson.

OPENING LEADS

The defending side has the first move in the play of the cards, in that it launches the offensive by making the opening lead. An understanding of the basic principles involved in this initial offensive by the defenders is most important: it has been estimated that almost half of all game contracts are either made or defeated on the opening lead! Although this figure cannot be proved, the fact remains that a correct versus an incorrect opening lead will often mean the difference between victory and defeat.

Nobody, not even the top-flight expert, makes the best opening lead all the time. This is because the selection of an opening lead is not an exact science—and it will never be—since the dummy is unseen until after the opening lead has been made. Nevertheless, there are certain basic principles which, if observed, will enable you to find the proper lead a very high percentage of the time.

On the principles to be presented, only general advice will be offered in many of the situations—that is, you will not be told "always" to lead something or "never" to lead something. However, you should not deviate from these fundamental principles unless you have good cause to do so.

Here are the various types of leads, classified into five categories. These leads are not arranged in order of efficiency—that is, (I) is not necessarily better than (II), and so on.

I. Lead your partner's suit.
II. Lead from a sequence of touching high cards.
III. Lead the fourth-highest in your longest and strongest suit.
IV. Lead a short suit; a singleton, a doubleton, or a tripleton.
V. Lead a trump.

I. Leading Your Partner's Suit   Whenever your partner bids, it is usually best to lead his suit. Whether he opens the bidding, or whether he overcalls, your first impulse should always be to lead his suit, and probably 99 per cent of the time, if you obey that impulse, you will make the best possible lead. Especially does this apply when partner has overcalled, for his overcalls are always based on good suits (as opposed to opening bids, which are frequently made on weakish suits).

Generally speaking, the only occasions on which you will not lead his suit will be where you have what figures to be a superior lead, e.g., A K Q x, or K Q J in your own suit. Most of the time you will not have the above-mentioned good leads of your own, and so will lead your partner's suit.

Let us see which card of partner's suit you should lead from various types of holdings.

If you have two or three worthless cards in partner's suit, lead the highest card. Likewise, when you have a sequence of high cards in a partner's suit, lead the highest card.* If you have just two cards of partner's suit, worthless or otherwise, lead the higher card. In all other situations, the proper lead is a low card.

LEADING PARTNER'S SUIT

The correct card to lead is shown in bold face.

---

* There is just one exception: whenever you have the A-K-x, A-K-x-x, etc., of partner's suit, the king is led. Where you have, specifically, the A-K doubleton, the ace is led first, conventionally, and then the king.

2 cards	3 cards	4 cards (or more)
A 2	A 5 3 (*)	A 5 3 2 (*)
K 3	A K 2	A K 3 2
Q 4	K Q 3	Q J 5 4
J 5	Q J 4	K 9 4 2
10 6	J 10 5	Q 8 5 3
3 2	K 6 3	J 9 6 4
A K	Q 7 4	10 6 5 3
K Q	J 8 5	6 4 3 2
Q J	10 7 5	8 7 5 3 2
J 10	8 5 3	J 10 6 3 2

Note that, against either a suit or no trump, the lead of the ace before the king shows exactly a doubleton, A K.

Note also, that from three worthless cards in partner's suit (8, 5, 3), the highest card is the proper lead. (However, many players prefer to lead low from three small ones. This is purely a partnership matter, necessitating prior partnership agreement.)

Let us now discuss those situations where partner has not bid. You are called upon to make an opening lead "in the blind." As your guide, you should follow the principle discussed below.

In choosing among blind opening leads, a vital distinction is whether the contract is in a suit or in no trump. One type of lead will work best against a suit contract, while another type is preferable against a no-trump contract.

II. Leading from a Sequence of Touching High Cards
A long suit topped by a sequence of three touching high cards affords the most efficient lead available against either a suit or a no-trump contract. For example:

AKQxx   KQJxx
QJ10xx   J109xx

The correct lead is the highest card, except that the king is led from A K (with three or more cards in the suit).

---

* If the contract is in a suit, and you have either the A x x or the A x x x of partner's suit, the correct lead is the ace. If the contract is no trump, and you hold either the A x x or the A x x x of partner's suit, the correct lead is the third-best or fourth-best, as shown in the table.

235

This lead from a triple sequence is highly desirable because it forces out a high card (if any) held by declarer, and at the same time rarely jeopardizes a high card (if any) held by partner. In fact, the lead from such a suit of your own is often preferable to opening a suit bid by your partner.

When the sequence is tripleton (not accompanied by any small cards), it still is a desirable lead against a suit contract. But against no trump, the general principle of opening one's long suit takes precedence. This matter is discussed in the next section.

A lead from two touching high cards is of course not so desirable as a lead from three. But it is often the best of unhappy choices in blind leading. Against a suit contract, the correct lead is the top card (except that the K is led from A K):

A K x x	K Q x x
Q J x x	J 10 x x

The same lead may be made against a suit contract whether the suit comprises two, three, or more cards. Against no trump, the suit should not be opened blind unless it comprises at least four cards, and the correct lead is the fourth-best:

A K x x	K Q x x
Q J x x	J 10 x x

III. Leading the Fourth-Highest in Your Longest and Strongest Suit In blind leading against a no-trump contract, the general principle is to open a long suit. Let us see why this is so.

In order to defeat a three no-trumps contract, your partnership must win five tricks. You're never going to win five tricks by cashing three aces and two kings, for when the opponents get to three no trumps, you and your partner won't have three aces and two kings between you.

Your hope of defeating them, then, rests in establishing and cashing winners out of little cards in your long suit. To this end your longest suit is opened—and when the high cards will be removed from circulation, your little ones will remain as winners.

North
- ♠ Q 10 x x
- ♡ 8 7 x
- ◇ x x x
- ♣ A K x

West
- ♠ x x
- ♡ Q 10 6 3 2
- ◇ A x x
- ♣ Q J 10

East
- ♠ A x
- ♡ J 9 5
- ◇ x x x x
- ♣ x x x x

South
- ♠ K J x x x
- ♡ A K
- ◇ K Q J
- ♣ x x x

Suppose that South arrives at the incorrect contract of three no trumps, and that you incorrectly open the queen of clubs. As you can see, you will in time make a winner out of your ten of clubs. But all you and partner will make, all in all, will be your ten of clubs, the ace of spades, and the ace of diamonds, for declarer will establish and cash his spade and diamond suits. By incorrectly opening the queen of clubs, all you created was one club trick.

But suppose that you correctly open the three of hearts, the fourth from the highest, which declarer would win with the king. Declarer will then play a spade, to establish his own long suit. Your partner, upon winning with the ace, will return hearts, forcing declarer to take his ace. Your Q 10 6 of hearts will now be established as winners, and when you subsequently obtain the lead with the ace of diamonds, you will cash them.

But had declarer been in the proper four-spade contract, the queen of clubs would be the proper lead, to build up one club trick (although, on this deal, no lead can defeat four spades). To open the fourth from the highest heart would accomplish nothing, as you can see. True, after declarer's ace and king of hearts have been removed, West's Q 10 6 of hearts would all be high—but when they were played, declarer would trump them.

What it comes to is this: there is little point in opening your longest suit against a suit contract, in order to establish the little cards; they will not generally be cashable, since declarer will trump them. Hence, sequences are opened against suit contracts, to establish quick, cashable winners. Against no trump, however, your low-card winners cannot be trumped: therefore establish as many of them as you can.

As to why the "fourth-best" is led (rather than the lowest or any other), the purpose is to let partner obtain additional information through two simple principles:

(a) If the leader has more than four cards of the suit, such additional cards must be lower than the card led. When a two is led, partner knows that the leader has just four cards; when a three is led, he watches for the two to ascertain whether the leader had four or five cards; etc.

(b) The so-called "Rule of Eleven" may give information of value as to the high cards of the suit. The rule is: subtract the denomination of the card led from 11; the difference is the number of cards of the suit, higher than the lead, held by the other three players. Since leader's partner sees two of the three hands, his own and dummy, he will always know how many cards *higher than the card led,* are held by declarer.

Let us put this in diagram form.

North
♠ K 10 7 5
♡ K Q 6
♢ Q J 2
♣ 9 5 4

West
Leads ♠ 6

East
♠ Q 9 3
♡ J 8 3 2
♢ 9 5 3
♣ 8 7 2

The contract is three no trumps by South, and your partner (West) opens the six of spades, upon which the seven is played from dummy. If you apply the Rule of Eleven, you will know that the play of the nine-spot will win the trick. Six from 11 leaves 5; that means that in the North, East and South hands there are *exactly* five spades higher than partner's six-spot. Three of these higher cards are in dummy, and two are in your hand. Therefore, declarer can have none. So why waste the queen to win a trick, when the nine-spot will do.

Let us take a look at some illustrations of the situations thus far presented. The contract is three no trumps, and you are on lead, holding each of the following hands:

(1)	(2)	(3)
♠ Q J x	♠ x x	♠ x x x
♡ Q 10 6 3 2	♡ K Q x	♡ x x
◊ A x	◊ K 10 8 5 3	◊ Q J 10 7 5
♣ x x x	♣ x x x	♣ K Q x

(4)	(5)	(6)
♠ x x	♠ K 10 6 3	♠ 10 7 5 3 2
♡ x x	♡ K 8 6 3	♡ Q J 6
◊ Q 9 7 4 2	◊ x x	◊ J 10 5
♣ J 10 6 3	♣ x x x	♣ K Q

(1) Lead the three of hearts. Against a suit contract, say three clubs, the correct lead would be the queen of spades.

(2) Lead the five of diamonds. Against a suit contract, say four clubs, the king of hearts would be proper.

(3) Lead the queen of diamonds, informing your partner that diamonds is your longest suit, and that the suit contains Q J 10, else you would have led the fourth-best.

(4) Lead the four of diamonds.

(5) Lead the three of spades. With two suits of equal length, lead from the stronger of the two.

(6) Lead the three of spades. The length-lead takes precedence over the sequence-lead at no trump.

The lead of the fourth-best from a long suit is not particularly good against a suit contract; experience indicates it to be distinctly inferior to the opening of partner's suit, to the sequence lead, and generally to the lead of a singleton. But, in the absence of the foregoing possibilities, the blind lead of a fourth-best serves as a decent lead.

IV. Leads Short Suit When your partner has not bid, and you don't have a sequence, and your only good suit has been bid by the opponents, you have a problem what to lead; there is nothing "good" to choose from. In these cases, a lead of a singleton or from a doubleton or tripleton is sometimes made (sometimes a trump, as discussed in the following section).

Let us now look into the matter of leading a singleton, a doubleton, or a tripleton.

Suppose you hold the following hands, and in each case the opponents have bid both spades and hearts, and have purchased the contract for four spades:

(1)	(2)	(3)
♠ J x x x	♠ Q x x	♠ Q x x
♡ K J x x	♡ K J x x	♡ K J x x
◇ 7 5 3	◇ 8 5 4	◇ 8 6 5 3 2
♣ 4 2	♣ 7 6 2	♣ 3

(4)	(5)	(6)
♠ Q J x	♠ Q J x	♠ x x x x
♡ Q J x x	♡ Q J x x	♡ Q x x
◇ x x x x	◇ x x x	◇ Q 6 2
♣ 8 3	♣ Q J x	♣ Q 6 2

(1) Whenever you lead any suit, it is with the fond hope of building up a trick or more in that suit. When the opponents have bid your best suit, the hope of building up tricks in *their* suit will have diminished, if not vanished altogether. What is done in these cases is to select a "substitute" suit. On this hand, then, it becomes a matter of whether a diamond or a club should be led—a pure guess, even to the world's best players. On some days, the diamond lead will turn out nicely; and on other days the club lead will turn out better. Whichever suit you elect to lead, your lead should be the highest card in that suit: the seven of diamonds or the four of clubs. Probably the preferable lead, in the long run, is the four of clubs, for that offers a better hope of eventually being able to win a trick by trumping.

(2) Lead either the eight of diamonds or the seven of clubs as the "top of nothing." Which to choose is, of course, an out-and-out guess. The highest card is led from these short holdings to help partner read that it is not a fourth-best lead from a long suit.

(3) Here again, the choice is between leading from a worthless diamond suit, or leading the singleton club. The lead of the singleton, in this case, is highly recommended, for you can trump the second lead of clubs.

(4) Lead the eight of clubs, hoping that clubs is your partner's best suit. Whatever you have coming to you in spades or hearts you'll get, since these are the opponents' suits. Lead against possible weakness, not indicated strength.

(5) Lead the queen of clubs, a solid sequence lead.

(6) A trump lead (spade) is recommended in this hand, because you simply have no better positive lead to make. A heart lead is out because they have bid that suit; as between diamonds and clubs, it's a pure guess, and a wrong guess might be costly. However, if you feel the urge to lead one of the unbid suits, clubs and diamonds, lead the two-spot, treating the three-card suit as though it were a four-card suit, so that your partner will figure you for a high card in that suit. Don't lead the queen, for if you do your partner will assume that you are making a sequence lead from the Q, J.

Against no trump, a short-suit lead is of course most undesirable. However, if the opponents have bid your only long suit, you will be confronted with the necessity of leading a short suit. Which of your short suits should you lead?

(a) Never lead a singleton against no trump (except, of course, if your partner has bid the suit).

(b) Avoid leading from a doubleton against no trump if you can. To be profitable, such a lead necessitates "finding" that suit to be your partner's real good suit, which is, mathematically, highly unlikely.

(c) The lead from a tripleton, by elimination, offers the best hope when you are compelled to make a short lead. From a worthless tripleton (its highest card a nine or lower) lead the top card (9 6 3, 7 5 2, etc.).

But if your three-card suit is not worthless—that is, if it contains at least a ten-spot, such as 10 x x, J x x, Q x x, K x x or A x x—lead the lowest card. Admittedly, your partner may be misled, since he will assume you have at least a four-card suit, but at least you hold a high card in support of a continuation of the suit by him.

When the opponents have bid your long suit, and you therefore elect to make a secondary lead against their no-trump contract, the card in **bold face** is the proper one to lead:

A 8 **3**   K 7 **5**   Q 4 **2**   J 8 **3**   **K** Q 5   **Q** J 3   **J** 10 2   10 7 **3**

Note in the above that from the holdings headed by a sequence the correct lead is the top card. Again, your partner may be deceived as to the length of your suit, but at least he'll know you hold the card ranking directly below the card you led.

241

V. Trump Leads This lead is recommended in just two situations: (a) where the bidding has indicated that dummy may be able to trump some of declarer's losers, and that a trump lead will either diminish or eliminate this possibility, and (b) where you are apprehensive of making any other lead, for fear that the lead might present declarer a trick. Let me illustrate these points by two deals from actual play.

North
♠ 8 6 3
♡ 5 2
♢ 9 8 4 3
♣ 9 7 5 2

West
♠ A 9 4
♡ K J 9 7
♢ Q J 10
♣ 8 4 3

East
♠ 5 2
♡ 6 3
♢ K 7 6 5 2
♣ Q J 10 6

South
♠ K Q J 10 7
♡ A Q 10 8 4
♢ A
♣ A K

The bidding proceeded as follows:

South	West	North	East
2 spades	Pass	2 no trumps	Pass
3 hearts	Pass	3 no trumps	Pass
4 hearts	Pass	4 spades	Pass
Pass	Pass		

In the bidding, South has revealed lengths of at least five cards in spades and hearts. North, in the bidding, has revealed that he prefers spades to hearts. North, therefore, figures to be short of hearts.

So West opens the ace of trumps, followed by another trump. Then when West subsequently obtains the lead in hearts, he plays a third round of trumps, thereby effectively preventing North from trumping any of South's hearts. Declarer now goes down one, losing three heart tricks and the ace of trumps.

Had West made the "normal" opening of the queen of diamonds, declarer would have made his contract by simply playing the ace and another heart, which West would win. Even if West now (belatedly) shifted to the ace and another trump, declarer would be able to trump one heart, thereby robbing West of a heart trick.

The following deal illustrates the situation where a defender properly leads a trump because his ear has told him that any other lead might be dangerous.

North
♠ Q J 9 4
♡ A 10 4
♢ K 3 2
♣ J 3 2

West
♠ 8 6
♡ Q 7 5 2
♢ Q 9 4
♣ K 6 5 4

East
♠ 10 3 2
♡ 9 8 6
♢ 10 8 7 6
♣ 10 9 8

South
♠ A K 7 5
♡ K J 3
♢ A J 5
♣ A Q 7

The bidding:

South	West	North	East
2 no trumps	Pass	3 clubs (a)	Pass
3 spades	Pass	6 spades	Pass
Pass	Pass		

(a) The "club convention" over no trump, requesting opener to show a major suit.

Had West led a heart, a diamond, or a club, declarer would have made twelve tricks with ease, since any of those leads would have given declarer a trick in the suit.

But West knew that his partner had nothing, since the opponents figured to have 33 points out of the approximately 40 points in the deck, and West himself had 7 high-card points. So West, fearing to make an aggressive lead, made the "safe"

243

lead of a trump, a neutral lead. He then sat back and waited. Eventually, West made a club trick and a diamond trick.

The table on the following pages gives the correct lead in the various, frequently occuring situations enumerated. The assumption is that you have decided to open the specific suit indicated; the table indicates the proper, conventional lead in that suit.

TABLE OF OPENING LEADS

Holding in Suit	Against No Trump	Against Trump Bids
A K Q J	A	K
A K Q x x x	A	K
A K Q x x	K	K
A K Q x	K	K
A K x	K	K
A K J 10	A	K
A K J x	K	K
A K J x x	x	K
A K J x x x x	A	K
A K x x x x	x	K
A K 10 9 x	10	K
A K 10 9 x x	10	K
A K x x x	x	K
A Q J x x	Q	A
K Q J x x	K	K
K Q 10 x x	K	K
K Q 7 4 2	4	K
Q J 10 x x	Q	Q
Q J 9 x x	Q	Q
Q J 7 4 2	4	4
J 10 9 x x	J	J
J 10 8 x x	J	J
J 10 7 4 2	4	4
10 9 8	10	10
10 9 7 4	4	10
A Q 10 9 x	10(a)	A
A Q 8 7 4 2	7	A
A J 10 8 2	J	A
A 10 9 7 2	10	A
K J 10 7 2	J	J
K 10 9 7 2	10	10

244

Holding in Suit	Against No Trump	Against Trump Bids
A 7 4	4	A
K J 4	4(b)	4
K 7 4	4	4
Q 10 4	4	4
J 7 4	4	4
10 7 4	4	4
K 9 8 7	7(c)	7

(a) The queen is led when you suspect the king is in dummy. Your A 10 will then retain its ambushing position over declarer's presumed jack.

(b) An unattractive lead, but if the opponents' bidding indicates that a lead of this suit is called for, the third from the highest is led.

(c) The 9 8 7 is not considered a sequence, the latter always containing at least the ten-spot. If you lead the nine, partner will undoubtedly consider it to be a "top of nothing" lead.

PLAY BY SECOND HAND

One well-known bridge adage advises defenders to play "second hand low." Yet another maxim recommends that you "cover an honor with an honor." Bridge is too challenging a game to be reduced to slogans, so let us see if we can reconcile these apparently contradictory principles.

Second Hand Low If declarer or dummy leads a low card and you are next to play, it is usually best to play low. Retaining your honor(s) may enable you to capture an opponent's honor later on, or you may cause declarer to guess wrong. For example:

Dummy
♦ 7 4 3

Partner	*You*
♦ Q 10 9 8 5	♦ A 6 2

Declarer
♦ K J

Declarer, who would very much like to lose only one diamond trick, leads the three-spot from dummy. If you erroneously rush up with your ace, declarer has no problem. But if you properly play your deuce (without a revealing hesitation), declarer may go wrong by finessing the jack. Another example:

Dummy
♡ Q 7 4

You   *Partner*
♡ A 6 2   ♡ J 10 9 8

Declarer
♡ K 5 3

Declarer has the lead, and plays the three of hearts. If you clamber up with your ace, declarer plays low from dummy and gratefully collects two heart tricks. If instead you correctly play low, dummy's queen will win; but on the next lead of the suit you capture declarer's king with your ace, gaining two heart tricks for your side and limiting declarer to just one.

Most of the time, then, "second hand low" applies when declarer or dummy leads a low card. However, there are some exceptional cases where you should reject this rule and play high: if you have a solid sequence like K Q J (so that going up is unlikely to cost); if you can win the trick and then cash enough other winners to defeat the contract (your top priority as a defender); or if you deduce that an emergency exists (for example, you will lose your trick in this suit if you don't take it right away).

Covering Honors   If declarer or dummy leads an honor, it is often correct to cover with a higher honor if you have one:

Dummy
♠ Q 7

Partner   *You*
♠ 10 9 8   ♠ K 6 3

Declarer
♠ A J 5

Playing a no-trump contract, declarer leads the spade queen from dummy. Your proper play is to cover with the king. Declarer wins the ace and can cash the jack, but partner's ten will now prevent declarer from enjoying a third spade trick. If you play a low spade on dummy's queen, declarer will let it ride and then lead small to the jack, winning three spade tricks instead of two.

When do you *not* cover an honor with an honor? One instance occurs when you can, if you wait, cover an equal honor the next time the suit is led:

Dummy
♣ Q J 9

Partner   *You*
♣ 10 8 7   ♣ K 6 4 3

Declarer
♣ A 5 2

Dummy leads the club queen. If you make the mistake of covering with the king, declarer wins with the ace and finesses dummy's nine on the next round, winning three club tricks. But if you properly play low, and cover the jack when it is next led, you limit declarer to two tricks in this suit.

Another good time not to cover is when you can deduce that there is nothing to gain:

Dummy
◇ Q J 10 9

Partner   *You*
◇ 8 7 5 2   ◇ K 4 3

Declarer
◇ A 6

This contract is no trumps, and dummy's diamond queen is led. Even though you cannot see declarer's hand, you can tell that covering cannot win, for dummy will be high once the ace and king have been played. Thus your only chance is to play low, play low once again when the diamond jack is led, and hope that declarer must expend the ace too soon—as in fact happens. However, if you cover the queen with the king, declarer scores up four diamond tricks instead of two or three, if dummy has a reentry.

PLAY BY THIRD HAND

Third Hand High If your partner leads a small card and you can top dummy's play, the normal rule is to play your highest card:

Dummy
♠ 7 5 3

Partner　　　　　　　　　　*You*
♠ Q 9 8 6　　　　　　　　♠ K 10 4

Declarer
♠ A J 2

Partner leads the six of spades, and dummy plays low. Go right up with your king. If instead you play the ten, you will give declarer an undeserved spade trick. Similarly:

Dummy
♡ 7 6

Partner　　　　　　　　　　*You*
♡ K J 8 4 2　　　　　　　♡ A 10 5

Declarer
♡ Q 9 3

If partner leads the four of hearts, pop up with your ace; don't let declarer steal a trick with the queen. However, note that an exception occurs when you hold two or more equal honors: play the queen from K Q x, rather than the king. This obviously won't reduce your chances of winning the trick, and will make it easier for partner to deduce your holding in this suit. (If you play the king, partner will know you do not hold the queen.)

Finessing against the Dummy In the preceding examples, dummy held only small cards. If dummy has an honor in the suit led by partner, it is often best to finesse against the dummy:

Dummy
♣ J 6 3

Partner   *You*
♣ Q 9 8 5   ♣ K 10 4

Declarer
♣ A 7 2

Partner leads the five of clubs, and dummy plays low. You should play the ten, which limits declarer to one club trick. If instead you go up with the king, declarer wins the ace and gains a second club trick by leading up to dummy's jack. What if declarer held the queen instead of the ace, a possibility at a no-trump contract? Then declarer's side must win one trick in any event, so your play of the ten costs you nothing.

SIGNALING

Attitude Signals The laws of bridge strictly prohibit you from smiling broadly or nodding your head when partner leads a suit that you like, or from glaring at him when you don't care for his selection. Fortunately, there is a legal way to convey the same messages: the play of an unusually high spot card encourages partner to lead that suit, while a low spot card discourages the lead of that suit. For example:

Dummy
♠ 7 6 5

Partner   *You*
♠ A K J 10   ♠ 9 8 2

Declarer
♠ Q 4 3

Partner has the lead, and chooses the king of spades. A second spade lead will be disastrous for your side, as this will establish a trick for declarer's queen. Since you have nothing of interest in spades, you play your deuce—a discouraging signal—and partner is warned against the fatal continuation. (With something like the ace-king-queen of spades, partner will ignore your signal and continue the suit anyway, since here no help is needed from your hand.) Another example:

Dummy
◇ 6 5 3

Partner
◇ A 7 4

You
◇ K Q 9 2

Declarer
◇ J 10 8

Let us suppose that partner happens to lead the ace of diamonds. You know that partner has struck oil, but he doesn't! Thus he may shift to a different suit if left to his own devices, giving declarer a chance to discard diamond losers on winners in a different suit. To prevent this calamity, play your nine of diamonds—an encouraging signal. This unnecessarily high spot informs partner that you would very much like a diamond continuation.

The following example is somewhat more advanced:

Dummy

♠ 10 7 6 5
♡ 7 6 3
♢ A K Q J 10
♣ 10

Partner
♠ ?

You

♠ 4
♡ A K Q 8 2
♢ 9 7
♣ 7 6 5 4 3

Declarer
♠ ?

The contract is four spades, declarer having bid only spades while dummy mentioned the diamonds and then supported declarer's suit. Partner leads the nine of hearts and you win with the queen, declarer playing the four. You cash the heart ace, declarer follows with the ten, and partner plays the five. Partner has obviously led the top of a doubleton, so you now play the heart king. Declarer drops the jack, and partner discards the deuce of clubs.

What now? Without partner's discouraging signal, a club return would be the indicated play. If partner has the club ace, you'd better take it right away, lest declarer draw trumps and throw away all of his club losers on dummy's good diamonds (Actually, holding the club ace, partner should ruff your heart ace and cash the ace of clubs to prevent you from making a mistake. But that is an expert play.) What other lead can partner want? A trump is pointless, since partner will be able to score any spade tricks he must be given without your leading that suit. A diamond is also most unlikely to gain. So, warned away from the club lead by your partner's discouraging signal, you continue with—*a fourth round of hearts.* Right! The complete deal:

251

                        Dummy
                        ♠ 10 7 6 5
                        ♡ 7 6 3
                        ◇ A K Q J 10
                        ♣ 10

Partner   *You*
♠ J 9 8   ♠ 4
♡ 9 5   ♡ A K Q 8 2
◇ 6 5 3 2   ◇ 9 7
♣ Q 9 8 2   ♣ 7 6 5 4 3

                        Declarer
                        ♠ A K Q 3 2
                        ♡ J 10 4
                        ◇ 8 4
                        ♣ A K J

After your heart lead, if declarer ruffs low or discards, partner will ruff with the jack of spades and defeat the contract. But if declarer trumps with an honor, partner's spade jack will become the setting trick after the two remaining spade honors are led out. Conversely, if you return anything but a heart at trick four, declarer promptly draws trumps and easily makes four spades.

If partner did hold the club ace, he would instead discard the club nine as an encouraging signal (or take control by ruffing your high heart, as mentioned previously). And if partner doesn't have much in spades or clubs and cares very little what you lead next, he can just discard a diamond, announcing that he wishes neither to encourage nor to discourage the marked club lead.

Moral: Good defense requires good communications, in the form of signaling. (Also: trust thy partner!)

Suit-Preference Signals   In the following example, you are defending against a four heart contract:

Dummy
♠ 10 7 6
♡ J 10 9 3
◇ K Q J
♣ K Q J

Partner
♠ 3
♡ 7 6
◇ 10 7 5 4 2
♣ 10 7 5 4 2

You
♠ A 9 8 5 4 2
♡ 5 4
◇ A 6 3
♣ 8 6

Declarer
♠ K Q J
♡ A K Q 8 2
◇ 9 8
♣ A 9 3

Partner leads the three of spades and you win with the ace, declarer dropping the jack. You don't need an illegal peek to know that partner's lead was a singleton, as the correct lead from holdings such as queen-small or king-queen-small would be the top card. So you return a spade, which partner ruffs.

Now comes the moment of truth: if partner leads a club, declarer will win, draw trumps, drive out the ace of diamonds, and make the contract, and dummy will be eminently satisfied. But if partner leads a diamond, you will win with your ace and give partner another spade ruff to defeat the contract, and dummy will want to know why the partnership wasn't in three no trumps. Left to his own devices, partner will guess right approximately half the time—but the winning bridge player tries to improve on these odds.

The solution lies in the particular spade which you return at trick two for partner to ruff. If you want partner to lead the *higher*-ranking of the two remaining side suits (here, diamonds), play an unnecessarily high spade (such as the nine). If instead you would like partner to lead the *lower*-ranking side suit (clubs), play your lowest spade (the deuce). In our example, therefore, you should lead the nine of spades at trick two, whereupon partner will know that your all-important entry is in diamonds.

Count Signals Still another type of signal is illustrated by the following deal:

Dummy
♠ K 9
♡ 4 3 2
♢ K Q J 10 9
♣ 5 3 2

Partner
♠ ?
♡
♢
♣

You
♠ A Q 2
♡ 9 7 6
♢ A 6 4 3
♣ 9 6 4

Declarer
?

Declarer, who originally opened the bidding with one club, is playing three no trumps. Partner leads the four of spades, and dummy plays the nine. You win with the queen and cash the ace, partner playing the three, and you lead the deuce of spades to declarer's jack. Declarer now leads the five of diamonds, partner perforce playing low. What card do you play?

If declarer began life with a singleton diamond, you should take your ace immediately. Declarer will never again be able to enter the dummy, so the long suit will go to waste, and you can accomplish this desirable result without letting dummy win even one diamond trick. But if declarer started with a doubleton diamond, you must play low and win your ace on the second round of the suit to cut declarer off from dummy. And if declarer happened to start with three diamonds, you'll need to hold up your ace twice.

In such situations, count signals will save you from severe headaches and losing guesses. Partner plays high-low with an *even* number of cards in the suit, and the normal low-high with an *odd* number. To illustrate, suppose that partner plays the eight of diamonds on the first lead of the suit. The only missing cards are the seven and the deuce (remember, declarer led the five), and partner cannot have both of them (the correct signal from eight-seven-deuce would be the deuce, low from an odd number). Therefore, declarer must have at least one more diamond. And, therefore, you must duck the first lead of the suit. The complete deal:

Dummy
♠ K 9
♡ 4 3 2
◇ K Q J 10 9
♣ 5 3 2

Partner
♠ 10 8 6 4 3
♡ Q 10 8
◇ 8 2
♣ 10 8 7

You
♠ A Q 2
♡ 9 7 6
◇ A 6 4 3
♣ 9 6 4

Declarer
♠ J 7 5
♡ A K J 5
◇ 7 5
♣ A K Q J

Let us suppose that, after you duck the first diamond lead, declarer reenters his hand with a club and plays another diamond. When partner follows with the deuce, all of the missing diamonds are accounted for, so declarer can't have any more. You therefore win this trick with your ace, and regardless of whether you play back a heart or a club, declarer has only eight tricks and must go down one. (If instead partner showed out on the second diamond lead, you would know that declarer began with three diamonds—and that you must hold up your ace a second time.) Notice that, on this deal, you must win precisely the second diamond lead to defeat the contract.

Of course, declarer has a better play: leading the second round of diamonds from dummy. This forces you to make your decision before seeing whether or not partner can follow suit, so you must guess whether to take your ace now or hold it up once more. Nevertheless, count signals have markedly improved your chances of defeating this contract. Furthermore, you'll usually be right if you win the second diamond lead with your ace. Why? If partner did begin with a singleton eight, then declarer started with precisely 7 5 3, and not many players would lead the five from this holding on the first round of the suit. Conversely, with just 7 5, the lowest card is the natural play.

Helpful hint: When in doubt, assume that any signal is an *attitude* signal. The other types apply only when the attitude meaning is clearly inappropriate—as is the case here, since both you and your partner can easily tell (without signals) that neither of you can want a diamond lead.

FOUR-DEAL BRIDGE (CHICAGO)

"CHICAGO" is an increasingly popular form of contract bridge. Instead of the customary rubber, four deals—one by each player in turn—constitute the unit of play.

Perhaps if this form of contract had been introduced as "Speed-bridge" or some similar name promising the elimination of the "endless" rubber, it would already be more popular than rubber bridge. But Chicago, from the city where this game was first played, and 4-Deal, which describes its form, are the customary names so, as yet, its popularity is largely confined to American bridge clubs (it is often called "the club game"), to home games that include five or more players, and to commuter games which must stop when the train reaches its terminal. Despite the incursions of 4-deal bridge, the commuter trains remain a last haven of the ghoulish "Goulash," in which passed-out hands are not shuffled but are redealt by the same dealer in packets of 5, 5, and 3 producing, along with the desired speed, hideous freak distributions that require a strategy all their own.

Chicago, too, calls for a strategy that differs from the customary rubber game, but the differences are minor; the game is as like rubber bridge as possible, while affording certain major advantages:

—No "endless" last rubber to keep you playing longer and later than you had expected.

—No long sit-outs for the player who is waiting to get back into the five-hand or six-hand game.

—Equality of opportunity to score vulnerable bonuses or penalties, even though the opponents hold the better cards for the first couple of deals.

—A fairer break for the less able player, for a reason I will explain later.

—Experience in the kind of scoring that will be met if you take part in a duplicate game or tournament.

Perhaps the major reason why Chicago is almost exclusively an American game, despite these obvious advantages, is that, in British clubs for example, each of the tables playing at his chosen stakes is open to any out-player. Thus, the player who is cut out at one table is eligible to join the first table at which a rubber is completed. The conclusion of a rubber is signaled by the call of "Table up," and any member not then playing—either because he has just arrived or because he is cut out—may take a place at that table.

There is something to be said for the democracy of this practice, but Americans usually prefer to remain in the group where they have started, or with the players to whose games they are accustomed. Hence, Chicago has taken over at most of the larger American clubs and it is surprising that it has not swept to equal popularity in home games—especially when there are five players, but even when there are only four.

The 4-deal unit vs. the rubber

In Chicago, the playing of four deals corresponds to the conclusion of a rubber. If there is an out player, he comes in. If it is a cut-for-partners game or a pivot game, partners change in the agreed way, the same as they would at the conclusion of a rubber. The Chicago set of four deals may end with neither side having scored a game, or indeed having scored anything below the line.

Passed-out hands are not counted as part of the four-deal set. The same player re-deals until a contract has been played.

Part-scores carry over to the next deal, the same as in rubber bridge. Thus, a pair making a part score on an earlier hand, may convert it into a game by adding another score or scores on later deals which would bring the cumulative total to 100 or more. But a part-score is wiped out, just as in rubber bridge, if the opponents bid and make a game before the part-score has been converted.

There is one special rule about part-scores *bid* and made on the fourth and last deal: they are awarded a bonus of 100 points above the line. But a part score surviving from a previous deal does not receive this bonus.

The regular laws of Contract Bridge apply to 4-Deal with the exceptions covered by the Official Rules (see page 264), which may be described principally as follows:

Bonuses are awarded for individual games as made, not for two-game rubbers. The side that scores a game—whether by bidding and making it on a single hand or by converting an existing part score—receives 300 points above the line if not vulnerable *on that deal,* 500 points if vulnerable. Slam bonuses are the same as in rubber bridge; 500 or 750 for small slam; 1,000 or 1,500 for grand slam, depending upon vulnerability.

Penalties for setting the opponents are scored exactly as in rubber bridge, and are governed by vulnerability. But . . .

Vulnerability of each side is determined by the sequence number of the deal, *not* by previously having bid or made a game. (This feature tends to lessen the advantage of the side that first scores a game.) The bonus or penalty to be scored is determined by vulnerability *on that deal,* without regard to vulnerability that existed when a previous part score or game may have been made.

X marks the spot.

The scorekeeper (it is recommended that there be at least one for each side) draws an "X" at the top of the scorepad. (Some pads are printed with the "X" already in place.) The quadrants within the "X"-diagram represent the position of the dealer of each hand. Thus, if the scorekeeper deals the first hand, he places a figure "1" in the lower quadrant of the "X"—the quadrant representing his position at the table. If his partner dealt the first hand, the figure "1" would be placed in the upper quadrant. If an opponent deals, the number is placed in the left or right quadrant, accordingly. The second deal is indicated by placing a "2" in the next quadrant, moving clockwise, and so on. When three of the four deals of a Chicago set have been completed, the diagram kept by the original dealer will look like this:

It is now the deal of the player to *that* score-keeper's right. Note that each scorekeeper records the deal in relation to *his own* position at the table. If South was the first dealer, West's score, read facing him, would appear:

The sequence of vulnerability is determined by the position of the dealer and the number of the deal. Deal 1, neither side is vulnerable; deals 2 and 3, only the dealer's side is vulnerable; in deal 4, both sides are vulnerable.*

Effect on size of losses

It may seem that Chicago would tend to materially increase the size of the average rubber, but this is not true. Suppose that one side scores four consecutive games, making three no trumps on each. It would receive 400, 600, 400 and 600—a total of 2,000 points scoring two games when not vulnerable, two games when vulnerable. The same result in a rubber game would mean that one side won two rubbers, for each of which it would score a 700 point bonus, for a total of 1,800 points.

As against this, compare the result if one side were to win two games and the rubber, while the other side won one game. Assume this result were achieved in three deals, again by making three no trumps on each hand. In rubber bridge, the side winning the rubber would score 200 below the line, plus 500 above: 700. The other side would score 100, leaving the net gain to the winner + 600.

The same result in 4-deal bridge, assuming that the side making two games was vulnerable on only one, would give that side 300 + 500 for the two game bonuses + 200 for the trick scores: total, 1000. As against that, however, the other

---

* Some play the Cavendish variation of this method, so named because it was first adopted by the Cavendish Club in New York City. In this variation, the *non*-dealer's side is vulnerable on deals 2 and 3. This gives the non-vulnerable side an opportunity to bid—perhaps pre-emptively—before the vulnerable side has a chance to speak.

side would have scored either a non-vulnerable game, worth a total of 400 or a vulnerable game worth 600. Subtracting these amounts from the 1,000 total scored by their opponents would give the same amount as in rubber bridge: −600, or, if the losers made their game when vulnerable: −400. On average, therefore, 4-deal bridge would tend to reduce the swing on these three deals by 100 points.

Slam bonuses are the same as in rubber bridge, but in the second and third deals if the side bidding the slam is not vulnerable *on that deal,* they receive a smaller bonus; if they are vulnerable, their opponents are always not vulnerable and can sacrifice at advantageous non-vulnerability penalty rates.

Because the set ends automatically after four hands are played, there is no temptation to continue the "flag-flying" tactics (save the rubber at all costs) which sometimes make for very high-scoring rubbers.

To the weaker players in the game, 4-deal offers another advantage: his partner will not be tempted to sell out rather than take a profitable save which would continue to leave him at the disadvantage of continuing with the same partner. Each deal has an exact value and the term one serves with the low man on the relative-skill-poll continues for exactly four deals.

Strategy and tactics

Differences in tactics between 4-deal and the rubber game are principally concerned with relative vulnerability and with the 100 point part-score bonus on the fourth and final deal.

When only the opponents are vulnerable: After three passes, the non-vulnerable player in fourth seat should strive to open the bidding against vulnerable opponents even though he has little hope of making game with a passed partner. Why?

Suppose you pass out the hand; the same dealer re-deals, his side remains vulnerable and if they get a game or slam hand their bonus will be greater. If *you* get the good hand, your score will be at non-vulnerable rates. But if you open the bidding, the bonuses swing either in your favor or to equality on the next deal, depending upon whether that next deal is the third or fourth of the set.

Your extremely light fourth-hand bid exposes you to minimal

risk. Both opponents having passed, in most cases they will not be able to bid and make game. The chances are that your partner will have his share of the missing cards and that they are equally divided between the two sides. It will be more difficult for them to compete when they are vulnerable and you are not. If you are set, it will be at non-vulnerable rates. If you are able to make a part score, you will have an advantage on the next deal. If *they* make a part score, you have not lost much. Especially if you have the spade suit, or both majors, you have another advantage.

Note that, unlike rubber bridge, your object in bidding fourth hand is simply to make any plus score—not necessarily a game—or to incur only a small minus, in exchange for taking away the opponents' vulnerability advantage. Of course your partner must be equally aware that you may have opened a shaded bid and should not push toward game until you have confirmed the fact that you have a sound opening. Neither can he expect that, because you have opened fourth-hand, you will respect a one-over-one response or a new suit at the two level as a forcing bid. More than ever, he should try to raise your suit, either with a single raise or a double raise, and he must particularly avoid the shaded two no trumps response that he might otherwise give as a passed hand.

Beware of freak distributions

In considering a sub-minimum fourth-seat opening with a long suit, or with a two-suiter, remember that this is the dangerous kind of hand. If you and your partner locate a fit, the opponents will also have one. The hands on which they find increased values because of this fit are the ones they are more likely to have passed out and yet are able to bid and make a game. Therefore, unless you have a full bid, or unless you have the major suits, or unless you can open pre-emptively, you must exercise caution.

Here are some fourth-hand bidding examples in which only the opponents are vulnerable:

(a) ♠ A K x x x   (b) ♠ x   (c) ♠ A Q J x x
     ♡ K x x x x   ♡ x x   ♡ x x x
     ◊ x   ◊ A K x x x   ◊ Q J 10
     ♣ x x   ♣ K x x x x   ♣ x x

(d)	♠ A x x x	(e)	♠ Q J 10 9 x x	(f)	♠ x x x
	♡ K x x		♡ x x		♡ x x x
	◇ x x x		◇ A x x x		◇ A K x x
	♣ A J x		♣ x		♣ A x x

(a) Bid one spade. The likelihood of the opponents outbidding you is lessened by your possession of the majors; there is even some possibility of making a game if partner's pass includes just the right cards.

(b) Pass. Too much danger the opponents might discover a major-suit fit and make game.

(c) Bid one spade. Again you are influenced by the fact that you hold the highest-ranking suit. Swap the spade and diamond holdings and a bid would be very doubtful.

(d) Bid one club. Your defensive strength is such that the opponents are unlikely to make game. Your object is no more than a part score.

(e) Bid three spades. This is a stretch on a hand you could pass out, but it is obvious that partner must have about 10 points and you are unlikely to suffer any great penalty. On the other hand, it is essential to shut the opponents out.

(f) Bid one diamond. True your strength is only in the minors, and you have no great length to add distributional values. But you can tolerate any suit partner may name, and the fact that you have three defensive tricks in short suits is apt to insure that the opponents cannot make game. Of course you do not intend to rebid this hand.

Non-vulnerable openings in second position

There is no need to shade second-hand openings if you can rely on partner to bid fourth-hand on minimum values. Where there is any doubt, be conservative in second seat, but open minimum hands which include good defensive values even though they may not have much in the way of distribution.

Bidding close games on the fourth deal

Except in 4-deal bridge, where a part-score gets a bonus of 100 points, there is no agreement upon what owning a part score is worth on the next deal. The record of results in 1,000 deals where one or both sides had a part score, as kept by

Jean Besse of Switzerland, showed that a non-vulnerable partial of 40 or more was worth about 90 points; a vulnerable partial of 40 or more against non-vulnerable opponents was worth about 110 points; with both sides vulnerable, the partial was worth 220 points. However, while these factors apply to the first three deals in 4-deal bridge, they do not apply to the fourth where the bonus value is precisely 100 points.

It would seem that the wiser course is to stop short of game and earn the 100 point bonus on all fourth deals where game is doubtful. However, the odds (omitting the 100 point bonus) favor bidding game with a 43% chance of success when vulnerable. Therefore, you should settle in three hearts rather than go on to four only if you realize there is little or no play for the game, or if you take into account the possibility of being set more than one trick if you run into a trump stack. Otherwise, a 50-50 chance is enough to warrant bidding for game.

Many players think they don't care for Chicago bridge because they have never really tried it. There always exists some reluctance to try something new. However, I strongly recommend that you try 4-deal bridge next time you play. I think you will find it faster, more exciting and easier to calculate your tactics and potential profit or loss on every deal.

OFFICIAL RULES FOR
FOUR-DEAL BRIDGE*

Four-Deal Bridge is a form of Rubber Bridge much played in clubs and well suited to home play. Its effect is to avoid long rubbers of uncertain duration; a member never need wait longer than the time (about twenty minutes) required to complete four deals. The game is also called Club Bridge, and is often called Chicago for the city in which it originated.

* As prepared for the American Contract Bridge League.

A. BASIC RULES

The Laws of Contract Bridge and Rules for Club Procedure are followed, except as modified by the following rules.

B. THE RUBBER

A rubber consists of a series of four deals that have been bid and played. If a deal is passed out, the same player deals again and the deal passed out does not count as one of the four deals.

A fifth deal is void if attention is drawn to it at any time before there has been a new cut for partners or the game has terminated; if the error is not discovered in time for correction, the score stands as recorded. A sixth or subsequent deal is unconditionally void and no score for such a deal is ever permissible.

In case fewer than four deals are played, the score shall stand for the incomplete series unless attention is drawn to the error before there has been a new cut for partners or the game has terminated.

When the players are pivoting (forming new partnerships in a fixed rotation), the fact that the players have taken their proper seats for the next rubber shall be considered a cut for partners.

C. VULNERABILITY

Vulnerability is not determined by previous scores but by the following schedule:

First deal:	Neither side vulnerable.
Second and Third deals:	Dealer's side vulnerable, the other side not vulnerable
Fourth deal:	Both sides vulnerable.

D. PREMIUMS

For making or completing a game (100 or more trick points) a side receives a premium of 300 points if on that deal it is not vulnerable or 500 points if on that deal it is vulnerable. There is no additional premium for winning two or more games, each game premium being scored separately.

E. THE SCORE

As a reminder of vulnerability in Four-Deal Bridge, two

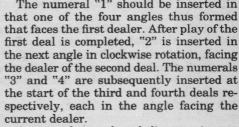

intersecting diagonal lines should be drawn near the top of the score pad, as shown:

The numeral "1" should be inserted in that one of the four angles thus formed that faces the first dealer. After play of the first deal is completed, "2" is inserted in the next angle in clockwise rotation, facing the dealer of the second deal. The numerals "3" and "4" are subsequently inserted at the start of the third and fourth deals respectively, each in the angle facing the current dealer.

A correctly numbered diagram is conclusive as to vulnerability. There is no redress for a bid influenced by the scorer's failure to draw the diagram or for an error or omission in inserting a numeral or numerals in the diagram. Such error or omission should, upon discovery, be immediately corrected and the deal or deals should be scored or rescored as though the diagram and the number or numbers thereon had been properly inserted.

F. PART-SCORES

A part-score or -scores made previously may be combined with a part-score made in the current deal to complete a game of 100 or more trick points. The game premium is determined by the vulnerability, on that deal, of the side that completes the game. When a side makes or completes a game, no previous part-score of either side may thereafter be counted toward game.

A side that makes a part-score in the fourth deal, if the part-score is not sufficient to complete a game, receives a premium of 100 points. This premium is scored whether or not the same side or the other side has an uncompleted part-score. There is no separate premium for making a part-score in any other circumstances.

G. DEAL OUT OF TURN

When a player deals out of turn, and there is no right to a redeal, the player who should have dealt retains his right to call first, but such right is lost if it is not claimed before the actual dealer calls. If the actual dealer calls before attention is drawn to the deal out of turn, each player thereafter calls in rotation. Vulnerability and scoring values are determined by the position of the player who should have dealt, regardless of which player actually dealt or called first. Neither the rotation of the deal nor the scoring is affected by a deal out of turn. The next dealer is the player who would have dealt next if the deal had been in turn.

H. OPTIONAL RULES AND CUSTOMS

The following practices, not required, have proved acceptable in some clubs and games.

(i) Since the essence of the game is speed, if a deal is passed out, the pack that has been shuffled for the next deal should be used by the same dealer.

(ii) The net score of a rubber should be translated into even hundreds (according to American custom) by crediting as 100 points any fraction thereof amounting to 50 or more points: e.g., 750 points count as 800; 740 points count as 700 points.

(iii) No two players may play a second consecutive rubber as partners at the same table. If two players draw each other again, the player who has drawn the highest card should play with the player who has drawn the third-highest, against the other two players.

(iv) Any player may announce, prior to the auction and before he has looked at his hand, which deal it is and who is vulnerable; or may, for his own information, inquire as to these facts when it is his turn to call. There is no redress if no announcement is made or if incorrect information is given.

(v) To avoid confusion as to how many deals have been played: Each deal should be scored, even if there is no net advantage to either side (for example, when one side is entitled to 100 points for undertrick penalties and the other side is entitled to 100 points for honors). In a result that completes a game, premiums for overtricks, game, slam, or making a doubled contract should be combined with the trick score to produce one total, which is entered below the line (for example, if a side makes two spades doubled and vulnerable with an overtrick, 870 should be scored below the line, not 120 below the line and 50, 500 and 200 above the line).

PARTY BRIDGE

IN THE two most popular forms of party bridge, players take part as fixed pairs throughout, or as individuals, changing partners at the end of each round (four deals) of play. Player or pair numbers are assigned by drawing of tally cards* (or score cards) for each individual or for each pair. The score of each set of four deals may be kept by scoring as in 4-Deal bridge, or as in regular rubber bridge, except that each round of play ends with the conclusion of four deals. The players then enter their net scores (in some games, players enter their total plus scores only without deducting their minuses) and change partners and/or opponents by progressing as described below.

Playing as individuals:

Each table (there may be any number from two upward) is formed by the North player taking the position indicated by the letter. He remains seated throughout. At the end of each round of four deals the numbered players pivot in clockwise

---

* Available at stationery or adult games retailers.

direction around North, player 1 taking the seat of player 2, 2 following 3 and 3 following 1. At the conclusion of three rounds of play, the lettered players remain seated and the numbered players exchange seats in accordance with the following chart:

A		B		C		D	
8	6	2	12	11	3	5	9
10		7		4		1	

The pivot rotation is then resumed. Allow approximately twenty minutes per round of four deals, or one hour for completion of play among the individuals at each table. Play may be halted after any agreed number of rounds, or at the conclusion of a fixed period of time elapsed. Prizes are then awarded to the highest net (or in some games, gross) scores achieved. At the conclusion of two hours, each player will have had six different partners. If longer play is desired for a two-table game, it is suggested that the players remain at the table at which they conclude the six rounds and play back, beginning with their last partner and moving counterclockwise in ensuing rounds.

Sub-dividing your game

There are several ways of separating players into classifications of relative skill, compatability, etc., depending upon the number in your party. If there are sufficient prizes, each table may have its own continuing competition. Four tables may be divided into two separate groups of two, the players moving only within their own group. In a three-table game, simply eliminate table d from the diagram shown earlier, players from table c moving to table a at the completion of three rounds of play (12 deals).*

Set Pairs Competition

If play is to be by set pairs of partners (as, for example, married couples or other regular partnerships), the partnership

---

* For play in duplicate style (allowing each player to play the same hands as every other) write for Easy Guide to Duplicate and/or Home Duplicate leaflet (both free on request accompanied by self-addressed stamped envelope) to American Contract Bridge League, P. O. Box 161192, Memphis, Tennessee 38131.

of odd players may be determined by drawing paired cards. The number of each pair is determined by lot, or by pre-assignment. It is suggested that the host(ess) and partner occupy the North-South position at Table 1, remaining seated throughout in a game of three or four tables, as per the seating diagrams that follow:

Rd. 3 table game

```
      6        5        3
1. 1 □ 1  2 □ 2  4 □ 4
      6        5        3

      6        1        4
2. 2 □ 2  3 □ 3  5 □ 5
      6        1        4

      6        2        5
3. 3 □ 3  4 □ 4  1 □ 1
      6        2        5

      6        3        1
4. 4 □ 4  5 □ 5  2 □ 2
      6        3        1

      6        4        2
5. 5 □ 5  1 □ 1  3 □ 3
      6        4        2
```

Rd. 4 table game

```
      8        6        7        4
1. 1 □ 1  3 □ 3  2 □ 2  5 □ 5
      8        6        7        4

      8        7        1        5
2. 2 □ 2  4 □ 4  3 □ 3  6 □ 6
      8        7        1        5

      8        1        2        6
3. 3 □ 3  5 □ 5  4 □ 4  7 □ 7
      8        1        2        6

      8        2        3        7
4. 4 □ 4  6 □ 6  5 □ 5  1 □ 1
      8        2        3        7

      8        3        4        1
5. 5 □ 5  7 □ 7  6 □ 6  2 □ 2
      8        3        4        1

      8        4        5        2
6. 6 □ 6  1 □ 1  7 □ 7  3 □ 3
      8        4        5        2

      8        5        6        3
7. 7 □ 7  2 □ 2  1 □ 1  4 □ 4
      8        5        6        3
```

```
     N
  W     E
     S
```

Player directions correspond to this diagram.

If each round consists of 4 deals, the three-table game will play 20 deals in all, while the four-table game would play 28. The number of deals in the larger game can be reduced by

271

playing three to each round, or by eliminating the final round of play; this would mean that each pair would meet six other pairs and miss meeting one other pair, for a total of 24 deals played. However, it should be pointed out that progression in these pairs movements will be held up on every round until the last table to finish has completed all its deals. A four-deal round will therefore take about one-half hour to complete and the time for which the game is planned should be estimated accordingly.

In order to avoid undue hold-ups, the North player at the first table (the host or hostess) should announce not later than five minutes before the time allowed for one round that no new deal should be started at any table. This may result in some tables playing fewer deals, but some such measure must be taken in order to bring the slower players back on schedule.

NOTE: Even in a game where only plus scores are counted, pairs should agree on and enter the actual result of each deal and the opponents against whom it was played. This will enable a check-up on claimed final totals before the award of prizes. Should there be an exact tie for a prize, it may be broken by awarding it on the result of the deals which the tied players played against each other. In the event that ordinary rubber bridge scoring is used, the totals of both sides for that *round* should be entered; it is not necessary to give the total for each deal.

TABLE CARD

Study of the progression schedules will reveal that every pair follows and takes the previous round's position of the next lower numbered pair, pair 1 following the next-to-highest numbered pair since the highest numbered pair is stationary throughout. If desired, guide cards can be placed on each table, including the table number and instructions where each pair is to sit next. For example: The guide card for table 1 in a three-table game would read:

Table 2's card would read: etc.

N-S remain	N-S move to Table 3 E-W
E-W move to Table 2 N-S.	E-W move to Table 1 E-W.

Guide cards for three- and four-table games can be purchased from the American Contract Bridge League or other duplicate accessory suppliers.

More than four tables

With more than four tables in play, the simplest progression is for the North-South pairs to remain seated and the East-West pairs to move at the end of each round to the next-higher numbered table (the E-W pair from the highest numbered table moving to E-W at table 1). This will provide at least 20 deals with five tables playing four deals each round. If desired, prizes can be given to the high North-South pair and the high East-West pair, but this is not essential in a game where the cards are mixed at the beginning of every deal and there is no duplication of the hands played.

TABLE OF PROBABILITIES

SUIT DIVISIONS

If you and your partner have together in one suit:	*The cards of that suit in opponents' hands will be divided*	
6 cards	4-3	62%
	5-2	31%
	6-1	7%
	7-0	Less than ½%
7 cards	4-2	48%
	3-3	36%
	5-1	15%
	6-0	1%
8 cards	3-2	68%
	4-1	28%
	5-0	4%
9 cards	3-1	50%
	2-2	40%
	4-0	10%
10 cards	2-1	78%
	3-0	22%
11 cards	1-1	52%
	2-0	48%

Digest of the Current Laws

IRREGULARITIES IN CONTRACT BRIDGE

THIS DIGEST of the most frequently invoked Laws of Contract Bridge, © 1981 by the American Contract Bridge League has been prepared with the valued assistance of Edgar Kaplan, co-chairman of the National Laws Commission. The most important changes—the first since 1963—involve the penalties for revokes; for cards exposed (penalty cards) before, during, or after the auction, whether inadvertent or through error; for calls out of turn and for leads out of turn. For the complete laws, see the *Laws of Contract Bridge,* published by the ACBL.

For the reader's convenience in referring to the laws, an effort has been made to present them during the appropriate time division of bridge play.

PRIOR TO THE BIDDING

New Shuffle and Cut　Before the first cut is dealt, any player may demand a new shuffle and cut. There must be a new shuffle and cut if a card is faced in shuffling or cutting.

Deal Out of Turn　The correct dealer may reclaim the deal before the last card is dealt; thereafter, the deal stands as though it had been in turn and the correct dealer loses his right to deal in that round.

Redeal　There must be a redeal if the cards are not dealt correctly; if the pack is incorrect; if a card is faced in the pack or elsewhere; if a player picks up the wrong hand and looks at it; or if at any time during the play one hand is found to have too many cards and another too few (and the discrepancy is not caused by errors in play). When there is a redeal, the same dealer deals (unless the deal was out of turn) and with the same pack, after a new shuffle and cut.

Incorrect Hand　If a player has too few cards and the missing card is found (except in a previous trick), it is considered to have been in the short hand throughout. If it cannot be found, there is a redeal. If it is found in a previous trick, see *Defective Trick*.

DURING THE BIDDING

Waiver of Penalty When a player calls or plays over an illegal call or play by his right-hand opponent; he accepts the illegal call or play and waives a penalty. The game continues as though no irregularity had occurred. However:

Retention of the Right to Call A player cannot lose his only chance to call by the fact that an illegal pass by his partner has been accepted by an opponent. The auction must continue until the player has had at least one chance to call.

Barred Player A player who is barred once, or for one round, must pass the next time it is his turn to bid; a player who is barred throughout must pass in every turn until the auction of the current deal is completed.

Change of Call A player may change an inadvertent call without penalty if he does so without pause for thought. Any other attempted change of call is canceled. If the first call was an illegal call, it is subject to the applicable law; if it was a legal call, the offender may either:

(a) allow his first call to stand, whereupon his partner must pass at his next turn; or

(b) substitute any legal call (including a pass, double, or redouble) whereupon his partner must pass at every subsequent turn.

Insufficient Bid If a player makes an insufficient bid, he must substitute either a sufficient bid or a pass (not a double or redouble). If he substitutes:

(a) The lowest sufficient bid in the same denomination, there is no penalty.

(b) Any other bid, his partner must pass at every subsequent turn.

(c) A pass, his partner must pass at every subsequent turn, and declarer (if an opponent) may impose a lead penalty. A double or redouble illegally substituted is penalized the same as a pass and is treated as a pass.

The offender need not select his final call until the law has been stated; previous attempts at correction are canceled.

Information Given by Change of Call In the case of an illegal call which has been canceled, if an opponent becomes declarer the illegal call may be subject to the special lead penalty described hereafter.

A Call Out of Rotation ("out of turn") may be accepted by the player next to call. If it is not accepted, the illegal call is

276

canceled and the auction reverts to the player whose turn it was. Rectification and penalty depend on whether it was a pass, a bid, or a double or redouble, as follows:

A call is not out of rotation if made without waiting for the right-hand opponent to pass, if that opponent is legally obliged to pass; nor if it would have been in rotation had not the left-hand opponent called out of rotation. A call made simultaneously with another player's call in rotation is deemed to be subsequent to it.

Pass Out of Turn If it occurs (a) before any player has bid, or when it was the turn of the offender's right-hand opponent, the offender must pass when his regular turn comes; (b) after there has been a bid and when it was the turn of the offender's partner, the offender is barred throughout; the offender's partner may not double or redouble at that turn; and if the offender's partner passes and the opponents play the hand, declarer may impose a lead penalty.

Call Out of Turn Any player may call attention to such a call, but the player to offender's left may accept it, in which case the auction continues without penalty. If not accepted, the following penalties apply:

I. If the illegal call was a pass:

a. When it was the turn of the right hand opponent, or before any player has bid, offender must pass at his first opportunity.

b. If any player has already bid, and it is the turn of the offender's partner, the partner may pass, bid a suit or no trump, but may not double or redouble. Offender is then barred for the balance of the auction.

II. If it was an illegal bid of a suit or no trump:

a. At partner's turn or at the turn of the dealer at offender's left, the illegal bid is canceled but partner must pass throughout. Should an opponent become declarer, lead penalties (q.v.) may apply.

b. At the right hand opponent's turn and:

1. Opponent passes, the bid out of turn stands and there is no penalty. (An insufficient bid must be corrected.)

2. Opponent makes any call other than a pass and offender then bids a sufficient number of the same suit, offender's partner must pass at his next turn. If offender substitutes any other bid, his partner must pass throughout. (Lead penalties may apply.)

DOUBLE OR REDOUBLE OUT OF TURN

I. When it was partner's turn to bid, offender's partner is

barred (must pass) throughout the auction. Offender may not double or redouble the same bid which he illegally doubled or redoubled. (Lead penalty may apply.)

II. When it was the turn of offender's right-hand opponent, if that opponent passes the double or redouble may be repeated without penalty.

III. When it was the turn of offender's left-hand opponent, who then makes any call except a pass, offender may make any legal call but offender's partner must pass at his next turn. (Lead penalty may apply.)

Impossible Doubles and Redoubles If a player doubles or redoubles a bid that his side has already doubled or redoubled, his call is canceled; he must substitute (a) any legal call, in which case his partner is barred throughout and if he becomes the opening leader declarer may prohibit the lead of the doubled suit; or (b) a pass, in which case either opponent may cancel all previous doubles and redoubles, the offender's partner is barred throughout, and if he becomes the opening leader he is subject to a lead penalty.

If a player doubles his partner's bid, redoubles an undoubled bid, or doubles or redoubles when there has been no bid, he must substitute any proper call, and his partner is barred once.

Other Inadmissible Calls If a player bids more than seven, or makes another call when legally required to pass, he is deemed to have passed and the offending side must pass at every subsequent turn; if they become the defenders, declarer may impose a lead penalty on the opening leader.

Call After the Auction is Closed A call made after the auction is closed is canceled. If it is a pass by a defender, or any call by declarer or dummy, there is no penalty. If it is a bid, double or redouble by a defender, declarer may impose a lead penalty at the offender's partner's first turn to lead.

A Card Exposed during the Auction becomes a penalty card (primary—an honor; or secondary—a spot card, as defined in the penalty card law, which see). In addition, the partner of the player with a primary penalty card must pass at his next turn to bid.

Review of the Bidding may be requested:

I. When it is a player's turn to bid. (The review should be given by an opponent, but if erroneous it may be corrected by any player.)

II. After the final pass, by any player (except dummy) *at his turn to play to the first trick*.

III. Any player may ask to have a call repeated if it is not heard distinctly.

THE PLAY

Dummy's Rights Dummy may give or obtain information regarding fact or law, ask if a play constitutes a revoke, warn any player against infringing a law, and, only when the play is over, may draw attention to an irregularity. Dummy forfeits these rights if he looks at a card in another player's hand.

If dummy has forfeited his rights, and thereafter

(a) is the first to draw attention to a defender's irregularity, declarer may not enforce any penalty for the offense;

(b) warns declarer not to lead from the wrong hand, either defender may choose the hand from which declarer shall lead;

(c) is the first to ask declarer if a play from declarer's hand is a revoke, declarer must correct a revoke if able but the revoke penalty still applies.

Revoke A revoke is the act of playing a card of another suit, when able to follow suit to a lead. Any player, including dummy, may ask whether a play constitutes a revoke and may demand that an opponent correct a revoke. A claim of revoke does not warrant inspection of turned tricks, prior to the end of play, except by consent of both sides.

Correcting a Revoke A player must correct his revoke if aware of it before it becomes established. A revoke card withdrawn by a defender becomes a penalty card. The nonoffending side may withdraw any cards played after the revoke but before attention was drawn to it.

Established Revoke A revoke becomes established when a member of the offending side leads or plays to a subsequent trick (or terminates play by a claim or concession). When a revoke becomes established, the revoke trick stands as played (unless it is the twelfth trick—see page 120).

Revoke Penalty The penalty for an established revoke is one trick (if available), in addition to the trick on which the revoke occurred if won by the revoking side, transferred at the end of play from the revoking side to the opponents. This penalty can be paid only from tricks won by the revoking side after its first revoke, including the revoke trick. If no trick is available, there is no penalty. (But see excerpt from "Proprieties" below.*)

---

*PROPRIETIES;

The Laws cannot cover every situation that might arise, nor can they produce equity in every situation covered. Occasionally, the players themselves must redress damage. The guiding principle: The side that commits an irregularity bears an obligation not to gain directly from the infraction itself. For example: South, declarer at 3 NT, will have nine tricks available if the diamond suit—ace-king-queen-sixth in dummy opposite declarer's singleton—divides favorably.

There is no penalty for a subsequent established revoke in the same suit by the same player.

A transferred trick ranks for all scoring purposes as a trick won in play by the side receiving it. It never affects the contract.

(For example, if the contract is ♡3 and declarer wins 9 tricks plus 1 trick as a revoke penalty, total 10 tricks, he can score only 90 points below the line and the other 30 points go above the line.)

Revokes Not Subject to Penalty A revoke made in the twelfth trick must be corrected, without penalty, if discovered before the cards have been mixed together. The nonoffending side may require the offender's partner to play either of two cards he could legally have played. A revoke not discovered until the cards have been mixed is not subject to penalty, nor is a revoke by any faced hand (dummy, or a defender's hand when faced in consequence of a claim by declarer). A revoke by failure to play a penalty card is not subject to the penalty for an established revoke.

Lead Out of Turn Defenders may accept declarer's lead out of the wrong hand, or request dealer to lead from the correct hand (if he can) a card of the same suit; if it was a defender's turn to lead, or if there is no card of that suit in the correct hand, there is no penalty.

If a defender is required to retract a lead out of turn, declarer may either treat the card so led as a penalty card, or impose a lead penalty on the offender's partner when next he is to lead after the offense.

Lead If a defender leads out of turn declarer may accept the lead; treat the card led as a penalty card; require the lead of that suit from the proper leader, or forbid him to lead that suit for as long as he holds the lead at that turn.

Premature Play If a defender leads to the next trick before his partner has played to the current trick, or plays out of rotation before his partner has played, declarer may require the offender's partner to play his highest card of the suit led, his lowest card of the suit led, or a card of another specified

---

The six missing diamonds are in fact split evenly, three-three, between East and West. However, West, who holds jack-third, shows out on the third round of diamonds, revoking. Thus, declarer wins only three diamond tricks instead of six, for a total of six tricks instead of nine. The established revoke is later discovered, so one penalty trick is transferred after play ends. But declarer is still down two.

Here, East-West gained two tricks as a direct consequence of their infraction. The players should adjudicate this result, scoring the deal as 3 NT making three. (Note, declarer is not given a penalty trick in addition; the object is to restore equity, to restore the result likely to have occurred had the infraction not been committed.)

suit. Declarer must select one of these options, and if the defender cannot comply, he may play any legal card. When declarer has played from both his hand and dummy, a defender is not subject to penalty for playing before his partner.

Exposed Cards Declarer is never subject to penalty for exposure of a card, but intentional exposure of declarer's hand is treated as a claim or concession of tricks.

A defender's card is exposed if it is faced on the table or held so that the other defender may see its face before he is entitled to do so. Such a card must be left face up on the table until played and becomes a penalty card.

Penalty Card In the case of a card prematurely or illegally exposed there are now two types of penalty card:

I. If the card is one of "secondary significance," i.e., a card below honor rank, that is inadvertently (accidentally) exposed, the offending player may substitute an honor card of that suit (or any legal card in another suit), but may not play any other card below honor rank in this suit until the penalty card has been played.

II. If the card is one of "primary significance" (an honor card not inadvertently exposed by a defender during the bidding or play), it must be played at the first legal opportunity. When offender's partner first obtains or holds the lead, declarer may demand or prohibit the lead of that suit, in which event the penalty card may be picked up and the offender may choose to play any card in the suit led. If declarer does not impose a lead penalty, the exposed card remains as a primary penalty card. (Note that under the revised laws declarer may no longer call for the lead of any other specified suit.)

Special Penalty A lead penalty incurred in the bidding: If the offender's illegal call was other than in a suit (i.e., a bid of no trump or a double or redouble), the declarer may bar the lead of a specified suit. (But he may NOT call for the lead of a particular suit.)

Two or More Penalty Cards If a defender has two or more penalty cards that he can legally play, declarer may designate which one is to be played.

Failure to Play a Penalty Card is not subject to penalty, but declarer may require the penalty card to be played, and any defender's card exposed in the process becomes a penalty card.

Inability to Play as Required If a player is unable to lead or play as required to comply with a penalty (for lack of a card of a required suit, or because of the prior obligation to follow suit) he may play any card. The penalty is deemed satisfied, except in the case of a penalty card.

Declarer Claiming or Conceding Tricks If declarer claims or concedes one or more of the remaining tricks (verbally or by spreading his hand), he must leave his hand face up on the table and immediately state his intended plan of play.

If a defender disputes declarer's claim, declarer must play on, adhering to any statement he had made, and in the absence of a specific statement he may not "exercise freedom of choice in making any play the success of which depends on finding either opponent with or without a particular unplayed card."

Following curtailment of play by declarer, it is permissible for a defender to expose his hand and to suggest a play to his partner.

Defender Claiming or Conceding Tricks A defender may show any or all of his cards to declarer to establish a claim or concession. He may not expose his hand to his partner, and if he does, declarer may treat his partner's cards as penalty cards.

Correcting the Score A proved or admitted error in any score may be corrected at any time before the rubber score is agreed, except as follows: An error made in entering or failing to enter a part-score, or in omitting a game or in awarding one, may not be corrected after the last card of the second succeeding correct deal has been dealt (unless a majority of the players consent).

Effect of Incorrect Pack Scores made as a result of hands played with an incorrect pack are not affected by the discovery of the imperfection after the cards have been mixed together.

MISCELLANEOUS

Opening Lead Out of Turn When based on misinformation from an opponent, there is no penalty.

If, after an opening lead out of turn, declarer exposes one or more of his cards as if he were dummy, partner then becomes declarer.

Declarer may accept an incorrect lead by playing a card or, if he accepts it verbally, he may see dummy before playing from his own hand.

Simultaneous Leads

I. By defender:

a. If only one of two cards is visible, it is played.

b. If two or more cards are exposed, the offender may name which one is played, but the other card so exposed becomes a penalty card.

II. By declarer: He designates which card is played; the other card is returned to the proper hand.

GOREN'S CONTRACT BRIDGE PRIMER

(Revised to Conform to His Recommendation of Five-Card Majors)

INTRODUCTION: Contract bridge is a card game for four players, competing as two partnerships. Partners sit across from each other. The game is played with a deck of cards. A standard 52-card deck, without jokers, has 13 cards in each of the four suits: spades (♠), hearts (♡), diamonds (♢), clubs (♣). In each suit, the cards rank ace (high), king, queen, jack, 10, 9, 8, 7, 6, 5, 4, 3, and 2 (low).

LESSON 1: *Getting started:* Deal the entire deck face down, one card at a time. Each player gets 13 cards. Pick up and sort your hand into suits.

The game begins with the *bidding* or *auction.* Then comes the *play.* However, before you bid you want to know what you are trying to buy, so let us first talk about how the cards are played.

You win at contract bridge by scoring points. You score points mainly by winning *tricks.* A *trick* is a round of four cards, one from each player in turn. The first card played is the *lead.* The *leader* may play any card in his hand. Each of the others must play a card of the same *suit* as the *lead,* if he can do so.

If everyone follows suit, the trick is won by the highest card played. For example: West leads a spade jack. Each player in turn tries to win the trick for his side by playing a higher spade: *N*-Q; *E*-K; *S*-A. South's ace, being highest, wins the trick.

(Suppose East had played a low spade instead of his king.

North's queen would be high enough to take the trick. South, his partner, could play a low spade, saving his ace to win a later trick.)

If you do not have a card of the suit led, you may play any card of any suit. This gives you another way to win a trick, because every card of the suit that was named by the high bidder is a *trump*. When you play a card of that suit, you win the trick by *trumping*, because *a trump wins a trick against any card but a higher trump*. For example: Having won the first trick, South chooses to lead another spade, the nine. All the higher spades have been played, so West's 10 will win this trick if no one plays a trump. However, North does not have another spade. Diamonds were trumps, so North plays a 7 of diamonds in order to win the trick for his side.

East does not have any spades left, either. He can win the trick by *over-trumping* if he plays a higher diamond. He could not win it by playing a higher heart, because hearts were not trumps. A player who cannot follow suit *discards* when he plays any card except a trump. A *discard* cannot win a trick.

LESSON 2: *The bidding.* In order to *bid,* you name a number from one to seven and a *suit* which you would like to make trumps, or *no trump,* which means you would like to play the hand without any trump suit.

The first six tricks the bidder wins, called the *book,* do not count toward his bid. Your lowest possible bid, one club, undertakes to win seven tricks if clubs are trumps. Your highest possible bid, seven no trumps, proposes to take all thirteen tricks—a grand slam.

The highest bid in the auction becomes the *contract.* If you are able to fulfill your contract, your side scores points for every trick over your book. If you fail (are *set*), the opponents will collect penalty points for each trick by which you fall short. (See Scoring Table.)

The auction: The dealer speaks first. He may *bid* or *pass.* Thereafter, each player in turn may *pass, bid, double* an opponent's bid or *redouble* an opponent's double.

Each new bid must be higher than the last. In bidding, the suits rank: clubs (low), diamonds, hearts, spades. You can bid one diamond over one club; one spade over any other suit. No trump is the highest bid, so one no trump beats any bid of one in a suit. However, a bid for a greater number of tricks outranks any bid for a lesser number. Example: four clubs over a bid of three no trumps.

A double or redouble does not raise the level of the last bid; it merely increases the points scored for each trick if that bid becomes the final contract.

After any new bid, double or redouble, each other player gets another turn. Three successive passes after any bid are like the auctioneer's "Going, going, gone!" The third pass ends the bidding.

After the auction: If your side did not make the high bid, you and your partner become the *defenders*. The opponent who first bid the suit (or no trump) which became the final *contract* is the *declarer*. The *defender* sitting at declarer's left opens the *play* by selecting a card from his hand and placing it face up in the center of the table.

After the *opening lead,* declarer's partner places his entire hand face up in front of him. In turn thereafter the declarer will play the cards from this hand (called the *dummy*) as well as the cards from his own hand.

When each hand has played, the *trick* is complete. It is gathered up and placed face down, in a separate bundle, before one player of that side that won it. One partner keeps all the tricks for his side.

LESSON 3: *How to win points.* You win a large number of points in contract bridge: when your opponents bid too high and you collect a big penalty; and when your side, as declarer, makes a *game* and wins a *rubber*.

To win the *rubber* and earn the bonus it carries you must win two *games* before your opponents win two. To win a game, you must score 100 points or more "below the line" that runs horizontally across the bridge score. And the only points you may enter "below the line" are those you earn for the tricks your side has *bid for and made*.

You need not make the entire 100 points in a single deal. If you earn 60 points on one deal, you can claim the *game* by adding 40 points or more on a later deal—provided the opponents don't beat you to it by scoring 100 first. Whenever one side earns 100 or more "below," another horizontal line is drawn across the score and both sides start again at zero on the next game.

If you make more tricks than you have bid for, you get credit for them "above the line" where they do not count

toward game. That is why you should bid enough to score the
points you need for a game any time there is a good chance
you will make it.

WE	THEY
	(a) 60
(b) 100	(a) 60

(a) On the first deal
THEY bid 2 spades
and made 4. The 60
points for tricks
they didn't bid had
to be scored above
the line.

(b) On the next hand,
WE bid and made
3 no trump.

You are ready now to study the Scoring Table.

SCORING TABLE

FOR TRICKS BID AND MADE:

	Contract	Not Doubled	Doubled	Re-Doubled
Each trick over 6	♦ or ♣	20	40	80
	♠ or ♡	30	60	120
1st trick over 6	No trump	40	80	160
Each add'l trick	No trump	30	60	120

These points are scored below the line, and are
the only ones that may be counted toward game.

FOR TRICKS OVER 6 MADE BUT *NOT* BID:

	Not Vul. Trick value	Vulnerable* Trick Value
Undoubled	100	200
Doubled (each)	100	200
Redoubled (each)	200	400

* A side is Vulnerable when it has won a game.

BONUSES:

For making doubled or redoubled contract	50	50
Small slam (12 tricks) bid and made	500	750
Grand slam (13 tricks) bid and made	1000	1500

For winning rubber before opponents make 1 game 700
For winning rubber after opponents make 1 game 500
For honors: (A, K, Q, J, 10 of trumps)
    Four in one hand   100
    Five in one hand   150
    (In No Trumps) Four Aces in one hand   150

PENALTIES

For failure to make contract:	Not Doubled	Doubled	Re- Doubled
First undertrick Not Vulnerable	50	100	200
First undertrick Vulnerable	100	200	400
Each add'l undertrick Not Vulnerable	50	200	400
Each add'l undertrick Vulnerable	100	400	600

You will see that, in order to make 100 points or more in a single deal you must bid three no trumps, four spades or hearts, five clubs or diamonds.

Of course, if the opponents *double* your bid, you will score the doubled value of tricks under the line if you make your contract. But you will also pay a much heavier penalty above the line if you are defeated; heavier still if your side has already scored a game and you are therefore *vulnerable*.

The next lessons will tell you how to value your hand so that you will neither underbid nor overbid.

LESSON 4: *Valuing your hand for a bid.* You have seen that some tricks are won by high cards and others are won by trumping. In order to measure these different kinds of trick-winning values, let us reduce them to the simple common denominator of *points*. (Do not confuse these points with the kind you enter on the score. You use them only to estimate how much you can afford to bid.)

Your high cards count: Ace = 4, King = 3, Queen = 2, Jack = 1. The high cards of each suit total 10 points.

For suit bids your short suits count: Doubleton (only 2 cards in a suit) = 1; Singleton (only 1 card in a suit) = 2; Void (none of suit) = 3. (When your partner was first to bid the suit you are going to help him with, you may count a singleton as 3 and a void as 5.) The shorter the suit, the more tricks you are apt to win by trumping.

When you bid a suit, you count both your high-card points and your distributional points. When you bid no trump, you count *only* high-card points.

The magic number—13. There are 40 high-card points in each deal. The average hand will have 10. To make more tricks than the opponents, you must be stronger than average, so you do not open the bidding with a hand that counts less than 13 points. It is easy to remember this because there are 13 cards in your hand; 13 in each suit; 13 tricks in each deal. 13 is bridge's magic number.

With 13 points, you *may* bid one of a suit. With 14, you should consider it your duty to do so.

POINTS FOR HIGH CARDS

A = 4
K = 3
Q = 2
J = 1

POINTS FOR DISTRIBUTION
(Count for short suits)

As initial bidder		In support of partner
	DOUBLETON	
1	(2 cards in suit)	1
	SINGLETON	
2	(1 card in suit)	3
	VOID	
3	(none of suit)	5

COUNT THE POINTS IN THESE EXAMPLES:
Which of these hands is worth an opening bid?

(a)	(b)	(c)
♠ A Q 10 5 4	♠ 2	♠ Q J 6 5 4
♡ A 3	♡ A K 10 8	♡ A Q 9 6 2
◇ 6 5 4	◇ J 7 5 4	◇ K 5 4
♣ 7 6 2	♣ A 9 8 6	♣ —

Only (a) does not qualify as an opening bid. It counts but 11 points, 4 each for two aces; 2 for queen; 1 for doubleton heart.

(b) Counts 14, 12 for high cards, 2 for the singleton spade.

(c) Counts 15, 12 for high cards, plus 3 for void in clubs.

LESSON 5: *Opening bid of one in a suit.* The side that opens the bidding (a pass is not a bid) has an advantage. Therefore you should not pass a hand of 14 points or more and you should always try to find an opening bid of one in a suit whenever you have 13 points and a *biddable suit.* The high-card requirements in a *biddable suit* are:

With 4-card length: Queen-jack or better (3 points or more).

With 5-card length: Jack or better.

With 6-card length: No high card in suit required.

Do not bid a major suit shorter than four cards, even though it is strong in high cards. Three-card minor suits may be opened if your major suits are unbiddable, or if you are opening a major suit only when it contains five or more cards—the method that I now strongly recommend instead of the traditional method of opening on a four-card major.

BIDDABLE:	*NOT BIDDABLE:*
Q J 8 4	Q 8 5 4
K 9 6 2	J 8 4 2
A 8 5 3	10 6 5 3
J 8 7 6 5	9 7 4 3 2
9 7 6 5 4 2	A K

Choosing the suit: Sometimes your hand will include more than one biddable suit. Follow these guides in deciding which to bid first:

If they are of unequal length, bid the longer suit:

	♠ 7 6		♠ J 9 7 6 4 = Bid 1 ♠
	♡ A K J 8		♡ 9 2
	◇ 8 4		◇ A K Q 7
Bid 1 ♣ =	♣ A 10 7 6 5		♣ A 8

Between two five-card or six-card suits, choose the higher ranking (not necessarily the stronger).

	♠ 7		♠ A
Bid 1 ♡ =	♡ J 8 7 5 3		♡ —
	◇ A K J 4 2		◇ Q 7 6 5 4 2 = Bid 1 ◇
	♣ A 6		♣ A Q 7 6 5 2

With more than one biddable suit, select the suit next lower in rank to your shortest suit. (Remember, we have elected to consider a four-card major suit as not a good opening bid, even though it may otherwise meet the high-card requirements.)

A	B	C
♠ A 7 2	♠ A Q 7 2	♠ 7
♡ Q J 9 5	♡ A K 7 2	♡ Q J 9 5
◇ 7 2	◇ Q 6 2	◇ K 10 8 3
♣ A K 5 4	♣ 7 2	♣ A K 5 3

A. Bid 1 Club.
B. Bid 1 Diamond.
C. Bid 1 Diamond.

Your proper choice of the opening bid is important because

your purpose in opening the bidding is to explore the possibilities of making game. If you and your partner have, in your combined hands, a total of 26 points, you will be correct to bid for game in no trump or in a major suit—hearts or spades. If your partner has 13 points, he must be able to rely upon you to have 13 or more for your opening bid.

When you open the bidding you promise that you have at least 13 points, that your suit is biddable and also that you will bid once again if partner makes what is called a *forcing* response.

LESSON 6: *Responding to opening suit bid.* When partner opens the bidding with one of a suit, you have many possible responses. Of these, let's consider first the one which you should consider last—the *pass*. Remember, your first aim is to bid for game if there is a good chance to make it. Partner may have only 13 points, but he may have as many as 21. Therefore, pass only if you have fewer than 6 points.

Let's assume partner has opened with 1 heart. With from 6 to 10 points you may:

—Raise partner's suit from 1 to 2. (Bid 2 ♡)

1 pt. =	♠ 8 6		3 pts. =	♠ 2
5 pts. =	♡ A J 5			♡ 10 7 6 5
	◇ 9 7 3 2		3 pts. =	◇ K 8 4
3 pts. =	♣ K 7 6 4			♣ 10 8 7 5 3

— Bid 1 no trump lacking support for partner's suit.

4 pts. =	♠ A 9 8		3 pts. =	♠ K 8 6
	♡ 7 6			♡ 8 5
2 pts. =	◇ Q 5 4 3		1 pt. =	◇ J 5 4 2
1 pt. =	♣ J 9 6 2		2 pts. =	♣ Q 8 6 3

—Bid one in a new suit.

3 pts. =	♠ K 9 7 6 4	♠ 9 5 4	(This hand must be passed because it is not strong enough for 2 ◇ and it counts only 5 points at no trump.)
1 pt. =	♡ 8 2	♡ 8 2	
2 pts. =	◇ Q 6 5	◇ K 9 7 6 4	
	♣ 9 5 4	♣ Q 6 5	

291

With 11-12 points, you may:

—Bid one or two in a new suit, as required:

Bid 1 ♠ = ♠ A 10 7 4   ♠ 7 6
       ♡ A 2   ♡ A 7 2
       ◇ Q 8 2   ◇ J 8 2
       ♣ 10 6 3 2   Bid 2 ♣ = ♣ A Q 9 7 6

With 13 points or more, you may choose:

A jump raise in partner's suit. Bid 3 hearts with adequate trump support, preferably four or more, headed by an honor, and from 13 to 15 points, counting both high cards and distribution.

A jump takeout in no trump. Bid 2 no trumps with 13, 14, 15 points; 3 no trumps with 16, 17, 18 points. Hand must be evenly balanced and have protection in all three unbid suits. For example:

Bid 2 no Trumps   Bid 3 no trumps
   ♠ A Q 10   ♠ A Q 7
   ♡ 9 8   ♡ Q 7 2
   ◇ K Q 7   ◇ A J 6
   ♣ K 7 4 3 2   ♣ K J 8 3

A jump bid (one more than necessary) in a new suit. At least 19 points in your hand will put your combined hands in the slam zone, for a small slam bid is justified with 33 points in the combined hands if either partner's hand can furnish support for the other's suit.

   Bid 3 ♣   Bid 2 ♠
   ♠ A 8 3   ♠ A K Q J 7 5
   ♡ K Q 7 5   ♡ J 2
   ◇ 6   ◇ A 8
   ♣ A Q J 7 4   ♣ A Q 7

These jump bids all require partner to continue bidding until game has been reached or an opponent's bid is doubled.

LESSON 7: *No trump bids.* No trump hands are easy to recognize and easy to bid. You count only your high-card points because no trump means exactly what it says—NO trumps. You never bid no trump with a void or a singleton, and to bid no trump with a hand that includes a doubleton, this short suit must be headed by the ace or the king.

A bid of one no trump shows 16, 17, 18 points with at least three suits *protected*. (A-2, K-2, Q-3-2, or J-4-3-2 is minimum.)

A bid of two no trumps shows 22, 23, 24 points, four suits protected.

A bid of three no trumps shows 25, 26, 27 points, all suits protected.

Responding: When your partner opens with a bid in no trump, you get such a clear picture of his hand that you can tell at once where many hands should play. Adding your points to the maximum his bid can show, you know, for example, that if partner bids one no trump you will not make a game if your hand totals 7 points or less, since you usually need 26 to have game-going material.

If partner's opening bid is 1 no trump and you hold:

7 points or less: Pass with a normal type hand, but bid two of a long suit with a hand that will not play well at no trump. For example:

♠ 9 5   ♡ 6   ♢ K 9 7 6 5 4   ♣ Q 10 6 2   Bid two ♢

8 or 9 points: Bid 2 no trumps. If partner has a minimum 16, you may be unable to make 3 no trump. But if he has 17 or 18 he will go on to game. Or respond 2 clubs (Stayman Convention) if you wish partner to show a four-card major, in which your distributional values may offer a better play for game. Lacking a four-card major as good as J x x x, opener responds 2 diamonds.

10 to 14 points: Bid three no trumps, or jump to three (a forcing bid) in a five-card or longer suit.

15 or 16 points: Raise to four no trumps. If partner has better than a minimum, your combined hands may include the 33 points needed to justify bidding for a small slam.

17 points: Jump to six no trumps, or skip to three in your long suit. Even if partner has a minimum, you are assured of small slam material.

If partner's opening bid was 2 no trumps:

With 3 points or less: Pass. Do not take out in a suit unless you want to bid for game.

With 4 to 7 points: Bid three no trumps.

With 11 or 12 points: Jump to six no trumps.

If partner's opening bid was 3 no trumps:

With less than 6 points: Pass. Any bid over three no trumps is a slam try.

LESSON 8: *Powerhouse hands and slam bids.* If you are lucky enough to be dealt a hand so powerful that you want to play it at a game contract even if partner has less than 6 points, you can make sure your partner does not pass you out below game by opening with a bid of two in a suit. This opening bid says, "Partner, no matter how little you have, don't worry. I have at least 25 points of the 26 it takes to make game."

Strictly speaking, such a hand need not be measured only in points. With so much strength concentrated in one hand, it is usually easy to see whether you are within one trick of game. You should be able to win nine tricks in your own hand to open with two spades or two hearts; ten tricks of your opening bid is two clubs* or two diamonds.

However, here is the formula for a two bid in terms of points.

With a good five-card suit ..... 25 points   ⎫ Holding a sec-
With a good six-card suit...... 23 points   ⎬ ond good five-
With a good seven-card suit ....21points   ⎭ card suit: 1 pt.
                                              less will suffice

Examples:

(a)	(b)	(c)
♠ A	♠ 5 4	♠ A 8 6
♡ A K Q 7 6	♡ A K Q J 7 6	♡ A K Q J 5 4 2
◇ K Q 10 2	◇ A 9	◇ A 5
♣ A K 2	♣ A K 8	♣ 7

Each of these hands is worth an opening bid of 2 hearts. *Responding:* Whatever you do, if partner opens with a bid of two in a suit do not pass. Let us assume that partner has bid two hearts:

With 5 points or less: Bid two no trumps. This does not mean you want to play at no trump. It denies high-card strength.

With 6 points or more: Make a *positive* response. For example:

---

* Some play, and I recommend, that a bid of 2 clubs replaces the strong two bids in other suits, freeing other two bids for other uses. The negative response to 2 clubs is 2 diamonds, *not* 2 no trumps. The 2 clubs bid is artificial and does not show a club suit.

Raise to three hearts: ♠ 5 2 ♡ Q 10 6 3 ◇ K J 9 ♣ 7 6 5 4
Bid new suit: ♠ 5 2 ♡ 7 6 ◇ K Q 10 7 5 ♣ K 6 5 2 (Bid 3 ◇)

Jump to three no trumps:
 ♠Q 6 5 4   ♡ 8 2   ◇ K 7 4 2   ♣ K 10 9
Since two no trumps would deny as much as 6 points, you show this 8-point hand by a positive response of three no trumps.

Rebids: The opener does not have to jump the bidding to make sure his partner bids again. Both players are obligated to keep bidding until at least a game has been bid, or until a penalty double of the opponents' bid promises an equally satisfactory score.

Slam Convention: There is a thrill to bidding a slam; there are also some handsome bonuses. However, in order to make a slam, you must be sure that your side holds sufficient aces and kings. For this purpose, there is a special conventional bid of FOUR NO TRUMPS—the Blackwood Convention. A bid of four no trumps asks for aces. Partner responds conventionally: With no ace: 5 clubs; one ace, 5 diamonds; 2 aces, 5 hearts, *etc.* If the player who bid four no trumps then bids five no trumps, it announces that all the aces are present, and requests partner to give information about kings in the same manner: no kings, 6 clubs, one king, 6 diamonds, etc.

Two words of caution: Don't call on the Blackwood Convention unless you are almost sure you can make a slam. And, until you have had more experience, don't bid a slam without calling on the Blackwood Four-Five No Trumps Convention.

LESSON 9: *Defensive bidding.* When an opponent makes the first bid, your side's entry into the auction is called a *defensive bid.* The Scoring Table warns you that defensive bids may be costly. You lose 500 points if you are doubled and are set two tricks when vulnerable or three tricks when not vulnerable. 500 points is approximately the value of game *if* the opponents bid *and* make it.

For this reason, a defensive bid should never risk more than 500 points. And there is no reason to take *any* risk if you have a hand that can win three or four tricks against the opponents' bid. You pass because the chances are they will not be able to make game.

Confine your defensive bids to two kinds of hand:

Overcall (make the lowest possible bid in your long suit) with a hand that will win many tricks if you are declarer; few if your opponent plays the hand.

Double the opening bid of one of a suit with a hand that is so strong both in high cards and distribution that you hope to make game despite the opponents' announced strength. This double is a specialized bid. It does not mean that you want to play for penalties; it means that you want partner to bid his best suit. Therefore your hand should be strong in all the suits not bid by the opponents, or you should have a very powerful suit of your own.

Overcalls are not based on points; more important is the number of tricks you can expect to win with one long, strong suit or a two-suit hand if you are able to name the trump suit.

For example:

(a)	(b)	(c)
♠ J 8 4	♠ K 10 9 7 5	♠ 6 5 3
♡ A 7	♡ 7	♡ A 2
◇ A Q 6 4 2	◇ A J 9 7 2	◇ K Q J 9 8 4
♣ Q 6 3	♣ Q 2	♣ 7 4

East opens the bidding with one heart. Neither side is vulnerable. What should South bid next with each of these three hands? (a) Pass. This hand is not good enough for a takeout double, and the suit is too weak to provide safety for an overcall. Don't overcall at the level of two when you might lose three tricks in your own trump suit. (b) Bid one spade. If your spade bid is doubled, you can retreat to two diamonds, for which partner may have good support. (c) Bid two diamonds. Your suit promises five tricks, plus your ace of hearts.

A Takeout Double must be as strong as an opening bid—at least 13 points, located mostly in suits the opponents have not bid. After East's opening bid of one heart, South holds:

(a)	(b)	(c)
♠ A Q J 2	♠ 7 2	♠ A 6 2
♡ 7 2	♡ A Q J 5	♡ 10 9 7 5
◇ A 9 7 3	◇ A 9 7 3	◇ A Q 4
♣ K 6 3	♣ K 6 3	♣ K 6 3

Hand (a) a takeout double; better than an opening bid and support for any suit other than hearts. Hand (b) pass; too much strength is in the opponents' suit. Hand (c) pass; with no distributional assets, your chance of making game is poor—but so is your opponents'.

Responding to a Double: As partner of the player who has doubled for a takeout, the one thing you should not do is pass. The weaker your hand, the more important it is for you to obey your partner's request that you respond by showing your best (longest) suit.

For example:

(a)	(b)	(c)
♠ J 9 5 4	♠ J 9 5 4	♠ A 10 7 5 4
♡ 10 7 6 3	♡ 7 6	♡ 6 3 2
◇ K 4 2	◇ K J 8 6	◇ K Q 2
♣ 3 2	♣ 5 3 2	♣ Q 6

Your partner's takeout double of West's one heart bid is passed by East. As South, what should you do with each of these hands? (a) Bid 1 spade. Don't even consider leaving the double in because you have four hearts and a weak spade suit. (b) Bid 1 spade. Partner will prefer to hear the "other major suit"; besides, your stronger diamond suit would require bidding at the two level. (c) Bid 2 spades. This jump response shows partner that you are responding with a good hand.

The Exception to the rule about passing partner's takeout double occurs when you are so strong in the opponents' suit that you will win about three trump tricks in it. Usually, you are asking partner to lead a trump.

For example: ♠ 7 2 ♡ Q J 10 8 7 ◇ A 5 4 ♣ 7 6 5

With this hand, if partner made a takeout double of one heart you would be correct to pass and play for penalties.

LESSON 10: *Play of the Cards.* You win tricks in three ways: with high cards; by trumping; and by making little cards into winners by exhausting all the higher ones.

Below, you see part of all four hands: all of the cards in two suits, hearts (trumps), and spades. You, South, have won the lead and are now ready to play.

For example:

```
                    ♠ 6 5
                    ♡ A 7 6 5

   ♠ J 10 9              N              ♠ Q 8 7
   ♡ J 10            W       E          ♡ Q 9
                         S

                    ♠ A K 4 3 2
                    ♡ K 8 4 3 2
```

You play a low heart and partner's ace wins. You lead another heart from dummy (North) and win a trick with the king. Now East and West have no more trumps.

You win tricks with the ace and king of spades. Then you lead the four of spades. North trumps this trick, capturing East and West's high cards. Now, when you regain the lead, you will be able to win tricks with the two lowest spades. In all, you win five tricks in the spade suit: two with high cards, one by trumping, two by establishing low cards.

The Finesse: Suppose that your hand was the same as shown with just one change. Instead of the king of spades, you have the queen and East has your king. If you played the same way, you would lose a trick when you led the second spade from your hand. So, this time, you take the king of hearts first. Then you lead a low heart and let North's ace win the second heart trick. Now North has the lead. When North plays a spade, if East played the king, you would capture it with your ace and win the second spade trick with your queen. Instead, East plays the seven, following the advice "second hand low." Instead of playing the ace, you play the queen. If West had the king, of course he would capture your queen. But East has the king, so your queen wins the trick. This is a *finesse*.

Plan: The best general advice for declarer is: When you see the dummy, count the tricks you are sure to win. If they are not sufficient to make your contract, see where you might win the extra tricks you need by trumping, by finessing or by establishing long cards.

Defender's Play: Do not be hasty about cashing aces. Play to establish other tricks, hoping to regain the lead with the ace.

For example:

```
                    ♠ K Q J 10
                    ♡ A 5 4 3

♠ A 5 4 3              N              ♠ 9 8 7 6
♡ K Q J 10          W   E            ♡ 2
                       S

                    ♠ 2
                    ♡ 9 8 7 6
```

Again you see only part of the hands—the cards in each hand in just two suits. South is playing with diamonds as trumps. West has the lead. If West leads his high card, the ace, when North wins the ace of hearts he will cash the three high cards in spades and South will discard his three hearts. But if West leads the king of hearts instead of the ace of spades, when North wins the ace of hearts and leads a spade, West will be able to capture the spade trick and cash three good tricks in hearts before South has achieved his discards.

BIDDING VALUATION
AT A GLANCE

HIGH-CARD POINTS	DISTRIBUTIONAL POINTS		
	In opener's hand		In support of partner's suit
Ace = 4			
King = 3	1	Doubleton	1
Queen = 2	2	Singleton	3
Jack = 1	3	Void	5

For no trump bidding, count only high-card values
For suit bidding, add high card and distributional points

To bid for	Combined hands should total
GAME at no trump or major suit	26 points
GAME at minor suit	29 points
SMALL SLAM	33 points
GRAND SLAM	37 points

OPENING BID REQUIREMENTS

1 of a suit: 13 points with a strong suit, or any hand with 14 points.

2 of a suit: 25 points or more. (23 with a good six-card suit; 21 with a good seven-card suit.)

1 no trump: 16-18 points; balanced hand (no singleton) and stoppers in at least three suits.

2 no trumps: 22-24 points; balanced hand, stoppers in all four suits.

3 no trumps: 25-27 points; balanced hand, stoppers in all four suits.

RESPONSES: TO SUIT BIDS

0-5 points:	Pass.
6-10 points:	Bid one no trump.
7-10 points:	Raise partner to 2 with trump support.
6-18 points:	Bid one in a new suit.
10-18 points:	Bid two of lower-ranking new suit.
13-15:	Raise partner to 3 of his suit, with strong trump support.
19 or more:	Jump bid in a new suit.
13-15:	Jump to two no trumps with stoppers in unbid suits.
16-18:	Jump to three no trumps with stoppers in unbid suits.

RESPONSES: TO NO TRUMP BIDS

8-9 points:	Raise to two no trumps. (Exceptionally, with 7 points and a five-card suit)
10-14 points:	Raise to three no trumps.
15-16 points:	Raise to four no trumps.
17-18 points:	Raise to six no trumps.
19-20 points:	Bid three of a suit; then 6 no trumps.
21 points:	Raise to seven no trumps.

A response of 2 ♣ (or 3 ♣ over 2 NT) is conventional and asks opener to bid a 4-card major or deny one by rebidding 2 (or 3) ◇.

A response of 2 in any other suit shows less than 9 points, at least a 5-card suit and an unbalanced hand.

A response of 4 spades or 4 hearts shows a long suit (six or seven cards) with less than 10 points in high cards.

A response of 3 in any suit shows a hand with 10 or more points and a good suit.

CONTRACT BRIDGE SCORING TABLE

FOR TRICKS BID FOR AND MADE
(Score below the line)

	Undoubled	Doubled	Redbld
Spades or hearts, each	30	60	120
Diamonds or clubs, each	20	40	80
No Trump (first trick)	40	80	160
(each subsequent trick)	30	60	120

Game = 100 points scored below the line. The 100 points need not be scored in a single deal. When one side reaches 100 points below, the opponents' partial score no longer counts toward game; both sides start from scratch to score points below the line toward the next game.

BONUSES AND PENALTIES (Score above the line)

For winning Rubber: 500 to the winner of two games out of three
700 to the winner of two games to none

Slams:	*Not Vulnerable*	*Vulnerable*
Small slam (12 tricks)	500	750
Grand slam (13 tricks)	1,000	1,500
Honors: 4 trumps honors in one hand	....	100
5 trumps honors in one hand	....	150
4 aces in one hand at no trump	....	150

For making doubled contract: 50 points (no additional bonus if contract is redoubled)

OVERTRICKS:

	Not Vulnerable	*Vulnerable*
Not doubled	Trick value	Trick value
Doubled	100 per trick	200 per trick
Redoubled	200 per trick	400 per trick

PENALTIES:

	Undoubled		Doubled	
	Not Vul.	Vul.	Not Vul.	Vul.
First undertrick	50	100	100	200
Each subsequent undertrick	50	100	200	300

(The penalty for undertricks in a redoubled contract is twice that for a doubled one.)

ABOUT THE AUTHOR

RICHARD L. FREY, in addition to being an acknowledged master in the art of playing bridge, is a master of writing about the game. His non-fiction articles on many subjects have appeared in leading magazines; his daily newspaper articles on bridge appeared non-stop for a record thirty-five years.

Back in the mid-thirties, Ely Culbertson hailed Frey as "one of the greatest tournament players of all time and one of my favorite partners."

Today, Alan Truscott, bridge editor of the *New York Times*, says: "As this book so clearly shows, Dick Frey is superb both as bridge player and bridge writer."

For Charles H. Goren's opinion, see the introduction he wrote for this book.